A BIBLE HANDBOOK TO
REVELATION

A BIBLE
HANDBOOK TO
REVELATION

MAL COUCH
GENERAL EDITOR

kregel
PUBLICATIONS

Grand Rapids, MI 49501

A Bible Handbook to Revelation
Mal Couch, General Editor

Cover design: John M. Lucas

Library of Congress Cataloging-in-Publication Data
Couch, Mal.
   A Bible handbook to Revelation / Mal Couch.
     p.   cm.
   Includes bibliographical references.
   1. Bible. N.T. Revelation—Criticism, interpretation, etc.
I. Title.
BS2825.52 .C68   2001   228'.06—dc21   00-062947
                                       CIP

ISBN 0-8254-2358-9

Printed in the United States of America

1 2 3 4 5 / 05 04 03 02 01

CONTENTS

FOREWORD

A Bible Handbook to Revelation is a valuable contribution to the literature on the last book of the Bible. In addition to a verse-by-verse commentary, half of the volume deals with important doctrinal issues related to the book of Revelation. Part 1 of this volume deals with the place of Revelation in the New Testament canon, problems of interpretation, and its literary structure. A high level of scholarship that brings in considerable detail necessary to consider these subjects exhaustively characterizes the discussion. Part 2 deals with the theology of the book of Revelation as the book relates to various divisions of theology, including Christology, pneumatology, hamartiology, and Israelology. The general editor is supported by a series of contributing authors who deal with many of the issues surrounding the book of Revelation.

The verse-by-verse exposition provides the reader with the necessary facts to interpret the book of Revelation from a premillennial and pretribulational point of view. Hundreds of footnote references support quotations and cite the literature in the field bearing on the subject and will be an invaluable door to considering all possible views as compared to the correct view. Because of its in-depth introduction and its verse-by-verse analysis supplemented by extensive footnoting, *A Bible Handbook to Revelation* is an outstanding contribution to the literature on this important book of the Bible.

—JOHN F. WALVOORD

PREFACE

IT HAS BEEN BOTH A BLESSING and privilege to teach through the book of Revelation about twenty times during my ministry. The first time was when I was a Bible college student at a small country church in Arkansas. I can remember relying heavily on the notes in my *Scofield Reference Bible*. I also recall that I taught a number of passages whose meanings were not always clear to me.

But those days have come and gone. And for almost forty years now I have translated the book about four times. No, I still have not "arrived" in my understanding of the Apocalypse. And yes, I have many questions about some of the more complicated verses in Revelation. Any honest Bible teacher, no matter what his interpretive persuasion, would have to admit the same. Yet my convictions on what the book is all about have deepened.

After studying the book from every theological position, and after examining countless opinions about the book throughout church history, I am convinced that Revelation makes sense only from a premillennial point of view. In other words, the majority of the events described will take place in the future.

Some will argue that I was imprinted as a young ministerial student by the Scofield Bible and that I have not broken away from that influence. But I trust that, after four decades of biblical research both in the broad area of theology as well as in the study of prophetic truth, I have become even more objective in my understanding of the book of Revelation. My convictions now are based on much better evidence. I pray my heart is right as I search Scripture.

For those who claim the same objectivity but come to different conclusions about the book of Revelation, I simply urge them to read this book thoroughly. I hope that we all want to better understand the Scriptures and are willing to follow wherever the truth leads us. Finally, it must be remembered, that to all of us who open the pages of Revelation, John the apostle writes, "Blessed is he who reads and those who hear the words of the prophecy, and heed the things which are written in it; for the time is near" (1:3).

—Mal Couch
General Editor

CONTRIBUTORS

Mal Couch, Th.D., Ph.D., D.D., is founder and president of Tyndale Theological Seminary and Biblical Institute, Fort Worth, Texas.

Larry V. Crutchfield, M.Phil., Ph.D., is professor of early church history and culture at Columbia Evangelical Seminary, Longview, Washington.

Harold D. Foos, B.A., Th.D., is professor of Bible and theology and chairman of the department of theology at Moody Bible Institute, Chicago, Illinois.

Robert P. Lightner, B.A., M.L.A., Th.D., is professor emeritus of systematic theology at Dallas Theological Seminary, Dallas, Texas, and a visiting professor of theology at Tyndale Theological Seminary, Fort Worth, Texas.

Russell L. Penney, M.A., D.Sc., Th.D., is a professor of theology and director of post-graduate studies at Hebron Theological Seminary in Santa Cruz de la Sierra, Bolivia.

Todd Virnoche, Dip. Th.S., is a Bible teacher and a computer consultant for IBM.

PART 1

INTRODUCTION TO
THE BOOK OF REVELATION

CHAPTER 1

WHY IS REVELATION IMPORTANT?

MAL COUCH

What Is the Book of Revelation About?

THE BOOK OF REVELATION HAS been rightly labeled the grand and noble conclusion to our Holy Bible, the crown jewel of canonical literature inspired by the Spirit of God. The book is the last of five Bible books written by the apostle John. Revelation concludes the books of the New Testament and of the entire Word of God.

Doctrinally, like no other book of the Bible, Revelation shows the living relationship between Christ, the Son of God, and His heavenly Father. Revelation also closes the door on this old and dying world. It records the final pains creation will experience, and at the same time it sheds brilliant and glorious light on the new and eternal state to come. The pangs and death throes of this sinful world will be suddenly replaced by a new, radiant, and sinless paradise. In Revelation, the rule of the generations of the first Adam is replaced by the reign of the Second Adam, Christ Himself.

Seiss gives a succinct description of the Apocalypse and what the book is all about: ". . . the great theme and subject of this Book is the Coming of Christ, the Apocalypse of Himself, His own great Day of the Lord. . . . A tremendous Revelation is therefore brought before men in this Book."[1]

Why Is the Book of Revelation Significant?

Unfortunately most Christians have little idea of the value, purpose, and importance of the book of Revelation. For those brave enough to try to read the apostle John's last letter to the church, the effort seems too great and they stop after studying only a few chapters. Others make no attempt at grasping the message of the book. The word has already gone forth that "Revelation is too mysterious to try to understand!"

Also many are told that scholars themselves are woefully divided as to the meaning of this prophecy. And if godly men who study God's Word cannot figure out its meaning, how can the average Christian? With such a comprehensive and interpretive mountain to climb, Revelation unfortunately remains a closed book to many people.

But ponder for a moment about the books you have in your study. What keeps most of them in a tidy, neat row? The bookends! Consider the books of Genesis and Revelation. They are the "bookends" of the Word of God. Without these two great inspired volumes, the rest of the books of the Bible would make little sense. The book of Revelation is necessary because it explains and summarizes how world history, God's history, will come to a conclusion. Revelation reveals the darkest times ever to fall on mankind, but it also sheds light on how, through the Lord Jesus Christ, there is a final and glorious victory for those redeemed and saved by His sacrificial death on the cross!

Since this volume is part of God's Word, it demands a hearing from all who love the Lord. Here are eight reasons why Revelation is so important.

The Book of Revelation Is God's Word

Though most Christians struggle to understand the book, still today the average believer has no problem accepting it as one of the inspired books of Scripture. And for centuries Revelation has been accepted as part of the canon of the New Testament and as part of the Word of God. Internally, maybe more than any other book of Scripture, it contains overwhelming evidence of inspiration.

And though it was questioned by some for the first few hundred years of church history, the book was clearly and almost universally accepted as a unique feature of the inspired New Testament. It was seen as that final bookend of revelation. Walvoord writes:

> The revelation recorded by John the Apostle is presented as having a solid historical basis in his exile on the Isle of Patmos. . . . In the literature of the second half of the second century, evidence begins to reveal wide circulation of the Apocalypse.[2]

Walvoord quotes Thiessen, that "the early church, in spite of certain objections, generally accepted the book of Revelation by the end of the second century and the eastern church soon followed suit. Among conservative scholars, there is little disposition to exclude the book of Revelation from the canon."[3]

More will be said about this in chapter 4.

Jesus Is the Direct Divine Author

Though the Holy Spirit is the One who inspired the sacred writers of the Bible, the book of Revelation has another important dimension to it. John the apostle was the human penman, but the message came directly from Jesus Christ Himself. The first line in the book reads, "The Revelation of [literally, 'from'] Jesus Christ" (Rev. 1:1). Jesus was passing on to His disciples a direct message from God the Father, who "made it known by sending his angel to his servant John" (NIV).

Larkin writes, "Thus we see that the canon of Scripture would be incomplete without this message [of Revelation] from Jesus to His Church after His return to Heaven. While the Apostle John is the writer of the Book he is not the author or composer. The Author was the Lord Jesus Himself. The Apostle was only a 'scribe.'"[4]

Revelation Is Worldwide in Its Scope

The book of Revelation is important to us because it portrays the world as a global village. Entering the twenty-first century, no better expression describes our earth and its people. Besides a mushrooming population, other factors are pushing all humanity together, such as an interlinking economy, jet age transportation, and satellite communications. After chapter 6, most of what is described in the book is universal in scope.

For example we read of peace taken from the earth (6:4); a fourth of the earth killed (v. 8); avenging those who dwell on the earth (v. 10); the asteroids falling to the earth (v. 13); all green grass burned (8:7); the moon and stars smitten (v. 12); a third of mankind killed (9:18); the "rest" of mankind did not repent (v. 21); many peoples, nations, tongues (10:11); those of all peoples, tribes, tongues, nations will look on the dead bodies of the two martyrs and prophets (11:9); "those who dwell on the earth will rejoice . . . and they will send gifts to one another, because these two [godly] prophets tormented those who dwell on the earth" (v. 10). Many other verses further illustrate the global events taking place in Revelation. As Lange observes:

> Revelation, in accordance with its . . . world-historical character, takes in the entire breadth of the world, the entire length, heighth, and depth of its course, in a manner of which we find scarcely the faintest idea in classical historiography. . . . the Kingdom of God occupies in the foreground, arrayed for the final decisive combats with the world-power, whose advances become constantly bolder and more threatening.[5]

Because we live in a world so interconnected, every believer, and even nonbelievers, should be interested in its frightening yet positive final message.

Revelation Summarizes the Judgments Found in the Old Testament

Because the book of Revelation is global in scope, the judgments in it are also broad. God's wrath will overtake all unbelieving humanity (Rev. 6), coming on the world from both God the Father and Christ the Lamb (vv. 16–17). This was prophesied in Isaiah 2:19 and 34:2–4.

> And men will go into caves of the rocks,
> And into holes of the ground,
> Before the terror of the LORD,
> And before the splendor of His majesty,
> When He arises to make the earth tremble. (2:19)

> And His wrath against all their armies;
> He has utterly destroyed them,
> He has given them over to slaughter.
> So their slain will be thrown out,
> And their corpses will give off their stench,
> And the mountains will be drenched with their blood.
> And all the host of heaven will wear away,
> And the sky will be rolled up like a scroll;
> All their host will also wither away,
> As a leaf withers from the vine,
> Or as one withers from the fig tree. (34:2–4)

These are but a few examples of Old Testament verses that show God's anger against the sins of humanity; all of them are fulfilled in Revelation. Because the world will reject Jesus Christ, the Lord will have no other choice but to send judgment.

In one of the judgments God will send plagues of demons on an unrepenting population (Rev. 9:20). Instead of turning from sin, the nations are "enraged" with anger. No wonder, then, that the Lord will pour out His unrelenting fury (11:17–19)!

Revelation concludes with judgment on great Babylon the harlot (18:2–3), on all unbelieving earth dwellers (19:18), on the Beast (Antichrist) and the False (religious) Prophet (v. 20), and on Satan and his followers (20:7–10).

But the ultimate and the most pitiful judgment described in the book will be the spiritual condemnation pronounced on the lost and the unrighteous of all generations past. This Great White Throne judgment will conclude earth's history as we know it. Those not found written in the Book of Life will be "thrown into the lake of fire" (20:15).

In a sober tone Seiss describes this final adjudication in which Christ has no other choice but to condemn the lost. He writes, "There is not a song, not a voice of gladness, not a note of exultation, for it is simply and only the administration of retributive justice, which consigns the unsanctified to their final perdition, and which has nothing whatever of gladness about it."[6]

In view of this backdrop of sin and evil, the only hope is in the saving grace of the Lord Jesus Christ.

Revelation Describes the Final Demise of Satan

Revelation also predicts Lucifer's last efforts to overthrow the impending kingdom of Jesus Christ. In Revelation Satan is seen as extremely active, and he is described in many ways. He could be the "star" that fell from heaven (9:1) and the king and angel of the abyss (v. 11). He is described as the great red Dragon who will control the ten-nation confederacy (12:3), and he is called the Serpent, the Devil, and Satan, the one who deceives (v. 9).

In chapter 13, Satan can grant power and cause men to worship him. And in this same chapter he will make the world believe that the Beast is the promised Messiah!

Satan's final judgment will come in two stages. He will be bound for a thousand years in order to keep him from influencing the nations during the millennium (20:1–3). But he will be released at the end of the kingdom, Christ's millennial reign, and will bring about a rebellion against Christ (vv. 7–8), in which he will be defeated. His final confinement is eternal (v. 10).

Since he is the author of evil, it is significant that Revelation shows us his last days and his final doom. Swete tells us why this is so important. "St. John intends at least to teach that the forces, personal or impersonal, which have inspired mankind with false views of life and antagonism to God and to Christ will in the end be completely subjugated, and, if not annihilated, will at least be prevented from causing further trouble. From the Lake of Fire there is no release."[7]

Revelation Fulfills the Final Stages of Daniel's Seventy Weeks

"The Seventieth Week of Daniel. This term is based on Daniel 9:24–27, where Daniel was informed that God was going to have seventy weeks (490 years) of special dealings with Israel in order to accomplish six great purposes. The final week of seven years (the Seventieth Week) is yet future and is commonly called the Tribulation."[8]

When Daniel was praying for his people (Dan. 9), the angel Gabriel came to him from the Lord and revealed that some 490 years would be "determined upon" Israel. Since a "week" was seven years, seventy "weeks" total 490 years. These would be special years in which God would deal with the nation. But Daniel was told that after the sixty-ninth "week" was finished and before that final seventh week took place, some very important events would transpire.

The Messiah or promised King would be "cut off" or hindered from carrying out His great reign, and the temple of Jerusalem would be destroyed. The sixty-nine weeks have passed. Though risen from the dead and seated in heaven by His Father, the Lord Jesus is not reigning now on His earthly, Davidic throne. And as Daniel prophesied, the great temple was destroyed. This took place in A.D. 70.

The final week (or seven years of horrific Tribulation) is yet to take place! Even the world understands that some terrible days may be coming on the earth. At the end of the twentieth century, Hollywood produced more than three major movies on Armageddon! (But of course these were distortions of the book of Revelation, and the gospel certainly was not presented.) Revelation 6–20 deals with these years. "The seventieth week of Daniel's prophecy is yet to be fulfilled. When that is accomplished, Daniel's inquiry will be fully realized for Israel will be back in her homeland with her Messiah."[9]

This subject will be discussed further in chapter 15.

Revelation Reveals the Second Coming of Jesus the Messiah

The Old Testament prophetic books are filled with descriptions of *two* comings of the One called the Anointed, or the Messiah. His lineage, place of birth, nature of His birth (by a virgin), and the fact that He will die for the sins of His people (Isa. 53) are all predicted, and these were fulfilled in His first coming.

His second coming as the King over Israel and the world is also clearly foretold. In fact, hundreds of verses describe this coming and its impact on the Jews, the Middle East, and all humanity. Whole chapters describe how the land will be changed, nature harnessed, evil punished, health increased, and that the nations will truly know God and His Messiah. These themes occupy much of the contents of the major and minor prophets.

But a question is raised by those who deny the historic return of the Messiah: "If that return is literal and fulfills Old Testament messianic kingdom prophecies, why are there only a handful of verses describing this event at the end of the book of Revelation?"

This is an important question, but it is easy to answer. It is true that only Revelation 19:11–20:9 describe this return and the one-thousand-year reign of the Messiah. But that reign is seen as a literal time period with a beginning and an ending. It is described as earthly and not simply as some figurative or nonliteral happening.

The simple answer is that hundreds of verses need not be repeated in order to verify a fulfillment. The verses in Revelation 19–20 are enough to show that what was promised will come to pass! Many details of what will happen in that kingdom reign are all prophetically documented in the Old Testament.

Revelation Vividly Describes the Blessedness of the Coming Eternal State

Defying our present human senses, Revelation 21–22 tells of the new heavens and the new earth. The new Holy City, Jerusalem, will descend from above and will become the eternal dwelling place of the redeemed. Those in the city will know they are in the presence of God Almighty in the person of the Lamb, the Son of God (21:22–23; 22:3–5). In fact, evidence for the deity of Christ in these chapters is strong.

In poetic yet literal wording, these final verses of Revelation tell us of the eternal presence of Christ with all the saved, the eradication of sin, and the unfathomable joy and peace experienced by those who belong to the Lord.

In reference to these final chapters and the deity of Christ, Lange writes:

> The relation betw[een] God and the Lamb comes out distinctly in ch. xxi. 23, where it is declared that the glory of God lightens the City of God, and the Lamb is the light thereof; i.e., Christ the visible image, the perceptible manifestation of God (see ch. xxii. 3, 5). . . . Christ is adorned with all the features of the glorified God-manhood. The revelation of God is also the revelation of Christ. Grace proceeds from Him, as from Jehovah. His titles and traits combine His heavenly glory with His earthly work of redemption and salvation.[10]

Yet with so much truth and glory pouring forth from its pages, the question is asked again, "Why is Revelation still misunderstood?" How the book is to be interpreted remains the great divide among Bible scholars.

CHAPTER 2

REVELATION IN THE NEW TESTAMENT CANON

LARRY V. CRUTCHFIELD

WHEN THE CHURCH BEGAN ON the Day of Pentecost, Scripture consisted solely of the writings of the Old Testament. Over a period of some twenty years the apostles communicated Christ's teachings orally to the early church. Irenaeus (A.D. 120–202) believed that there was a body of oral "tradition which originate[d] from the apostles, [and] which [was] preserved by means of the successions of presbyters in the Churches."[1] He spoke of "elders" or "presbyters" who "were disciples of the apostles."[2] And he took special note of "the elders who saw John, the disciple of the Lord."[3] Of these, Irenaeus specifically mentioned Polycarp[4] and Papias.[5] That Irenaeus held this tradition in high regard is evident by the fact that he frequently drew from it and by the honor he bestowed on those who transmitted it.

Not until the end of the first century were all twenty-seven books of the New Testament available in written form. The first book was Paul's epistle to the Galatians, most likely penned around A.D. 48. The last book written was the Revelation to John, composed in A.D. 95 or 96. While all of the New Testament writings were in existence at the end of the first century, it was almost four hundred years before the many segments of the church reached agreement on the composition of the New Testament canon. (See chapter 4, page 52, on the dating of Revelation.)

There was considerable disagreement among early church leaders about the value of certain ecclesiastical writings (e.g., *Epistle of Barnabas*), which were eventually rejected because they lacked apostolic authority and divine inspiration. But there were also disputes over some books (e.g., Hebrews, 2 Peter, and Revelation) which are now included in the New Testament and universally regarded as inspired. However, the canonical fortunes of no book hinged more on personal prejudice and theological bias than that of the Revelation of John.

Revelation and the Criteria for Canonicity

In the earliest years of the church, believers had little incentive to make a collection of New Testament books. The apostles and those who heard their teaching were still alive to preach the gospel and to perpetuate the sayings of Jesus. Even into the middle of the second century, when all the apostles were dead, the church was content to circulate a loosely agreed-on body of writings attributed to the apostles or their disciples. In the last half of the second century, however, heretical teachers (e.g., Marcion) began to appear in the church. These false teachers either distorted existing orthodox doctrine or set forth different doctrinal principles under the banner of "new inspiration." As heretical teaching gradually made inroads into Christendom, increasingly greater thought was given to the concept of gathering together the genuinely inspired and authoritative New Testament writings.

Several criteria have been suggested as the early church's guiding principles in selecting canonical works.

- *Apostolic authority*. Did an apostle write the book?
- *Inspirational declaration*. Did the author claim divine inspiration?
- *Chronological priority*. Was the book written in the first century?
- *Doctrinal fidelity*. Are the book's teachings consistent with orthodox doctrine?
- *Ecclesiastical receptivity*. Was the book widely circulated and generally received by the church?

While some New Testament books did not meet all five criteria for canonicity (e.g., Mark and Luke were not apostles), according to the virtually unanimous opinion of the earliest church leaders after the apostles, the book of Revelation did.

Revelation and the Second-Century Church

The Fathers' Acceptance

The opening verse of Revelation states that the source of the message is an angel sent by Jesus Christ (cf. Rev. 1:2; 2:11, 19). The recipient of the vision is identified as the Lord's "bond-servant John" (1:1; cf. 1:4, 9; 22:8), who recorded what he saw during his confinement by Domitian on the island of Patmos (1:9) in the waning years of the first century. In the earliest references to Revelation, church fathers testified that the author was the apostle John, the disciple whom the Lord loved. Such was the belief of Justin Martyr (ca. A.D. 100–165),[6] the most prominent Christian apologist of the second century; Irenaeus (120–202),[7] the most important second-century polemicist; and Tertullian (150–225),[8] the great African moralist, apologist, and theologian. Nevertheless a few later church leaders either challenged the apostolic authorship of Revelation or rejected the earlier fathers' interpretation of its content.[9]

It is impossible to understand the Apocalypse's significance to the early church and its rocky road to full canonical acceptance without reference to the book's teaching on the millennium and how that prophecy and others were interpreted. The most explicit reference in Scripture to the thousand-year millennial reign of Christ is found in Revelation 20. It is a significant fact that the early adherents of premillennialism (or chiliasm, as it was first called), either had direct contact with John, the longest living apostle, or with his most famous disciple Polycarp. Tradition says that John spent the latter portion of his life at Ephesus in Asia Minor.[10] The origin of the views of perhaps seven early fathers who have been named with varying degrees of confidence as premillenarians may be traced in some way to Asia Minor and to the apostle who reportedly survived until the time of Trajan (98–117).[11]

Papias (ca. 60–130), one of the earliest premillennialists, has been called by some the "father of millenarianism." Irenaeus affirmed that Papias was "the hearer of John, and a companion of Polycarp."[12] Papias furnished the earliest extrabiblical witness to the millennial doctrine taught by the Apocalypse. He came from the same Asiatic background as John. Papias is often credited with influencing many of the early fathers to accept the premillennial view of Revelation.

From the close of the apostolic period, there was a settled belief among the early fathers that Jesus Christ would soon return to earth to establish the millennial kingdom of a thousand years. Attested to by John in Revelation 20, the doctrine of the premillennial advent of Christ was included among the tenets of early Christian orthodoxy. Justin Martyr stated, "I and every other completely orthodox Christian feel certain that there will be a resurrection of the flesh, followed by a thousand years in the rebuilt, embellished, and enlarged city of Jerusalem, as was announced by the Prophets Ezechiel, Isaias and the others."[13] Justin then supported his millenarian position by referring to Genesis 2:17; Isaiah 65:17–25; 2 Peter 3:8 (cf. Ps. 90:4); and John's explicit statement in Revelation 20:4–6.[14]

Irenaeus stated in even stronger terms than Justin that the premillennial doctrine was "traditional orthodoxy."[15] He spoke of "certain orthodox persons" whose opinions were "derived from heretical sources," and asserted that "they are both ignorant of God's dispensations, and of the mystery of the resurrection of the just, and of the [earthly] kingdom."[16] Twice Irenaeus insisted that the prophecies related to these future events could not be allegorized away.[17]

The early church fathers believed in a literal, thousand-year, earthly reign of Christ because they interpreted the teachings of Revelation in a normal rather than mystical way. Justin was one of the earliest fathers to present the case for a literal interpretation of prophecy. He regarded fulfilled prophecy as the authenticator of Christ's ministry,[18] an aid to faith,[19] and the guarantee that future events will be fulfilled.[20] Justin expected the coming millennial age to be the time when God's covenant promises to Abraham and David would be literally fulfilled.

Irenaeus was also a staunch supporter of the literal, plain method of biblical interpretation, especially with respect to eschatological matters. Furthermore he espoused principles that today are regarded as essential to any sound hermeneutical method. For example, he stressed the importance of context and the necessity of interpreting what is ambiguous in Scripture by what is clear. Irenaeus also insisted that Christ, "by His plain announcements freely imparts gifts to all who come to Him," and that "the entire Scriptures, the prophets, and the Gospels, can be clearly, unambiguously, and harmoniously understood by all, although all do not believe them."[21] At the same time, while Irenaeus placed great emphasis on a plain, clear, natural interpretation of Scripture throughout, he also made a distinction between figurative (or symbolic) and nonfigurative elements in the Scriptures.[22]

Tertullian was another church father who clearly stated his belief in a literal millennial kingdom. He wrote: "But we do confess that a kingdom is promised to us upon the earth, although before heaven, only in another state of existence; inasmuch as it will be after the resurrection for a thousand years in the divinely built city of Jerusalem, "let down from heaven" [Rev. 21:2]. . . . This both Ezekiel had knowledge of [Ezek. 48:30–35] and the Apostle John beheld [Rev. 21:10–23]."[23]

On the proper method of interpreting prophecy Tertullian stated:

> Now, to upset all conceits of this sort, let me dispel at once the preliminary idea on which they [heretics] rest their assertion that the prophets make all their announcements in figures of speech. Now, if this were the case, the figures themselves could not possibly have been distinguished, inasmuch as the verities would not have been declared, out of which the figurative language is stretched. And, indeed, if all are figures, where will be that of which they are the figures? How can you hold up a mirror for your face, if the face nowhere exists? But, in truth, all are not figures, but there are also literal statements.[24]

As stated by Wordsworth, "There is scarcely a book in the whole Bible whose genuineness and inspiration were more strongly attested on its first appearance than the Apocalypse. No doubts whatever seem to have been entertained on these points. Suffice it now to say, that . . . eminent teachers in the Church, in the next age to that in which it was written—proclaim that its writer was St. John, the beloved disciple of Christ. Such was *then* the voice of the Church."[25]

The Heretics' Challenge

In addition to the influence of orthodox Asiatic fathers on the eschatological views of future church leaders, Asia Minor became the spawning ground for less-than-orthodox apocalyptic notions as well. Among these were the teachings of the Gnostic Cerinthus, who resided in Ephesus around the turn of the first century. Included in his heretical potpourri of doctrines was the notion that at Christ's second coming a millennium characterized by sensuous pleasures would be established.[26]

In the middle of the second century the heterodox teachings of Montanus[27] precipitated the first substantial opposition to the Apocalypse of John. The views of this newly converted Christian were first enthusiastically embraced in the Phrygian town of Pepuza in southwestern Asia Minor. Montanus, who believed himself to be a prophet of God, claimed divine inspiration for his prophecies. In response to one of his supposed heavenly mandates, Montanus called for his followers to prepare for Christ's second coming by withdrawing from the world. Because Montanus appealed to the book of Revelation for support of his extreme views, Montanism cast a dark shadow of doubt over the book of Revelation.

Revelation and the Third-Century Church

The Premillenarian Proponents

The two most important fathers in the western church in the first half of the third century were Cyprian (ca. 200–258) and Hippolytus (died ca. 236). Cyprian was taught by Tertullian and succeeded him as bishop of Carthage. After studying under Hippolytus, Irenaeus served as a presbyter and teacher in Rome. Both church fathers quoted extensively from the book of Revelation and cited the apostle John as its author.[28]

Early in the third century the ardent anti-Montanist Caius (or Gaius) of Rome rejected both the gospel of John and the Revelation of John. He claimed that both books were written by the heretic Cerinthus. In Caius' summation of Cerinthus' carnal characterization of the millennial kingdom, he charged the heretic with getting his views from "revelations which he *pretends* were written by a great apostle."[29] Caius's rejection of the Johannine authorship of the fourth gospel and Revelation were challenged by Hippolytus in a work no longer extant. That Hippolytus was successful in his rebuke of Caius is seen in the fact that the Johannine authorship of Revelation (and the gospel of John) continued to be upheld in the western church from the beginning of the third century onward.

The earliest extant commentary on the book of Revelation was written by Victorinus (died ca. 304), Latin exegete and bishop of Petau. Victorinus stated that the apostle John wrote the book while "he was in the island of Patmos, condemned to the labour of the mines by Caesar Domitian" and that when he was set free, he "subsequently delivered the same Apocalypse which he had received from God."[30] All three of these fathers of the Western church, Cyprian, Hippolytus, and Victorinus, subscribed to the millenarian doctrine.

The Alexandrian Opponents

The most significant opposition to Revelation, and not surprisingly, to the doctrine of premillennialism, arose in the Eastern church at the end of the second century and beginning of the third. Running concurrently with the trend toward literal interpretation among premillenarian fathers was the rise of the distinctly Christian allegorism of the school of Alexandria. Begun by Pantaenus (died ca. 190), it was carried forward by Clement of Alexandria (ca. 155–ca. 220), Origen (ca. 185–ca. 254), and Dionysius of Alexandria (died ca. 264). The aim of this school was to unite philosophy and revelation. While Clement and Origen both accepted the book of Revelation as the inspired work of the apostle John,[31] Dionysius agreed that it was canonical Scripture, but he denied its apostolic authorship[32] and pointedly attacked the book on that basis.

Whether the Alexandrian fathers regarded John the apostle as the author of Revelation or not, none of them could or would accept the materialistic elements often associated with its teaching, particularly regarding the millennial kingdom. To these leaders in the Eastern church, millennialism was nothing more than a Jewish concept that appealed to Christians' baser sensual appetites rather than to their higher spiritual nature.[33] Consequently Origen became the first church leader of stature to challenge the premillennial orthodoxy of the early church. Dedicated to the allegorical method of interpretation like his mentor, Clement of Alexandria, Origen spiritualized virtually every Christian doctrine. Under Origen's influence, the blessed hope of the Christian apologists—belief in Christ's imminent return to establish His kingdom—began to yield to the "spiritual" hermeneutics of Alexandria.

Dionysius' views on the doctrine of the Millennium and the Revelation of John, according to the church historian Eusebius, were contained in a two-volume work called *On the Promises*.[34] Dionysius was motivated to write these books, Eusebius said, because of the Egyptian bishop Nepos's millenarian teaching "in a more Jewish manner" which included the idea of "bodily luxury upon this earth."[35] In just one of the many expressions of Eusebius' personal bias against millennialism he declared: "As he [Nepos] thought that he could establish his *private opinion* by the Revelation of John, he wrote a book on this subject, entitled Refutation of Allegorists."[36] This work apparently challenged the practice of those like Origen who attempted to explain away the physical earthly elements of the prophecies in Revelation by giving them allegorical or spiritualized meanings. Unfortunately no portion of Nepos's work remains. All we know about this Egyptian church leader and his views are found here in Eusebius, a staunch opponent of the millenarian doctrine.

Dionysius was distressed because Nepos's teaching did "not permit our simpler brethren to have [the] sublime and lofty thoughts concerning the glorious and truly divine appearing of our Lord, and our resurrection from the dead" taught by the allegorists. Instead, Dionysius asserted, simple-minded Christians were being led by millenarians "to hope for small and mortal things in the kingdom of God, and for things such as exist now," an earthly material kingdom instead of a heavenly spiritual one.

Dionysius attempted to refute this error in his *On the Promises*. He reportedly did the same in person while visiting Arsinoe where "this doctrine has prevailed for a long time, so that schisms and apostasies of entire churches have resulted." Dionysius reported that in front of the church leaders from all the surrounding villages he presented a three-day rebuttal of the millenarian doctrine and Nepos's book. The result was that all those present agreed completely with Dionysius' position, and they did so in a most congenial and harmonious manner. Unlike the distress Dionysius experienced over the "simple brethren" who were so easily led astray by the millenarians, on this occasion the Alexandrian bishop was able to rejoice "over the constancy, sincerity, docility, and intelligence of the brethren" with whom he met. More importantly, Coracion (ca. 230–280), Nepos's successor as bishop of Arsinoe and the chief expositor of his millenarian views, was so impressed by Dionysius that he promised "he would no longer hold this opinion, nor discuss it, nor mention nor teach it, as he was fully convinced by the arguments against it."[37]

While Dionysius followed the Alexandrian practice of allegorizing the teachings of Revelation in opposition to the literalistic interpretations of the millenarians, he took the assault against that doctrine one step further by disputing the apostolic authorship of the Apocalypse.[38] Dionysius first stated that "some" earlier writers had completely rejected the book of Revelation, "pronouncing it without sense or argument, and maintaining that the title is fraudulent. For they say that it is not the work of John, nor is it a revelation, because it is covered thickly and densely by a vail of obscurity." After mentioning the view by some that Cerinthus wrote the book, Dionysius admitted that he was unable to completely reject it because "many" others held it "in high esteem."[39]

According to Eusebius, Dionysius examined the book and "proved that it is impossible to understand it according to the literal sense." Therefore one has to look for a "deeper sense" which "lies beneath the words." In spite of Revelation's obscurity in places, Dionysius concluded that its author was "a holy and inspired man" named John, but he could not "readily admit that he was the apostle, the son of Zebedee."[40] Dionysius attempted to prove this theory by pointing out vocabulary, grammatical, and stylistic differences between the book of Revelation and gospel of John, and by alleging errors and discrepancies between the two books.[41] Dionysius' objections have been ably answered by many Bible scholars and linguists.[42]

On the basis of his "private opinion," Dionysius "pretended" to present irrefutable evidence that another John other than the apostle must have written the Apocalypse. This Alexandrian father presumptuously dismissed the Johannine authorship of Revelation even though a majority of the orthodox fathers who preceded him accepted it. From Dionysius onward, some continued to question the apostolic authority and canonicity of the Apocalypse. One of these was Eusebius, noted church historian, bishop of Caesarea, and ardent antimillenarian.[43]

Revelation and the Fourth-Century Church

Eusebius and Papias

Eusebius is significant here because he recorded his estimation of the New Testament canon as it stood in the early part of the fourth century.[44] He classified books then being used as Scripture as "accepted" (e.g., "the Gospels"), "disputed" (e.g., "the so-called epistle of James"), or "rejected" (e.g., "the Acts of Paul"). Eusebius was uncertain, however, as to how to classify the Apocalypse of John. The book was accepted by past fathers and by most of the churches, especially those in the West. However, "some" leaders in the Eastern churches rejected it, and that was the opinion that Eusebius himself held. So he decided to include Revelation in both the "accepted" and "rejected" categories.

> The tradition of the church in the time of Eusebius, the beginning of the fourth century, still wavered between acceptance and rejection [of Revelation]. But of the two oldest manuscripts of the Greek Testament which date from the age of Eusebius and Constantine, one—the Sinaitic—contains all the twenty-seven books [of our present New Testament], and the other—the Vatican—was probably likewise complete, although the last chapters of Hebrews (from 11:14), the Pastoral Epistles, Philemon, and Revelation are lost.[45]

Eusebius followed Dionysius in suggesting that the author of Revelation was not the apostle John, but a "presbyter John" mentioned by Papias.[46] But more than one commentator has suggested that the proposed two Johns were one and the same.[47] Schaff states that it is "more likely that Eusebius misunderstood Papias, and is responsible for a fictitious John, who has introduced so much confusion into the question of the authorship of the Johannean Apocalypse."[48]

Like Dionysius, Eusebius championed an allegorical interpretation of the book of Revelation. He referred to Papias's "apparent" weakness of intellect as evidenced by his "misunderstanding of the apostolic accounts" of the millennial age. The error, he insisted, was due to Papias's failure to perceive "that the things said by them were spoken mystically in figures." Eusebius credited Papias alone with leading Irenaeus and others astray on this point.[49]

A.D. 300 New Testament Used by Eusebius*	A.D. 400 New Testament Fixed for the West by the Council of Carthage
Four Gospels	Four Gospels
Acts	Acts
Paul's letters:	Paul's letters:
Romans	Romans
1 & 2 Corinthians	1 & 2 Corinthians
Galatians	Galatians
Ephesians	Ephesians
Philippians	Philippians
Colossians	Colossians
1 & 2 Thessalonians	1 & 2 Thessalonians
1 & 2 Timothy	1 & 2 Timothy
Titus	Titus
Philemon	Philemon
	Hebrews
	James
1 Peter	1 & 2 Peter
1 John	1, 2, & 3a John
	Jude
Revelation of John (authorship in doubt)	Revelation

Figure 1

---

*From Tim Dowley, ed., *Eerdman's Handbook to the History of Christianity* (Grand Rapids: Eerdmans, 1985), 95. Used by permission.

Not until the middle of the fourth century was the issue of the New Testament canon of Scripture taken up by a church council. The first such council to propose a list was the Council of Laodicea (A.D. 367). Compared to our present New Testament, its twenty-six-book canon excluded only the Revelation of John.

Athanasius and Augustine

Athanasius' Easter Letter to his congregations (A.D. 367)[50] listed the twenty-seven books of our present New Testament. The Athanasian letter generally fixed the canon in the East. However, there were still some who rejected the book of Revelation, most likely because of its teaching on the Millennium.

As the allegorical method gained greater influence in the East, belief in a literal millennial reign of Christ began to wane. The doctrine was virtually dead by the time the literal method of interpretation reached its apex in the school at Antioch. Even though literalism naturally leads to a belief in premillennialism, the doctrine was not discussed by Theodore of Mopsuestia (ca. 350–428), Chrysostom (354–407), or Theodoret (386–458), the Antiochene school's three most prominent teachers.[51]

Perhaps the legalization of Christianity by Constantine, the cessation of persecution brought by his Edict of Milan (313), and a continuing anti-Jewish sentiment, taken together, made it easy for the Antiochene fathers to dismiss the future "Jewish" millennium as fable while embracing the "Christian" empire of Constantine as the eschatological ideal. Interestingly the Apocalypse as the subject of homily or commentary was uniformly ignored by the three chief representatives of the Antiochene school.

The Council of Hippo (393) and the Third Council of Carthage (397), both influenced by Augustine,[52] fixed the New Testament canon in the western churches of Rome, Gaul, Asia Minor, and North Africa. Thus by the end of the fourth century, the book of Revelation was included in all the New Testament canons officially sanctioned by the church councils. When Jerome, at the direction of pope Damascus I, completed his Latin translation of the Old Testament and the twenty-seven books of the New Testament (together known as the Vulgate) in 404, the question of the New Testament canon was settled in the West.

While Augustine accepted the book of Revelation as Scripture, he fell prey to the Alexandrian method of interpretation. Early on, Augustine held millenarian views. But he abandoned that doctrine for the superficial reason that some millenarians had envisioned a kingdom age of unparalleled fruitfulness featuring banquet tables set with excessive amounts of food and drink.[53] He favored instead the position of his contemporary, the Donatist and lay theologian Tyconius,[54] who offered a spiritualized interpretation of the Apocalypse. Proceeding from this position, Augustine articulated an amillennial view in which no future thousand-year earthly millennium was expected.[55]

Augustine's allegorical interpretation of Bible prophecy dominated the understanding of eschatology during the medieval period. It found acceptance also with the Roman church and among the leaders of the Reformation. Even today, Augustinian eschatology is held by large segments of the Christian church.

Revelation from the Fifth Century to the Reformation

In the East, the Syriac church was the slowest to accept the book of Revelation in its canon of New Testament Scripture. Rabbula, elected bishop of Edessa in 411, edited the Peshitta, which became the standard version of the Bible for fifth-century Syriac-speaking Christians. The New Testament consisted of only twenty-two books. The books of 2 Peter, 2 John, 3 John, Jude, and Revelation were excluded. In A.D. 508 the Monophysite theologian Philoxenus revised the Peshitta and included the five missing books. This "Philoxenian revision" represented the fixed state of the Syriac canon.

The Revelation of John finally received official acceptance in the Eastern church at the Third Council of Constantinople (A.D. 680). According to Robert Mounce, "This favorable opinion was due in part to the first Greek commentaries on Revelation, which appeared about the sixth century." The oldest existing Greek commentary on the Apocalypse was authored by Oecumenius, a rhetorician and philosopher. Mounce says, "He held it to be divinely inspired and canonical, relevant for his day as well as important for an understanding of both past and future."[56]

While the Council of Carthage affirmed the New Testament canon of twenty-seven books, there were some isolated incidents involving the status of Revelation. One of these was a canon produced by Nicephorus (ca. 758–829), the patriarch of Constantinople, who listed the Apocalypse as a disputed book. However, Photius, who apparently succeeded Nicephorus, said it was Scripture. Arethas, who wrote a commentary on Revelation in the tenth century, also recognized it as inspired Scripture.[57] According to Guthrie:

> The most significant feature of this whole period was the ecclesiastical monopoly on the interpretation of Scripture, which virtually meant that the canon had ceased to be supported by common usage of the churches, but was buttressed by the hierarchy of the Roman church. It was this approach that led to the condemnation of Tyndale and others who produced Bibles in the language of the people. Authority which had earlier rested in Scripture had now been transferred to the Church. Such was the medieval background against which the opinions of the Reformers on the canon must be considered.[58]

Revelation and the Reformation Church

Erasmus and Luther

The Protestant Reformers were somewhat subjective in their opinions about the New Testament canon, and they were clearly influenced by decisions of former church leaders. When it came to the book of Revelation, unfortunately the negative assessments of earlier leaders carried the most weight. The antimillenarians Dionysius of Alexandria and Eusebius of Caesarea, for example, had regarded the Apocalypse as Scripture but they denied that it was written by the apostle John. Likewise, while the Dutch reformer Desiderius Erasmus, German reformer Martin Luther, and Swiss reformer Ulrich Zwingli were not inclined to excise Revelation from the New Testament canon, they all regarded it as a nonapostolic work. All three did so largely because it teaches a literal thousand-year earthly reign of Christ. Essentially, John Calvin and Luther simply ignored John's Revelation.

The same arguments were put forth by Erasmus and for the same reason. And like Eusebius, who placed Revelation both in the "accepted" category because it was widely recognized by the church as inspired Scripture and among the "rejected" books mainly because he favored the minority who had little use for it,[59] Erasmus, too, experienced a similar conflict. Revelation had official acceptance in the church, but his own personal evaluation rendered a contrary view. Even though Erasmus bowed to ecclesiastical authority on this subject, the fact that he even questioned the Johannine authorship of Revelation earned him condemnation at the Theological Faculty of Paris in 1526.[60]

Martin Luther, unlike Erasmus, gave higher priority to his own personal evaluation than to the official position of the church. For that reason the German Reformer did not hesitate to rearrange his New Testament into sections which reflected his own attitude about the various books. In the front of his New Testament he placed those books he valued most.[61] Another section, which he placed in the back of his Bible, included the New Testament works he felt had relatively little value (Hebrews, James, Jude, and Revelation). With reference to these four books Luther said, "They have from ancient times had a different reputation" and therefore should not be included with the "true and certain chief books of the New Testament."[62] A third division of Luther's Bible contained the books not included in the other two sections.

In reference to Revelation, Luther wrote in 1522 that he could find "no trace" of evidence that the book "was written by the Holy Spirit." In other words, he rejected its divine inspiration. Apparently Luther was merely stating his own personal opinion on this issue without necessarily expecting others to accept it.[63] Some years later Luther offered a somewhat different but qualified evaluation of the Apocalypse of John. "In 1530 [Luther] replaced the completely negative 1522 *Preface to the Revelation of St. John* with another which interprets the book in terms of the history of the church and shows its continuing value for the church. But for the rest of his life, he continued to put a different value on the books which he had put together at the end of his Bible than on the 'main books.'"[64]

Although Cardinal Caietan opposed Luther in 1518 at Augsburg, he shared the Reformer's attitude toward the canon. On Jerome's authority but without the same conclusion, Caietan disputed the canonicity of Hebrews, 2 Peter, 2 and 3 John, and Jude. While Cardinal Caietan accepted Second Peter, he rejected the book of Revelation.[65] Jerome had expressed some ambivalence at times about the Apocalypse, but later he accepted it.

The views of church leaders like Caietan and the Reformers, especially Luther, precipitated the decrees on the canon pronounced by the Council of Trent in 1546. As Guthrie explains:

> There was considerable difference of opinion over the classification of the canonical books, but the importance of the Council lies in its final decisions. For the first time, the Bible became an article of faith of the Church, accompanied by an anathema upon all who questioned any part of it. . . . It is worth noting that in a list of books prepared by Sixtus Senensis, whose opinions were representative of the majority opinion at the Council, a kind of deutero-canon is mentioned, comprising Hebrews, the minor Catholic epistles, the Apocalypse, and three separate passages (Mark 16:9–20; Luke 22:43, 44 and John 7:53–8:11). These books, at first only permitted to be read, came at last to be adopted as Scriptures of indisputable authority. The Church alone, according to this view, had the right to pronounce what is canonical.[66]

Zwingli and Calvin

Among the Swiss reformers, Zwingli seems to have been disinterested in discussing the canon of the New Testament. The only book he apparently excluded from the canon was the Apocalypse. Oecolampadius, while accepting all the New Testament writings, expressed the view that James, 2 Peter, 2 John, 3 John, Jude, and Revelation were inferior to the other books. These again were among the disputed books of earlier centuries.[67]

John Calvin placed greater importance on his own opinion of the New Testament canon than on the opinions of the church fathers. While he believed the testimony of the fathers had value, he did not regard their views as determinative. As for the authorship of the Apocalypse, Calvin suggested John Mark as a good candidate.[68]

The attitude of Calvinistic churches in general toward the book of Revelation was stated by the Westminster Confession composed in 1643. Article three rejected it as canonical Scripture. Today, however, virtually every Bible scholar who accepts the Johannine authorship of Revelation also accepts the book as inspired canonical Scripture. Conversely, belief in the inspiration of Revelation is almost always coupled with an acceptance of the apostle John as the book's author.

Conclusion

Perhaps the best conclusion to the whole question of the canonicity of the last book in our New Testament is set forth by Ned Stonehouse. He writes:

> Particularly in the period beginning with Origen we note an emphasis placed upon the thought that the New Testament, including the *Apocalypse,* was handed down from the church of preceding generations. This factor is closely related to that of apostolicity, for the thought is that these writings were handed down to the fathers by the eye-witnesses and ministers of the Word, as Athanasius expresses it.
>
> The Apocalypse was used and highly regarded as filling an inner need. . . . the church was conscious that in those writings which came from those who had been granted the inestimable privilege of associating with the Lord, and had been chosen by him for a work of abiding significance, satisfied its need far better than any others. For the same reasons the apostolic writings received a place in the cultus not granted to other literature.
>
> But with all our historical investigation we cannot say that the development of the New Testament Canon, and the history of the Apocalypse as a member of it, has been fully explained. For we cannot but recognize that behind and through this historical process there was a guidance of the Spirit of God. There was a higher guarantee than all the historical factors we have mentioned that the church would receive the New Testament writings including the *Apocalypse* as divinely authoritative and worthy of use on a level with the Old Testament Scriptures.[69]

CHAPTER 3

HOW HAS REVELATION BEEN VIEWED INTERPRETIVELY?

MAL COUCH

What Did the Early Jewish Rabbis Think of the Book of Revelation?

AS THE YEARS PASSED FOLLOWING the destruction of the temple in A.D. 70, it seems as if some Jewish rabbis looked with favor on the book of Revelation. Some may dispute this, but the evidence brought out by Jewish scholar Raphael Patai seems to confirm this idea.[1]

Patai shows a great amount of expectation between Jewish prophecy and what is written in Revelation. He writes, "Entirely within the spirit of these Jewish apocalypses (early Jewish writings) is the vision of the heavenly Jerusalem contained in Revelation . . . chapter 21."[2] He adds, "The Book of Revelation was written—in Hebrew, Aramaic, or Greek—late in the first century CE. Its author was a Judeo-Christian, well versed in the Scriptures, who, while he believed in the Messiahship of Jesus (whom he calls 'the Lamb'), expected his return in the Future to Come, and described the heavenly Jerusalem in Jewish apocalyptic . . . terms."[3]

Patai then points out striking details of how early Jewish writings also envisioned the messianic Jerusalem descending from heaven with thousands of towers, fortresses, and pools. Its streets will be covered with stones and jewels, its radiance will light up the entire new world, and it will rise up to God's throne of glory.[4]

The Messiah will cause built-up Jerusalem to descend from heaven, the rabbis write.[5] And though the foundation of this new heavenly Jerusalem will have twelve precious stones (21:19–20), Rabbi Milhamot Melekh haMashiah describes just ten.[6]

Though sometimes confusing the one-thousand-year millennial kingdom blessings with the new, eternal Jerusalem and the new heavens and new earth, the rabbinical authors seem to have borrowed many of their descriptions from the book of Revelation.

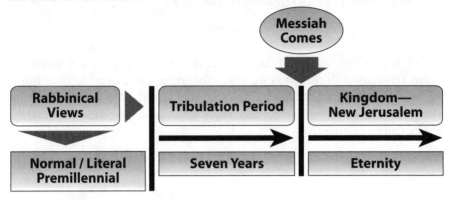

Figure 2

Without doubt, early Jewish rabbis cultivated an appreciation for the book of Revelation and recognized the parallel prophecies that had their genesis in the writings of the ancient prophets. In time, antagonisms would sprout like weeds between Christians and Jews so that any lasting blessing for the rabbinical community from John's apocalyptic writing would be smothered.

How Did the Medieval Church View the Book of Revelation?

Early on, Origen (ca. 185–254) was one of the first church fathers to turn against premillennial thinking. He and Clement of Alexandria were committed to the allegorical method of interpretation. With a "spiritualized" hermeneutic, they turned from the idea of Christ returning to establish His kingdom.

This departure from the literal approach to Bible interpretation drastically affected the interpretation of the book of Revelation in later years. By the time of Augustine (A.D. 354–430) the growing Roman Church was rapidly moving into amillennialism. In fact, in that prophetic view, the church was viewed as the kingdom. Therefore people were not taught to look for a literal millennial reign of Christ ruling on earth from Jerusalem on the throne of David. In fact, beginning in the Middle Ages, "Catholic theologians have argued the church is the kingdom on earth and have taught an amillennial view of the kingdom promises."[7]

Figure 3

To Catholic theologians of the Middle Ages, the descriptions of judgment in the Tribulation (Rev. 6–18) were simply poetic pictures of terrible times that were befalling the church. Some said the "tribulation" events were the Mongol hordes invading Europe, and others said they pictured the rise of Islam and its dangers to the Christian world.

Figure 4

Some pious teachers, however, turned the events of Revelation against the church and charged the pope with being the Antichrist. At best, the book of Revelation, in all of this interpretative darkness, was seen as confusing.

Medieval scholastic theologians also looked for excuses to find Mary, the mother of Jesus, in unsuspecting places. They saw her in Revelation 12, where they envisioned her incorruptibility and bodily transfiguration. Clothed with the sun, that woman, they said, is "the transfigured mother of Christ."[8]

But generally speaking, during the Middle Ages Augustine's views of the kingdom and the book of Revelation dominated. His two cities from his book *City of God,* show an earthly realm in which people lust for domination, and a heavenly city that glories in the Lord. The heavenly city, according to Augustine, is the church and the kingdom.

However, when the Franks came to power in the West, this churchly interpretation of the kingdom of God was made completely political. Charlemagne was the new David who took control of the royal lordship of the church. The pope took the role of Moses, "while remaining himself the sovereign who shared in the reign of Christ and of God."[9]

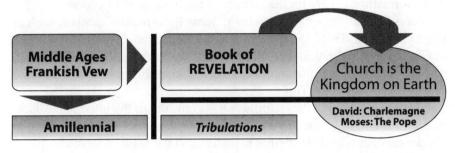

Figure 5

However, many efforts to relate events in the book of Revelation to events of that day came to an end in the early part of the fourteenth century. After the event described below took place, the church became more silent about apocalyptic happenings occurring then.

> Apocalyptic notions were . . . added to the political. The kingdom of the Franks along with that of the Romans was regarded as the "third kingdom" mentioned in the seventh chapter of Daniel, following the kingdoms of the Greeks and the Persians. Thus, the world awaited a last ruler to restore the empire to its glory and lay down his crown in Jerusalem, before the coming of the Antichrist. The most direct opposition to this imperial notion of the Kingdom of God was formulated by Pope Boniface VIII's bull, Unam Sanctam (1303), in which he declared that the pope alone has supreme authority over the whole world.[10]

Most Catholic theologians in the Middle Ages said that the millennial kingdom extended from Christ's first appearance down to the end of the tenth century. This idea greatly affected thousands, who at that time thought Jesus would return. They also expected the speedy coming of the Antichrist and the end of the world.

Since this did not happen, the interpretation was changed. The number one thousand was seen as a symbolic figure denoting an indefinite age.[11]

How Did the Reformers Understand the Book of Revelation?

Luther set a new pattern for interpreting Revelation by regarding the book as a compendium of church history. He said the Antichrist is papal Rome. Almost all the commentaries on Revelation written in the days of the

Reformation held the same view. But John Calvin and others stayed away from the book.

The Catholic approach to Revelation was similar to that of the leaders of the Reformation, except for the identity of the Antichrist, of course!

Others held still other strange views. Some Reformation scholars, such as Hugo Grotius (1583–1645), thought that the Millennium began with the Edict of Constantine in the year 311. Bossuet said the Roman emperor Diocletian was the Antichrist and that the loosing of Satan at the end of the thousand-year period pictured the Turks.

Interestingly, though the Reformers had come out of the interpretive darkness into the light of literal and historical hermeneutics, they still clung to allegorical details in their attempt to understand the book of Revelation.

Basically the Reformers said Revelation gives a symbolic presentation of all church history, ending with the second advent of Christ. This led to what later came to be known as postmillennialism, or the historical approach. This view gained popularity because it identified the pope and the papacy with the beasts of Revelation 13.

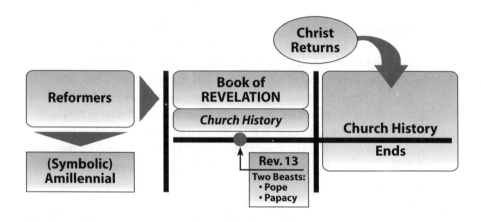

Figure 6

Included among those who held this view were John Wycliffe, Martin Luther, Joseph Mede, Isaac Newton, William Whiston, Charles Elliott, Johann Bengel, and others. These scholars' interpretations focused so tightly on their own generation that the events in the book of Revelation kept coming to a dead end in their own day.

By mixing the current history of their times, symbolism, and allegorical interpretation into a nonsystematic approach to prophecy, Revelation became impossible to expound plainly. As Walvoord writes:

As many as fifty different interpretations of the book of Revelation therefore evolve[d], depending on the time and circumstances of the expositor. . . . The very multiplicity of such interpretations and identifications of the personnel of Revelation with a variety of historical characters is its own refutation. If the historical method is the correct one, it is clear until now that no one has found the key.[12]

How Did Dispensationalists View the Book of Revelation?

For generations, Bible scholars had observed various dispensations outlined in Scripture. Working from a literal and grammatical approach, they let the Word of God explain itself. But still coming out of the post-Reformation period, their observations were sometimes mixed with the thinking of some of the Reformed writers. English scholars such as John Edwards (1637–1716) and Isaac Watts (1674–1748) outlined the Scriptures dispensationally.

But it was not until Englishman John Nelson Darby (1800–1882) began promoting and systematizing dispensationalism that a true system emerged that tied the entire Bible together.

Trained as a lawyer, Darby had a keen and observant mind. But he abandoned law and became a minister with the Church of England. Because he could explain the Word of God so clearly, it was said that at one time between six hundred and eight hundred Catholics were coming to Christ every week.

Is dispensationalism just another scheme of things, a new interpretation that is simply a novel competitive approach that has its own strange twist on the Bible message? Not at all!

Dispensationalism is actually built on the idea of letting the Bible speak for itself with a normal, literal hermeneutic. If simple rules of grammar and observation are put into place, the Scriptures will begin to make sense, from Genesis to Revelation.

Though Darby became a Plymouth Brethren, his noncomplicated approach to making the Bible clear spread throughout England and then to America. Some of the best Bible teachers adopted this clear and simple approach to studying the different periods of biblical history. Now the Word of God, and especially the prophetic books, began to make sense. And this certainly included the "mysterious" final book of the New Testament.

With such a literal viewpoint making the Bible so much more understandable, Revelation started to make sense also.

Toward the end of the nineteenth century the persecuted Jewish people of Eastern Europe clamored to build a safe homeland for themselves in Palestine. This desire began to fire even more the imagination of students of the Scriptures. In all other schemes of interpretation the Jews were the missing link in trying to grasp an end-times scenario.

In most of the historic and postmillennial systems current events were "forced" into the book of Revelation in a vain attempt to make the book "work." But not with dispensationalism. Of special interest was the actual return of Israel to her promised land.

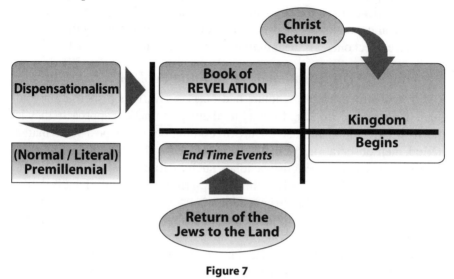

Figure 7

Dispensationalists take a futurist approach to Revelation. They are in good company with orthodox Judaism and also with the early church. This is the only approach that makes sense. Thomas, a dispensationalist, points out:

> The futurist approach to the book is the only one that grants sufficient recognition to the prophetic style of the book and a normal hermeneutical pattern of interpretation based on that style. It views the book as focusing on the last periods of world history and outlining the various events and their relationships to one another. This is the view that best accords with the principle of literal interpretation. The literal interpretation of Revelation is the one generally associated with the premillennial return of Christ and a view of inspiration that understands God to be the real author of every book of the Bible.[13]

What Is the Modern or Liberal View of the Book of Revelation?

The post-Reformation period was followed by a hard, cold rationalism and a critical spirit toward the Bible. This was especially true in Europe, where German thought dominated and ultimately destroyed trust in the Scriptures. Some critics held that Revelation portrayed various events in church history and contained numerous instances of numerology.

The critic Johann Semler held that the book was typical of Jewish millennial fanaticism. And the mention of Gog and Magog in Revelation 20:8 was the Jewish Bar Kochba revolt of A.D. 135. Others said Revelation is only a picture book of Christ's future kingdom. Still others wrote that it is a Greek drama.

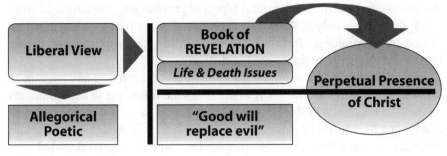

Figure 8

These views spread to North America toward the end of the nineteenth century, but they were modified and toned down somewhat for American churchgoers. *Ellicott's Commentary on the Whole Bible,* though sound in so many ways, reflects a liberal point of view, certainly on Revelation. The contributors often turn the difficult into poetry to explain away the obvious.

On Revelation, Carpenter wrote the following in *Ellicott's Commentary:*

> The "coming of Christ," viewed from the human side, is a picture which is not always to be held to one meaning; it is, in this aspect, analogous to the "Kingdom of God." Holy Scripture, beyond all doubt, recognizes potential and spiritual, as well as personal, "comings" of the Lord. There are many comings of Christ. Christ came in the flesh as a mediatorial Presence. Christ came at the destruction of Jerusalem. Christ came, a spiritual Presence, when the Holy Ghost was given. Christ comes now in every signal manifestation of redeeming power. Any great reformation of morals and religion is a coming of Christ. A great revolution, like a thunderstorm, violently sweeping away evil to make way for the good, is a coming of Christ.[14]

In his one-volume commentary on the Bible, J. R. Dummelow promotes the liberal view of Revelation in a similar way.[15] He writes that the purpose of Revelation is mainly to assure the perpetual presence of Christ for believers in their trials and difficulties. Being under persecution, the Christians were shown how to brace themselves and to endure. He says that Revelation dealt with life-and-death issues of those days in which it was penned.

The book gives "symbolical representations of good and evil principles, common to every age, and [is] to be understood spiritually."[16] It was written as a "secret" book "meant to be intelligible by those [only] to whom it was addressed, and would have arisen out of the circumstances of their state."[17]

One might call this an escapist approach to interpreting Revelation because it seeks to get rid of the supernatural aspect of prophesying the future. In other words the book is only a "naturalistic" rehearsal of the past couched in poetic or allegorical language. Revelation then is simply for the purpose of giving comfort to the godly in their times of difficulty.

Liberals today hold a similar view of Revelation, rejecting any attempt to espouse a futurist view. One such writer states the following in her comments on the four horsemen in Revelation 6: "The four horsemen of the Apocalypse ride among us, confronting us every day of the world. Thus is this text relevant for today, not as a book of secret prophecies that can only be decoded by a select group of alarmist paranoids, but as a constant reminder that the Divine is attentive to what we do and how we are with one another."[18]

CHAPTER 4

INTERPRETING THE BOOK OF REVELATION

MAL COUCH

MANY PEOPLE STILL WANT TO relegate this incredible book of prophecy to the junk heap of jumbled mysticism, designate it as a strange symbolic allegory of church persecution, or view it as a mysterious prophecy that has somehow already been fulfilled.

Even the world speaks of Armageddon, shuddering at the book's descriptions of future terror to come, and even those most skeptical of the book know of the "four horsemen of the Apocalypse."

Of course Revelation does require effort to understand its meaning. Yet many theologians still refuse to believe that God can predict the future through prophets like John. This chapter presents a brief history of various views on Revelation to illustrate how its interpretation has fared through the centuries.

The Interpretation of the Book of Revelation

C. I. Scofield observed that, as we near the time when the events recorded in the book of Revelation will occur, the things prophesied in it will become clearer. Most premillennialists would certainly agree. And most premillennialists hold to a futurist position, whether they understand the details of the predictions or not. But premillennialism has not been the dominant view in understanding Revelation. The amillennial view has dominated the history of the interpretation of the book, though this was not the view of the early church.

The Second and Third Centuries

Lange and Walvoord give a short history of how the book has been interpreted through the centuries.

Walvoord notes, "The second century like the first bears a sustained testimony to the premillennial character of the early church. Even the amillenarians claim no adherents whatever by name to their position in the second century except in the allegorizing school of interpretation which arose at the very close of the second century."[1]

Walvoord then adds, "Justin Martyr (100–168) is quite outspoken. He wrote: 'But I and whatsoever Christians are orthodox in all things do know that there will be a resurrection of the flesh, and a thousand years in the city of Jerusalem, built adorned, and enlarged, according as Ezekiel, Isaiah, and other prophets have promised.'"[2] Quoting *Herzog's Cyclopaedia,* Walvoord said, "Chiliasm constituted in the sec[ond] century so decidedly an article of faith that Justin held it up as a criterion of perfect orthodoxy."[3]

Then Walvoord observed the following about chiliasm in the third century: "The third century had its own continued witness to premillennialism, however. Among those who can be cited are Cyprian (200–258), Commodian (200–270), Nepos (230–280), Coracion (230–280), Victorinus (240–303), Methodius (250–311), and Lactantius (240–330). . . . Nepos early recognized the heretical tendencies of the Alexandrian school of theology, which was the first effective opponent of premillennialism, and he attacked it with vigor."[4]

From the "Old Catholic" Era to Gregory the Great (400–604)

Lange states that many people in these years "placed the time of the Millennial Kingdom in the period intervening between the first Coming of Christ in the flesh and the coming of Antichrist."[5] "Jerome interprets allegorically, e.g., he makes the Holy City denote the present world."[6] "Cassiodorus also reckoned the Millennial Kingdom from the birth of Christ; he held the first Resurrection to be significant of Baptism."[7]

From Gregory the Great to Innocent III (604–1216)

In the Middle Ages many people were certain that the events recorded in Revelation would begin in the year 1000, assuming that the millennial kingdom began at the first coming of Christ. Christians expected the Antichrist to come soon and that then the world would end. When the world did not come to an end in the year 1000, they modified their views and said the number 1,000 is a symbolic number, denoting an indefinite period of time. This was a historico-allegorical interpretation.[8]

From Innocent III to the Reformation (1216–1517)

Innocent III (1160–1216) said that Islam was the Antichrist and that Mohammed was the False Prophet. Pope Gregory IX (ca. 1145–1241) said Frederick II, the Holy Roman emperor (1194–1250), was the beast of the abyss, and Frederick retorted by applying the same appellation to the pope.

Joachim (ca. 1135–1262) said Rome is the carnal church and the new Babylon. Dante (1265–1321) said the papacy was anti-Christian. Nicholas of Lyra (ca. 1270–1340) regarded Revelation as a prophetic mirror of all of history.

The Reformation Era

In the Reformation era some thought the thousand years were past, whereas others said the thousand years had just dawned. Many felt Revelation was a prophetic compendium of church history and that it was a settled issue to interpret papal Rome as the Antichrist. Luther arranged the facts of Revelation to fit his view of church history. He said the thousand years extended from the time of the writing of Revelation to Gregory VII (ca. 1015–1085). Bossuet applied the number 666 to Diocletian, and he said the loosing of Satan at the end of the thousand years referred to the Turks.

The Eighteenth Century

In post-Reformation days many continued to see Rome as the Antichrist. William Whiston (1667–1752) felt Christ's coming would take place in 1715, and then later he said 1766. Isaac Newton (1642–1727) said that since Revelation was written during Nero's time the events in Revelation 12 had already come to pass.

Historico-Critical Period

With the influence of German rationalism, the true meaning of the Apocalypse was nearly destroyed. Johann Semler (1725–1791) thought the book presented Jewish chiliastic fanaticism. Others felt it represented enthusiastic idealization and/or Oriental figurative language. Others looked at the book as a novel, a poem, or some kind of illustration of the fall of Judaism.

Modern Times

Ernst Hengstenberg (1802–1869) felt the millennial kingdom had somehow come and gone. But during this period four ways of interpreting Revelation arose.

1. In the preterest view the prophecies in the Apocalypse were fulfilled in the early days of the church.
2. In the "continuist" or historical view Revelation is seen as presenting a symbolic view of church history. This was held by Martin Luther, Isaac Newton, Elliott, and others.
3. In the simple futurist view Revelation 4–22 present events that are yet future.
4. In what may be called the "extreme futurist" view, all of Revelation, including even chapters 1–3, are yet to be fulfilled.

What features of the book can help us understand how Revelation is to be interpreted? Does the book itself give us clues as to how to approach the message?

Literal or Symbolic?

Is Revelation to be interpreted literally or symbolically? From the Jewish and Christian premillennial perspective, Revelation is to be interpreted from a *literal* base but with the understanding that the book also includes *comparative language* that points to literal meanings.

Two Greek words that introduce comparative language are *hōs* and *homoios*. Both can be translated "like, as, likewise, it seemed to be, something like." *Hōs* is used almost seventy times in Revelation and more than four hundred times elsewhere in the New Testament. *Homoios* is used twenty-one times in the Apocalypse and twenty-four times in the rest of the New Testament.

In many of John's visions he was no doubt struggling to describe what he saw. Being spiritually transported into the future, he witnessed things and observed events he had never seen before. Take, for example, Revelation 8:8–9: "And the second angel sounded, and something like a great mountain burning with fire was thrown into the sea; and a third of the sea became blood; and a third of the creatures, which were in the sea and had life, died; and a third of the ships were destroyed."

When John wrote "'something like' [Greek, *hōs*] a great mountain burning . . . thrown into the sea," was he referring to an atomic cloud that boiled up into the atmosphere but then disintegrated into hot ash, rock, and dust as a massive gaseous fallout? Studying atomic mushroom clouds, one could see this possibility. Without doubt, when this great mountain or cloud falls on the sea, deadly pollution will follow. But what about the blood? The verse does *not* say the sea "became like" blood. Did it then actually become blood? No, because common sense comes into play, as in Exodus 7:17 when God said the Nile River would "become blood." Anyone reading these descriptions would understand the concept of pollution and would not be expecting the waters actually to become hemoglobin. But the literalness of pollution is retained, because in Revelation 8:9 sea creatures will die and ships will be destroyed. Unless otherwise indicated, literal interpretation should be accepted, with the understanding that comparative language may also be used.[9]

The Difficulty of Symbols

The best way to interpret symbols is to note the immediate context in which symbols are found.[10] In Revelation 1:12 the seven lampstands are explained in the context: They are churches (v. 20). In 20:2 "the dragon, that old serpent" is immediately identified as the "Devil and Satan." "Sodom and Egypt" in 11:8 are identified as the city "where also our Lord was crucified," that is, Jerusalem. And the star that fell from heaven (9:1) is identified as a personal being (v. 2).[11]

> It must be noted that not every word-picture in prophecy is a symbol. Many of these are plain, everyday figures of speech. When the angel in Revelation 19 invites the fowls to "the supper of the great God," figurative language is used. When Isaiah exclaims that "in the last days, the mountain of the Lord's house shall be established in the top of the mountains . . . and all nations shall flow unto it" (Isa. 2:23), the prophecy is not a symbol of the Christian church and world evangelization. The prophet Isaiah is using figurative language to describe the glory of the Jerusalem temple at the millennium.[12]

Milligan demonstrates how far amillennialists go in denying any literal sense in Revelation.

> One of the great lessons of the Apocalypse consists in this, that it unfolds such a *bright view, not of a world beyond the grave, but of this present world,* when we contemplate it with the eye of faith. . . . It may be doubted if in this respect there is one single picture of the Apocalypse applicable only to the future inheritance of the saints. What is set forth in its apparent visions of future happiness is rather the *present privilege of believers.*[13]

If one were on a desert island and read Revelation for the first time, how would he normally interpret the book? The answer would be "actual and literal," unless there was an amillennialist and allegorist around to say, "No, no, these events are not real! They have some hidden meaning that no one is sure of, but don't let that bother you!" The literal meaning, with comparative language, must be accepted unless there are other indicators that require that one read the verses some other way. Many Bible scholars look at the Apocalypse through the confusing system of interpretation called *allegorical interpretation.* The well-known *Ellicott's Commentary on the Whole Bible,* in its introductory remarks on Revelation, is an example of the allegorical approach. For example, W. Boyd Carpenter wrote,

> We are disposed to view the Apocalypse as the pictorial unfolding of great principles in constant conflict, though under various forms. The Praeterist may, then, be right in finding early fulfillments, and the Futurist in expecting undeveloped ones, and the Historical interpreter is unquestionably right in looking for them along the whole

line of history; for the words of God mean more than one man, or one school of thought, can compass. There are depths of truth unexplored which sleep beneath the simplest sentences. Just as we want to say that history repeats itself, so the predictions of the Bible are not exhausted in one or even in many fulfillments. Each prophecy is a single key which unlocks many doors, and the grand and stately drama of the Apocalypse has been played out perchance in one age to be repeated in the next. Its majestic and mysterious teachings indicate the features of a struggle which, be the stage the human soul, with its fluctuations of doubt and fear, of hope and love—or the progress of kingdoms—or the destinies of the world, is the same struggle in all.[14]

Nothing could be more unclear than to write, "for the words of God mean more than one man, or one school of thought, can compass." Without question, the spiritual depth of the Word of God can't be plumbed, and we're always comprehending more because of personal growth and increased Bible study; but Carpenter's statement implies that the Scriptures have hidden meanings. It implies that in each passage the Spirit of God had more than one message to give, messages that are secretly tucked away "behind" the words.

The second coming of Christ is a major theme in the book of Revelation. But Carpenter all but destroys this great historic truth.

The "coming of Christ," viewed from the human side, is a phrase which is not always to be held to one meaning: it is, in this aspect, analogous to the "Kingdom of God." Holy Scripture, beyond all doubt, recognizes potential and spiritual, as well as personal, "comings" of the Lord. There are many comings of Christ. Christ came in the flesh as a mediatorial Presence. Christ came at the destruction of Jerusalem. Christ came, a spiritual Presence, when the Holy Ghost was given. Christ comes now in every signal manifestation of redeeming power. Any great reformation of morals and religion is a coming of Christ. A great revolution, like a thunderstorm, violently sweeping away evil to make way for the good, is a coming of Christ.[15]

Although all allegorical interpreters may not be quite this confused, most of them still throw up their hands after attempting to explain the clear meaning of verses in Revelation.

Of course, both amillennialists and premillennialists may have difficulty grasping the meaning of a specific passage in Revelation, but amillennialists tend to allegorize the verses and to find spiritual, hidden meanings in the words.

Premillennialists, however, admit facing difficulty in understanding that same specific passage, but they seek to find the one intended meaning by means of a consistent hermeneutic.

LaHaye urges students of Revelation to start at the base—with literal interpretation. "When the plain sense of Scripture makes common sense, seek no other sense; therefore, take every word at its primary, ordinary, usual, literal meaning unless the facts of the immediate text, studied in the light of related passages and axiomatic and fundamental truths, clearly indicate otherwise. This rule . . . provides basic guidelines for properly interpreting the many signs and symbols in the book."[16]

Ellicott's Commentary concludes its "Introduction to Revelation" with these statements: "Jerusalem stands as the type of the good cause" and thus is "the Church of Christ. . . . We are thus taught, in this ever-deepening spirituality of the book, to look beneath the phenomena, to trace the subtle and unmasked principles which are at work. . . . The book of Revelation becomes the unfolding of a dream which is from God. [The book] is not meant to be a treasure-house of marvels for the prophetical archaeologist: it is a book of living principles."[17]

Why can't Revelation be a treasure house for the prophetical archaeologist if it is indeed a book of prophecy? Can't God write prophecy? Can't He give us the plan of the ages?

Some amillenarians say that John wrote Revelation in order to make martyrdom more attractive for early-church Christians. This view is propounded by Martin Rist in *The Interpreter's Bible*. He says Revelation was written "to sharpen the alternatives open to the Christians, of worshiping either Caesar or God, of being completely loyal to the state or wholly devoted to Christianity. Furthermore, he endeavored to make martyrdom, with its eternal rewards, so attractive, and worship of the emperor, with its eternal punishments, so fearsome, that his readers would quite willingly accept death as martyrs rather than be disloyal to Almighty God and his Christ by worshiping Rome and the emperors."[18]

Were the Early Church Fathers Premillennial?

Did the early church fathers view the Tribulation and the return of Christ as literal events? Were they still looking for His return even after A.D. 70 and the destruction of the temple in Jerusalem?

Lindsey lists several beliefs that were common among the early church fathers. (1) They believed that Israel was yet to be redeemed as a nation and would experience God's unconditional promises for her in the messianic kingdom. They held that the Second Coming would introduce God's kingdom on earth and that it would last a thousand years. (2) They believed that Christ could come anytime. (3) They believed the Tribulation, a time of great world distress, was yet future and would precede the Lord's second coming. (4) They believed that the Antichrist would appear during the Tribulation period. (5) They still held these views long after the destruction of Jerusalem in A.D. 70 and on into the fourth century.[19]

Lindsey adds, "These . . . prophetic views caused the early Christians to recognize the Jews as a chosen people to whom God will yet fulfill His promises. These views also promoted a compassion for the Jews because the Christians saw them as a demonstration of God's faithfulness to His Word."[20]

When Was Revelation Written?

The debate on how to interpret the Apocalypse turns on the dating of Revelation. Most, if not all, premillennialists hold that the book was written in A.D. 95 or 96, while many amillennialists place the date before A.D. 70 in order to say that certain events in the book predict the destruction of Jerusalem. However, the existence of the seven churches of Asia Minor (Rev. 2–3) clearly supports the late date. But Carpenter disagrees:

> The advocates of the later date rely much upon the degenerate state of the Asiatic churches, as described in the Epistles to the Seven Churches. The Epistles to the Ephesians, Colossians, and Philemon were written during the captivity of St. Paul at Rome, about the year A.D. 63. If, then, the Apocalypse was written in A.D. 69 or 70, we have only an interval of six or seven years to account for a striking change in the spiritual condition of the Asiatic churches. Can we believe that a Church which is so forward in love as that of Ephesus (Eph. iii.18) can have in so short a time left its first love? Can it be believed that the Laodicean Church—whose spiritual condition in A.D. 63 can be inferred from that of Colossae (Col. i.3, 4)— can have, in six brief years, forsaken their "faith in Christ Jesus and their love to all the saints," and become the "lukewarm" church (Rev. iii.15, 16) of the Apocalypse?[21]

Another argument given against the late date of the book, as Carpenter mentioned, is that the city of Laodicea was destroyed by an earthquake in A.D. 17 in the reign of Tiberius (A.D. 14–37) and again in A.D. 60 when Nero was emperor (A.D. 54–68). Therefore, it is argued, the city could not have been mentioned in Revelation if the book was written in A.D. 96. But as Unger points out, "the affluence of the city enabled its citizens to rebuild without help from Rome or the provincial government."[22] If the book was written in A.D. 96, over thirty years would have passed, whereby a thriving metropolis would have been reestablished with a wealthy but spiritually blind church in its place. Theodore Zahn, a respected New Testament scholar, affirms the date for Revelation. "The correctness of the date is also confirmed by all those traditions which refer the exile of John upon Patmos to his extreme old age, or which describe Revelation as the latest, or one of the latest, writings in the NT. On the other hand, all the differing views as to the date of the composition of Revelation to be found in the literature of the Church are so late and so manifestly confused, that they do not deserve the name of tradition."[23]

Most Bible scholars would agree that the church father Papias was wrong when he wrote that John was killed before A.D. 70. Clement of Alexandria (ca. 156–220) and Eusebius (ca. 260–390), on the other hand, both make the point that on Patmos John penned the Revelation around A.D. 96.

Even the renowned church historian Philip Schaff, an amillennialist, accepts the later dating of the writing of Revelation. "The traditional date of composition at the end of Domitian's reign (95–96) rests on the clear and weighty testimony of Irenaeus, is confirmed by Eusebius and Jerome, and has still its learned defenders."[24]

Other writers attempt to side-step the A.D. 96 dating by denying that the apostle John is the author. As Walvoord notes; "It is most significant that in many cases the theological bias against the chiliastic teaching of the book of Revelation seems to be the actual motive in rejecting the apostolic authorship [and the late dating] of the book."[25] Robertson agrees with the later date for the authorship of Revelation.

> The writer calls himself John (1:1, 4, 9; 22:8). . . . The traditional and obvious way to understand the name is the Apostle John. . . . Irenaeus represents the Apostle John as having lived to the time of Trajan, at least to A.D. 98. Most ancient writers agree with this extreme old age of John. Justin Martyr states expressly that the Apostle John wrote the Apocalypse. Irenaeus called it the work of a disciple of John. . . . On the basis of . . . slim evidence some today argue that John did not live to the end of the century and so did not write any of the Johannine books. But a respectable number of modern scholars still hold to the ancient view that the Apocalypse of John is the work of the Apostle and Beloved Disciple, the son of Zebedee.[26]

The testimony of the early church father Irenaeus is most significant in establishing the book's date and authorship.

> The later date was that which was accepted almost uniformly by the older theologians. In favor of this early tradition has been appealed to. The most important witness (in some respects) is Irenaeus, who says that "the Apocalypse was seen not long ago, but almost

in our own age, towards the end of the reign of Domitian." Other writers have been claimed as giving a support to this view by their mention of Patmos as the place of St. John's banishment; and it is plain from the way in which Eusebius quotes the mention of the Patmos exile by Clement of Alexandria, that he associated it with the reign of Domitian.[27]

Concerning Irenaeus, Lindsey observes; "Irenaeus was from Asia Minor, the region of the Apostle John's last ministry. He was discipled in the area around Ephesus where the Apostle John spent his last years. . . . the great Polycarp, trained by the Apostle John himself, was Irenaeus' spiritual mentor. So there was only one generation between Irenaeus and John. Therefore the quality of his evidence is as strong and reliable as any we have for any book of the New Testament."[28]

Lindsey also points out that Irenaeus was considered a careful scholar and defender of the faith. His answers against the Gnostics did much to halt the influence of this mystic heresy. In addition, because of his fair treatment of the Gnostics, "it is ludicrous to reason that Irenaeus would be less careful and accurate with facts about the book of Revelation which he held to be the Word of God."[29]

The majority of the early church fathers believed Revelation was written after the fall of Jerusalem. They looked for the events recorded in Revelation to take place beyond their own times. Schaff summarizes the premillennial view of many early church fathers.

> The most striking point in the eschatology of the ante-Nicene age is the prominent chiliasm, or millennarianism, that is the belief of a visible reign of Christ in glory on earth with the risen saints for a thousand years, before the general resurrection and judgment. It was indeed not the doctrine of the church embodied in any creed or form of devotion, but a widely current opinion of distinguished teachers, such as Barnabas, Papias, Justin Martyr, Irenaeus, Tertullian, Methodius, and Lactanius.[30]

However, Schaff reveals his bias for the preterist view of Revelation and against the futurist view when he says, "The Christian chiliasm [of the early church] is the Jewish chiliasm spiritualized and fixed upon the second, instead of the first, coming of Christ."[31] But to say that Christian millennialism is Jewish chiliasm *spiritualized* is not defensible because both Jews and Christians look forward to the Messiah's literal reign on the earth.

Figure 9

The preterist ("The Past") view holds that John was referring to events of his own day, about A.D. 96. This requires mental gymnastics that are quite unnecessary if one would apply the Golden Rule of Interpretation. The Roman emperors Nero or Domitian could scarcely fulfill the requirements of this book for the Antichrist.

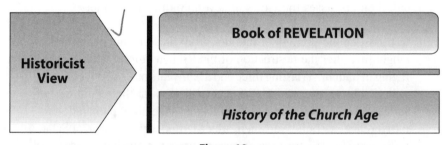

Figure 10

This historicist view suggests that John was describing major events that would take place during the history of the Church. It therefore suggests that we can see these events as we look back at history. This, of course, calls for the juggling of historical events to fit the prophecy. This is historically unsound and tends to distort the plain meaning.

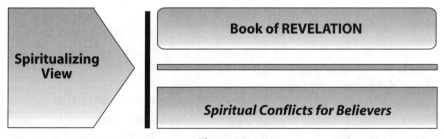

Figure 11

There are those who believe everything in the book should be taken figuratively or metaphorically, that John was talking about a spiritual conflict and not a physical experience. This view is held by most amillennialists and postmillennialists.

Schaff continues:

> Justin Martyr represents the transition from the Jewish Christian
> to the Gentile Christian chiliasm. He speaks repeatedly of the
> second parousia of Christ in the clouds of heaven, surrounded by
> the holy angels. It will be preceded by the near manifestation of
> the man of sin . . . who speaks blasphemies against the most high
> God, and will rule three and a half years. He is preceded by her-
> esies and false prophets. Christ will then raise the patriarchs,
> prophets, and pious Jews, establish the millennium, restore Jerusa-
> lem, and reign there in the midst of his saints; after which the
> second and general resurrection and judgment of the world will
> take place. He regarded this expectation of the earthly perfection
> of Christ's kingdom as the key-stone of pure doctrine.[32]

Schaff then discusses the views of several more early fathers:

> Irenaeus, on the strength of tradition from St. John and his disciples,
> taught that after the destruction of the Roman empire, and the brief
> raging of antichrist (lasting three and a half years or 1260 days), Christ
> will visibly appear, will bind Satan, will reign at the rebuilt city of
> Jerusalem . . . will celebrate the millennial sabbath of preparation for
> the eternal glory of heaven; then, after a temporary liberation of Satan,
> follows the final victory, the *general* resurrection, the judgment of the
> world, and the consummation in the new heavens and the new earth.
> [This is virtually what premillennialists teach today about the book of
> Revelation. It would seem as if they are in good company with the
> most outstanding teachers among the early fathers.]
>   Tertullian was an enthusiastic Chiliast. . . . After Tertullian . . .
> chiliasm was taught by Commodian toward the close of the third
> century, Lactanius, and Victorinus of Petau, at the beginning of the
> fourth. Its last distinguished advocates in the East were Methodius
> (d., a martyr, 311), the opponent of Origen, and Apollinaris of
> Laodicea in Syria.[33]

√ The Great Departure to Allegorical Amillennialism

What brought about the great departure from a literal, millennial position?
What led to the allegorical, mystical, and nonliteral interpretation of Scripture?
How did church leaders turn toward allegorizing the Scriptures, when most
early church fathers held to normal, literal interpretation? The story of
allegorical interpretation is fascinating, and this approach to the Bible has
strongly impacted the way many people view the book of Revelation.

In the sixth century B.C., the Greek philosopher Xenophanes denounced Homer's humanizing depiction of the Greek gods. In Homer's writings the gods were too human-like, even to the point of being licentious. Later Plato (ca. 428–347) and others began to interpret the deities' blatant hedonism symbolically or allegorically in an effort to make the gods less embarrassing and more readily acceptable. For example, Heraclitus (ca. 540–480) explained the bedroom scandals of the goddess Aphrodite by allegories. By viewing the stories of the gods simply as symbolic, children could again read their escapades.

Since Gentiles were critical of some of the frank statements in the Old Testament, Jewish rabbis in Alexandria, Egypt, began reinterpreting the Old Testament by means of allegories. This softened the harshness of the literal Law to make it more palatable to swallow. Origen (ca. A.D. 185–254), raised in Alexandria, could not help but absorb these cultural literary patterns around him.

Origen, more than anyone else, helped make allegorizing the key method of interpreting the Bible—a view that continued for more than 1,300 years into the Middle Ages. Trigg explains Origen's approach to the Bible.

> Origen's understanding of biblical inspiration was entirely consistent with a rigorously critical approach to the text. If the Bible is inspired by God but appears in places to be irrelevant to our condition, unworthy of God, or simply banal, we may take it for granted that we have failed to grasp its inner sense. If no spiritual significance is apparent on the surface, we must conclude that this surface meaning, which may or may not be factual, is intended symbolically. . . . It took no genius to recognize that such allegory was a desperate effort to avoid the plain meaning of the text, and that, indeed, is how Origen viewed it.[34]

For example, Origen tried to restate the conquest of Canaan as "Christ's conquest of the fallen human soul."[35] On interpreting the Old Testament as a whole, he saw Christ and the individual soul on every page. On the Lord's Prayer, Origen saw the hallowing of God's name and the coming of God's kingdom as referring to the believer's gradual sanctification. "We pray that God's name may be hallowed in our good works and that God's kingdom may come in our well-ordered life. There is not the slightest trace of apocalyptic eschatology, the notion that Christ will in fact reappear to establish God's reign on earth, in Origen's understanding of the kingdom of God."[36]

Trigg gives a clear explanation of Origen's allegorical scheme of interpretation and its watering down of the prophecies of the New Testament.

One of the most interesting features of the *Commentary on Matthew* [by Origen] is its tendency to psychologize the Gospel's apocalyptic eschatological imagery. Thus, when the Gospel predicts that Christ will come "on the clouds of heaven with power and great glory" (Matt. 24:30), it refers to his appearance to the perfect [or mature] in their reading of the Bible. Likewise, the two comings of Christ, the first in humility and the second in glory, symbolize Christ's coming in the souls of the simple when they receive the rudiments of Christian doctrine and his coming in[to] the perfect [the mature] when they find him in the hidden meanings of the Bible. The trials and tribulations the world must endure before the second coming symbolize the difficulties the soul must overcome before it is worthy of union with the Logos. The imminence of the second coming refers to the imminent possibility, for each individual, of death. Perhaps more radically, the two men laboring in a field, one of whom is taken and the other left when the Messiah comes (Matt. 24:40), represent good and bad influences on a person's will, which fare differently when the Logos is revealed to that person. Although Origen did not openly deny the vivid apocalyptic expectations such passages originally expressed and *still did for many Christians,* he tended by psychologizing them to make them irrelevant. Although that was far from Origen's intention, *the outcome of his work was to make the church feel distinctly more at home in the world.*[37]

Though not directly denying prophecy, Origen, by "rewriting the script" and ignoring future prophesied events, destroyed the truth intended by the passage.

A Sensual Millennium

As he described it in his *De Principiis,* Origen held a very sensuous idea of the millennial kingdom with numerous "marriages and luxuriant feasts." This sensual approach to the one-thousand-year reign of Christ caused many Christians to react against literal millennialism.

Though he is called "the father of critical investigation," Origen dealt the church a great blow with his allegorical teachings. When this system was fully developed by Augustine (354–430) the book of Revelation fell back into a darkness that persists among many even today. The door was shut on this most profound inspired prophetic work. It could well be argued that Satan is delighted to influence people to ignore the coming Tribulation, millennial reign, and judgment. Amillennialist Schaff is fair when he describes the great hermeneutical failings of Origen.

His great defect is the neglect of the grammatical and historical sense and his constant desire to find a hidden mystic meaning. He even goes further in this direction than the Gnostics, who everywhere saw transcendental, unfathomable mysteries. His hermeneutical principle assumes a threefold sense—somatic, psychic, and pneumatic; or literal, moral, and spiritual. His allegorical interpretation is ingenious, but often runs far away from the text and degenerates into the merest caprice.[38]

In the church in Alexandria, Egypt, a new school of interpretation was developed along the lines of pagan and "liberal" Judaism. Mounce explains:

In the Alexandrian church a spiritualizing approach was developing due in part to the influence of Greek thought, the fact that centuries had passed without the establishment of the awaited kingdom, and in reaction to the excessive chiliasm of the Montanist movement. Origen played a major role in the rise of an allegorical method of exegesis. The mysteries of the Apocalypse can be learned only by going beyond the literal and historical to the spiritual. The spiritualizing method was greatly advanced by the work of Tyconius, who interpreted nothing by the historical setting or events of the first century. Augustine followed Tyconius in his capitulation to a totally mystical exegesis. For the next thousand years this allegorical approach was normative for the interpretation of Revelation. . . . A new departure was taken in the twelfth century by Joachim of Floris. Since the rise of the allegorical approach it had been generally thought that the millennial reign had begun with the historic Christ.[39]

It is remarkable that present-day amillennialists, knowing this aspect of the history of hermeneutics, still cling to this system with confidence.

Influenced by Origen and by certain cultural factors, Augustine promoted the allegorical approach to Scriptures.

In Alexandria, Origen opposed chiliasm as a Jewish dream, and spiritualized the symbolical language of the prophets. . . . But the crushing blow came from the great change in the social condition and prospects of the church in the Nicene age. After Christianity, contrary to all expectation, triumphed in the Roman empire, and was embraced by the Caesars themselves, the millennial reign, instead of being anxiously waited and prayed for, began to be dated either from the first appearance of Christ, or from the conversion of Constantine and the downfall of paganism, and to be regarded as realized in the glory of the dominant imperial state-church. Augustine, who himself had formerly entertained chiliastic hopes, framed the new theory which reflected the social change, and was generally accepted. The apocalyptic millennium he understood to be the present reign of Christ in the Catholic church, and the first resurrection, the translation of the martyrs and saints to heaven, where they participate in Christ's reign. It was consistent with this theory that towards the close of the first millennium of the Christian era there was a wide-spread expectation in Western Europe that the final judgment was at hand.[40]

Amillennialism unwittingly opened the door for biblical liberalism. With such unsure and clouded meanings, it was easy for liberals to say the Bible was a mystical book full of wild human imaginations and thus an unreliable guide for humanity.

Interpretive Darkness

Some of G. B. Stevens's comments on Revelation in *The Preacher's Commentary* reveal a groping in interpretive darkness. "The aim of the book [of Revelation] was distinctly practical; it was written primarily for its own time. . . . The book is obscure because it deals with obscure themes—the program of the future and Christ's return to judgment. . . . And . . . the language of concealment (which the initiated would be able to interpret correctly) consists of Oriental symbols, largely derived from books like Ezekiel and Daniel, which are necessarily more or less enigmatic to the Western and modern mind."[41]

Though indeed there are certain practical sections in Revelation, especially the first three chapters, the main purpose of Revelation is to present a panorama of future events, and that in itself should impact believers as to how they need to live.

So what does Stevens mean when he says the book is "primarily for its own time"? No one yet has been able fully to correlate the events recorded in Revelation with specific events in the early church. What is the "language of concealment" which only "the initiated" can understand? And how does one get initiated? Why can't *Western* Christians understand Ezekiel, Daniel, and Revelation? Granted, all Bible study requires research. But did the Lord hide the meaning of these three books?

Cox reveals the same confusion in trying to explain the purpose of the Apocalypse.

St. John was not a prophet in the ancient and vulgar sense; he was not a mere seer of coming events, a mere student and interpreter of the shadows they cast before them. . . . And, hence, the Apocalypse of St. John is not a series of forecasts, predicting the political weather of the world through the ages of history; it is rather a series of symbols and visions in which the universal principles of the Divine Rule are set forth in forms dear to the heart of a Hebrew Mystic and poet. What is most valuable to us in this book, therefore, is not the letter, the form; not the vials, the seals, the trumpets, over which interpreters, who play the seer rather than the prophet, have been wrangling and perplexing their brains for centuries; but the large general principles which these mystic symbols of Oriental thought are apt to conceal from a Western mind. Whether or not, for example, the vision of an angel flying through heaven to proclaim an impending judgment was taken by St. John's first readers to indicate an approaching event of world-wide moment, is a question of comparatively slight importance to us; it is, indeed, mainly a question of curious antiquarian interest.[42]

It would be interesting to know the reaction of John the apostle at being labeled "not a mere seer of coming events." Or what would he think at being called a "Hebrew Mystic and poet," one who sets forth "symbols and visions" of universal principles of the "Divine Rule"? And on what basis can Cox say that the value of the book of Revelation is not in studying "the vials, the seals, the trumpets," but rather in noting the mystic "symbols of Oriental thought" that are concealed from Westerners?

It is more than of "slight importance" whether John is predicting "impending judgment"! These are not merely questions of issues greater than "curious antiquarian interest"! What is truly curious is how critics of premillennialism can argue that the literal, normative, prophetic interpretation of Bible prophecy, much less the book of Revelation, can be so foreign. The truth is that allegorical amillennialism stands as an unacceptable system for interpreting the book of Revelation.

Symbolic or Literal Interpretation?

Granted, the book of Revelation has many symbols and figures of speech. But these are approached differently by premillennialists and amillennialists. According to premillennialism, symbols and figures of speech are used to convey literal concepts behind them. Premillennialists reason forward to the fact that the symbols are used to explain something difficult to comprehend in normal language. This approach makes for consistency in understanding Revelation.

Amillennialists, on the other hand, approach the book of Revelation differently.

They tend to "spiritualize" the text, to see "hidden" truths behind normal language. "Everything contained in the Apocalypse is to be understood symbolically and spiritually [or spiritualized]."[43] Milligan misses the point, however, when he tries to illustrate *spiritualizing*: "When speaking of the fate of the two witnesses, he [John] says, in ch. xi. 8, And their dead bodies lie in the streets of the great city, which *spiritually* is called Sodom and Egypt—words clearly showing that, in this instance at least, we are not to interpret literally. Apart, however, from these particular words, literal interpretation must be admitted by all to be, at least in the main parts of the book, impossible."[44]

The rest of 11:8 reads, "where also their Lord was crucified." The "great city" then is clearly literal Jerusalem. But the city is described in a negative, illustrative, *spiritual* way by being called Sodom and Egypt. But speaking of something in a spiritual way is not the same as spiritualizing! Premillennialists have no problem seeing a spiritual description (in this case, Sodom and Egypt) attached to something distinctly literal (in this case, Jerusalem). Yet this differs from allegorical interpretation. For the latter implies there is a hidden, mystical meaning buried beneath the surface. An example would be to say that Sodom and Egypt represent evil forces that have persecuted Christian martyrs throughout church history. To premillennialists, the terms "Sodom" and "Egypt" vividly describe what Jerusalem will be like when these events transpire. Like Sodom and Egypt, Jerusalem will be ungodly, pagan, sensual, idolatrous, and hedonistic.

What the Jews Thought About a Literal Kingdom

Jesus taught that the kingdom would have godly and spiritual overtones, yet He also taught that the Messiah's rule would be literal and worldwide, with Jerusalem as the capital city. The yet-future rule of Christ on earth would follow the terrible seven-year Tribulation.

Some, however, try to *spiritualize* the references to the kingdom in the Gospels, arguing that the church has either replaced Israel forever in God's plans or that the prophecies in the Old Testament of Israel were really symbolic of the church. They say God is through with the Jews forever and has totally abandoned that nation, and that the church now fulfills God's promises to Israel in a spiritual way. But Jesus *never* abrogated the promised earthly, literal, and anticipated Davidic kingdom.

Neither John the Baptist nor Jesus redefined the basic structure of the kingdom, though they certainly stressed the fact that it would be spiritual in nature as well as historical.

What the Jewish leaders of Jesus' day believed about the Millennium is an important issue. Based on their knowledge of the Old Testament, the Jews *understood* that the coming millennium is to be a literal rule of the Messiah on the earth. And interestingly Jesus did not refute this belief of the Jews or correct their assumptions. Scholars of Jewish history have written about what the Jews thought about the kingdom and the Messiah. Peters, for example, makes the following statements about Jewish literal interpretation.

> There was no departure from the literal interpretation even among the Rabbinical party. . . . The allegorical interpretation of the Sacred Scriptures cannot be historically proved to have prevailed among the Jews from the time of the exile, or to have been common with the Jews of Palestine at the time of Christ and His apostles. . . . The Sanhedrin and the hearers of Jesus . . . give no indication of the allegorical interpretation. Even Josephus has nothing of it. The Platonic Jews of Egypt began, in the first century, in imitation of the heathen Greeks, to interpret the Old Testament allegorically. Philo was distinguished among those in that place who practiced this method and he defends it as something new and before unheard of, and for that reason opposed by the other Jews. . . . The Jewish method—evidenced by its exclusiveness and Messianic hopes—was adopted by the primitive Church, as witnessed e.g. by its application of prophecy, its Pre-millenarian views, etc. The ideal, presented in the system of Philo, was inaugurated into the Christian Church by the Alexandrian fathers.[45]

After the first century orthodox Jewish rabbis take literally the Old Testament statements about a future terrible time of trouble on earth (the Tribulation), the coming of the Messiah, and the establishing of the Messiah's reign on the earth. Can this be demonstrated by the writings and historic views of most of the rabbis, especially during the Middle Ages? The answer is yes.

Judaism and Millennialism

Jewish historians Michael Avi-Yonah and Zvi Baras write the following about the Jewish expectation of a literal kingdom.

> It was inconceivable that the promises should not be fulfilled and that the Kingdom of Heaven upon the earth should not arrive. All Jewish groups believed this implicitly. The disagreement among them concerned only the date of the fulfillment and the means of its accomplishment. Whereas the Sadducees did not carry forward the messianic hope of prophecy. . . . Even Christianity, essentially messianic . . . is the product of the great messianic promises. By reason of foreign influence, however, it sought the messianic Kingdom of God in a way other than that of Judaism. While Jewish messianism is firmly rooted in this world, in earthly life, even in

the "new world" of the days of the Messiah, Christian messianism is a "kingdom not of this world."[46]

The statement about "foreign influence" clearly refers to the pagan allegorical interpretation basically rejected by most orthodox Jewish scholars. Avi-Yonah and Baras also discuss the "Greek element" (i.e., allegorical interpretation) that influenced much of Christian thinking. "This renewed messianic idea, envisioned by the author of the Book of Daniel, was to be echoed in its essential thrust in the literature that took its clue from it. Its influence on Christianity is unmistakable. Once Christianity, however, introduced a Greek element into Jewish monotheism it changed the basic concept of the Kingdom of Heaven which it had borrowed from Judaism."[47]

This incredible statement shows that Avi-Yonah clearly understood the allegorical influence that makes amillennial Christian interpretation different from Judaism. (The editor of this work met professor Avi-Yonah in Israel shortly before his death. The two discussed the concern of evangelicals for Israel's future. Avi-Yonah said he shared this basic approach to a literal premillennial return of the Messiah.)

The Jewish View of the Seven-Year Period of Tribulation

Though Jewish scholars do not often admit it, they, as do Christian premillennialists, anticipate a seven-year Tribulation. Again, a literal/historical understanding of prophecy is the key. And looking at the Scriptures from a normative standpoint gives the Jews and Christians the same interpretation. Raphael Patai, quoting from the rabbinical writings, says, "Things will come to such a head that people will despair of Redemption. This will last seven years. And then, unexpectedly, the Messiah will come. . . . At the end of the seventh [year] the Son of David will come."[48]

The pangs of the Messianic times are imagined as having heavenly as well as earthly sources and expressions.

> . . . Awesome cosmic cataclysms will be visited upon the earth: conflagrations, pestilence, famine, earthquakes, . . . These will be paralleled by evils brought by men upon themselves: . . . corruption, oppression, cruel edicts, lack of truth, and no fear of sin. . . . Because of this gloomy picture of the beginnings of the Messianic era, which during Talmudic times was firmly believed in, some sages expressed the wish not to see the Messiah [because of such judgment coming]. . . . In any case, both the people and its religious leaders continued to hope for the coming of the Messiah.[49]

Quoting what the rabbis have always taught, Avi-Yonah and Baras continue:

All men, however, will suffer before the days of peace and tranquillity, the days of the Messiah, arrive. The greatest of all tribulations will befall Israel and its land during the period of the "pangs of the Messiah."[50]

The Day of the Lord [will come]. . . . The Kingdom of Heaven will be made manifest over all creation. Satan will then come to an end and with his disappearance sorrow will be banished from the world. God will arise from the throne of His Kingdom to take vengeance . . . The earth will tremble. . . . The sun will be turned into darkness and the beams of the moon will be broken. The moon itself will be turned into blood.[51]

The "pangs of the Messiah" are called "the time of tribulation."[52]

√ The Jewish View of the Kingdom/Millennium

New Testament scholars continue to argue whether the kingdom of God and the kingdom of heaven mentioned in the Gospels are the same. Avi-Yonah claims from rabbinical studies that the two terms describe the same thing— the earthly literal kingdom of the Messiah. He notes that after the four beasts of Daniel will come God's world dominion, "an everlasting kingdom—'to perfect the world under the Kingdom of God'—a Kingdom of Heaven upon earth."[53]

The rabbis of Christ's day saw from the Old Testament prophets not only the future kingdom's material well-being but also the spiritual treasures of heavenly blessings that God will open and shower upon the earth.

This description of material plenty agrees with that found both in the Syriac Baruch and in the tradition handed down by one of the Church Fathers, Papias, preserved by Irenaeus. It is this tradition that gave rise to the Christian belief in the Millennial Kingdom of Heaven (Millennium, Chiliasm). One must bear in mind, however, that these descriptions are to be found almost *verbatim* in early Tannaitic and midrashic sources.[54]

The Jews listened for the "Trumpet of the Messiah" that will bring in the blessed kingdom, as described in the Talmud:

At its sound, the dispersed of Israel will be gathered into their homeland and the tribes of Judah and Ephraim reunited, as in the days of David and Solomon. The land of Israel will attain to a condition of political strength, assuring peace and happiness. . . . The nations . . .

will stream in pilgrimage to this land and its [rebuilt] Temple. . . . Swords will be beaten into plowshares, following the final war against Gog and Magog. Even the wild beasts will disappear from the land and those that remain will no longer be injurious. Human beings will live to a ripe old age. The sick and maimed will be healed. The desolate cities will be rebuilt. . . . The boundaries of the land of Israel will be extended. The desert waste will be turned into fertile land. The King Messiah, offspring of the House of David, will rule the world by his holy [S]pirit.[55]

Israel will become the center of the world.

By the power of his [S]pirit, he expels the nations from Jerusalem and establishes a great kingdom in Zion that serves as the center of the world. The nations serve the God of Israel and the King Messiah. . . . The ingathering of the exiles . . . is a precondition of the coming days of the Messiah. Thus there is a political, national, and territorial aspect to the kingdom of the Messiah. The spiritual aspect, however, remains central.[56]

The Jews also have anticipated the reconstruction of the temple in Jerusalem.[57] Amillennialists throw stones at Christian premillennialists for saying the temple will be rebuilt, but this has always been a cardinal belief among those who understand biblical prophecy. "In the Days of the Messiah, a new heaven and a new earth will be created and all creatures will be renewed. The Temple of God will be raised aloft in Jerusalem on Mount Zion."[58]

It must be remembered that everything written in the preceeding sections is a summation of Jewish thought well known during the time of Christ, Paul, and the New Testament period. This material is compiled by recognized Jewish scholars who have spent years studying the past culture and history of their own people. And their statements fit exactly into a premillennial pattern.

The amillennial interpretation of Scripture is an aberration of all reasonable and historic approaches to biblical hermeneutics. Allegorizing destroyed a proper understanding of the Old Testament prophecies and mutilated a sound and reasonable understanding of the book of Revelation.

The irony is that, as the Jews looked at the Scriptures, they clearly saw the messianic kingdom. In fact, the Jews began to call the kingdom "the millennium," in the medieval writing called the *Zohar* (written between 1270–1300).[59] In the *Zohar* 1:119a we read, "Happy will be all those who will remain in the world at the end of the sixth millennium to enter into the millennium of the Sabbath." In *Zohar* 1:140a, Midrash HaNe'elam, we read, "The total saintly will arise at the rising of the dead of the Land of Israel . . . in the fortieth year of the ingathering of the exiles. And the last ones [will arise] in the . . . sixth millennium [in order to enter the last millennium]."

Interesting also is the reaction of Jesus to the high priest Caiaphas when Jesus was on trial. Caiaphas said to Jesus, "I charge you under oath by the living God: Tell us if you are the Christ, the Son of God" (Matt. 26:63 NIV). The Jewish leaders who were there well understood both expressions. "Christ" *(Christos)* is the Greek translation of *ha Měšîaḥ,* "the Anointed One," "the Messiah." And "Son of God" is the common expression for the Messiah taken from Psalm 2:7, paraphrased as "the Son who has a relationship with God." Jesus answered, "I tell you, hereafter you shall see the Son of Man sitting at the right hand of Power, and coming on the clouds of heaven" (Matt. 26:64). Using the title "the Son of Man," Jesus referred to Himself as the "Son who has a relationship to man." And by the words "sitting at the right hand of Power," Jesus spoke of His eternal position with God the Father in glory. These key expressions of the Messiah flashed before Caiaphas as he exploded in rage, "He has blasphemed!" (v. 65). The people agreed, "He is deserving of death!" (v. 66).

This incident tells us the Jews knew the Old Testament predictions about the Messiah's coming to earth. But they failed to see His predicted death, and they misunderstood His love for sinners and His care for hurting mankind. In other words, He did not fit their image!

Wilcock is typical of those who take the numbers in Revelation symbolically rather than literally. Regarding the 144,000 Jews in Revelation 7, he writes, "The figure is presumably another of the symbolic figures of Revelation, and indeed it looks too stylized to be anything else—the suspiciously tidy sort of number that is much more likely to be a symbol than a statistic. If we are to find ourselves described as 144,000 'Israelites,' when most of us are Gentiles, this is in line with the regular New Testament teaching which applies to the Christian church the titles and privileges of Israel."[60]

In Summary

Norman Cohn explains that by the time of Augustine (fourth century) the interpretive death knell had been tolled on a clear understanding of the book of Revelation. Allegory would cloud its message, and the meaning of the writing would be closed to countless generations. Only since the mid-nineteenth century has the book of Revelation been reopened.

> The third century saw the first attempt to discredit millenarianism, when Origen, perhaps the most influential of all the theologians of the ancient Church, began to present the Kingdom as an event which would take place not in space or time but only in the souls of believers. For a collective, millenarian eschatology Origen substituted an

eschatology of the individual soul. What stirred his profoundly Hellenic imagination was the prospect of spiritual progress begun in this world and continued in the next; and to this theme theologians were henceforth to give increasing attention. Such a shift in interest was indeed admirably suited to what was now an organized Church, enjoying almost uninterrupted peace and an acknowledged position in the world. When in the fourth century Christianity attained a position of supremacy in the Mediterranean world and became the official religion of the Empire, ecclesiastical disapproval of millenarianism became emphatic. The Catholic Church was now a powerful and prosperous institution, functioning according to a well-established routine; and the men responsible for governing it had no wish to see Christians clinging to out-dated and inappropriate dreams of a new earthly Paradise. Early in the fifth century St. Augustine propounded the doctrine which the new conditions demanded. According to *The City of God* the book of Revelation was to be understood as a *Spiritual Allegory;* as for the Millennium, that had begun with the birth of Christianity and was fully realized in the Church. This at once became orthodox doctrine.[61]

CHAPTER 5

THE LITERARY STRUCTURE OF REVELATION

MAL COUCH

For years Bible scholars have noted that the book of Revelation has a number of grammatical irregularities. In fact, this book has been characterized as "A Grammar of Ungrammar." In a number of places the apostle John departed from basic rules of grammar and syntax in his use of standard Koine Greek. As Swete writes, "But from whatever cause or concurrence of causes, it cannot be denied that the Apocalypse of John stands alone among Greek literary writings in its disregard of the ordinary rules of syntax. . . . The book seems openly and deliberately to defy the grammarian, and yet, even as literature, it is in its own field unsurpassed."[1]

Of course in inspiring the book, the Holy Spirit gave us the very message the Lord wants us to have, but it was written within the framework of the author's own style, education, age, and dramatic moment or situation. If the author had unusual expressions or writing style, this does not violate the fact of the book's divine inspiration.

Why did the apostle seem to depart from normal grammatical usage? Some have suggested that the message was so emotional and vivid that John struggled to keep up with the flashes of dramatic revelation coming on him. Others have said that the age of the apostle may have affected his thoughts and expressions as he wrote down what was communicated by the Lord and the Holy Spirit.

Others have noted that though John spoke Greek and lived among Greek-speaking people most of his life,[2] he was a Jew by birth and education. Could these facts account for his occasional out-of-the-ordinary Greek grammar? Even though the grammar may be different at times, still his vocabulary was fully adequate. "He lived long enough in the Greek cities of Asia to have ready to his hand all the Greek words that he needed for the purpose of his book. The Greek vocabulary of the Apocalypse does not suggest that the writer was crippled by a want of appropriate words. His store is ample for his needs, and it seems to have been chosen with care."[3]

The Unity of Revelation

Because Revelation has such an obvious literary plan in view (as discussed later), it is clear that there is also a literary unity in its composition. Though doubted by liberal scholars, conservatives have no problem detecting such unity from the first chapters all the way to the final paragraphs. "The book creates a prima facie impression that it proceeds from one author or editor. The first and last chapters claim to be written by the same person (i. I, 4, 9, xxii. 8)."[4]

Swete points to twenty-seven phrases in the early chapters that are matched up by nearly the same wording in the final chapters. "Such coincidences leave no doubt that the same writer has been at work" in chapters 1–3 and 20–22.[5]

Evidence shows that the author who announced his name in the prologue was at work throughout the book. He left his imprint and particular style in every part of the prophecy. "Everywhere the presence of the same creative mind has made itself felt."[6]

Symbolism, Type, and Illustration in Revelation

As noted in chapter 4, Revelation is full of comparative language: "as it were," "like," "as," "it appeared as." But most of these illustrations portray something real. These images are not to be understood allegorically. Instead these comparative statements and various symbols in the book are consistent with a literal hermeneutic. Much of the imagery comes from the Old Testament, especially the books of Daniel, Ezekiel, and Zechariah. "Symbolisms occur throughout Scripture as a vehicle for divine revelation, but it is undoubtedly true that the final book of the New Testament because of its apocalyptic character contains more symbols than any other book in the New Testament."[7]

Also a number of geographical allusions and religious items relate directly to the Old Testament. The golden lampstands of the churches of Asia Minor have some correspondence to the lampstand of the tabernacle and temple. Revelation also mentions the heavenly tabernacle, the ark, and the ceremonial censer. Places such as the Euphrates, Sodom, Armageddon, Jerusalem, Babylon, and Egypt all play important roles in the future. Old Testament characters, including Jezebel, Balaam, and Moses, are mentioned in Revelation. Walvoord notes, "It is nevertheless true that much of the imagery of the book of Revelation is new; that is, it is created as a vehicle for the divine revelation which John was to record. . . . It is also true that some items, while partially symbolic, may also be intended to be understood literally, as in numerous instances where reference is made to stars, the moon, the sun, rivers, and seas."[8]

He adds,

> It is inevitable therefore that any exposition of Revelation must have presuppositions based upon a study of the entire Word of God and involving the question as to whether prophecy should be interpreted with the same degree of literalness as other portions of Scripture. Though Revelation abounds in signs and symbols, it was intended to be interpreted with far greater literalness than has been commonly exercised. Such an approach yields a remarkable revelation of the end of the age which coincides with other prophetic revelation.[9]

The Use of the Old Testament in Revelation

Though a number of Old Testament places and names are referred to in the book, surprisingly all are allusions with no direct quotations. The 404 verses of Revelation include 348 allusions or indirect quotes of the Old Testament.[10] This makes this work unique, not only in the Scriptures but also among ancient secular writings.

Using the Greek Septuagint, John alluded to each of the five books of Moses, Joshua, Judges, 2 Samuel, 2 Kings, 1 Chronicles, Nehemiah, Psalms, Proverbs, the major prophetic books, and seven of the minor prophets—twenty-four books in all.[11] But he cited from Isaiah, Ezekiel, Daniel, and Psalms more often than the others.

Did John draw on the noncanonical Jewish apocalyptic literature he was probably aware of in his day, such as the writing called the book of Enoch? Swete answers that although the author possibly showed some knowledge of similar ideas in non-biblical writings that may have been popular during his time, he gives "no clear evidence of his dependence on Jewish sources other than the books of the Old Testament."[12]

Numbers in Revelation

"Why is the Book of Revelation so permeated with [an] emphasis on numbers?"[13] Though the same phenomenon is found elsewhere in Scripture, it is overwhelming in the Apocalypse. Morris believes this book reflects the natural world that is in itself so constructed with mathematical rules and laws. "God's inspired Word and His created world are consistent with each other."[14]

One cannot miss the numbers that stand out in Revelation. There are the two angels, the four (angelic) creatures, the twenty-four elders, the four horsemen, the number 666, the ten kings, two hundred million horsemen, the one-thousand-year millennium, the twelve gates, and many others.

But the one that is most obvious is the number seven. Morris has listed the twenty-four occurrences of this number in Revelation.[15]

1. Seven churches (1:4, 11, 20)
2. Seven Spirits (1:4; 3:1; 4:5; 5:6)
3. Seven candlesticks (1:12–13, 20; 2:1)
4. Seven stars (1:16, 20; 2:1; 3:1)
5. Seven lamps (4:5)
6. Seven seals (5:1; 5:5)
7. Seven horns (5:6)
8. Seven eyes (5:6)
9. Seven angels (8:2, 6)
10. Seven trumpets (8:2, 6)
11. Seven thunders (10:3–4)
12. Seven thousand killed (11:13)
13. Seven heads (12:3; 13:1; 17:3, 7, 9)
14. Seven crowns (12:3)
15. Seven angels (15:1, 6–8; 16:1; 17:1; 21:9)
16. Seven plagues (15:1, 6, 8; 21:9)
17. Seven vials (15:7; 17:1; 21:9)
18. Seven mountains (17:9)
19. Seven kings (17:10, 11)
20. Seven beatitudes (1:3; 14:13; 16:15; 19:9; 20:6; 22:7; 22:14)
21. Seven years of judgments (11:3; 12:6, 14; 13:5)
22. Seven divisions of each of the letters to the seven churches
23. Seven "I am's" of Christ (1:8, 11, 17–18; 21:6; 22:13, 16)
24. Seven doxologies in heaven (4:9–11; 5:8–13; 7:9–12; 11:16–18; 14:2–3; 15:2–4; 19:1–6)

Why are there so many "sevens" in the last book of the Bible? Most Bible students agree that seven is the number of completion. This is true in Scripture, and is also true in many spheres of life today. Many say seven is the "lucky" number or the "perfect" number.[16] Seven determines our calendar week, a fact that is universally true.

Ironically, a seven-day week has no basis in astronomy, as do the month and year, "nor does the number seven have a physiological basis like the number ten."[17] Why then have people followed a seven-day week? According to Morris, "The only real explanation why people have always followed a seven-day week and why the number seven has always symbolized fullness and completion is the divine decree of Genesis 2:3: 'And God blessed the seventh day, and sanctified it; because that in it he had rested from all his work which God created and made.' Once again, to understand Revelation we must return to Genesis."[18]

Koine Greek and Revelation

Some have argued that John originally wrote the Apocalypse in Aramaic, which was later translated into common or marketplace Koine Greek. The better view is that Revelation is good "Jewish Greek" used in Palestine in the first century. Evidence of this is seen in some Semitic words and phrases that are used in the book.

In fact, this may even explain some of the grammatical imperfections that crop up from time to time in the book. But this cannot be proven. John the author clearly knew Koine Greek and was also familiar with the Septuagint Old Testament, as were most godly prophets and apostles.

Height and Depth in Revelation

One of the unique features of this work is how the drama moves from the very heights of heaven to the abyss, where fallen angels are confined. Though that change of scene occurs from chapter to chapter, it often occurs from paragraph to paragraph! With this movement, Revelation is an adventure, a moving drama that leaves the reader wondering what is coming next.

The following shows the rapid changes of location in the book of Revelation.

On earth (Patmos): John visualized the glorified Christ (1:9–20)
On earth: The seven churches of Asia (2:1–3:22)
In heaven: The throne of God and the scroll (4:1–5:14)
On earth: The coming of the four seal judgments (6:1–8)
In heaven: The fifth seal opened; the martyrs of heaven (6:9–11)
On earth: Natural disturbance (6:12–17)
On earth: The sealing of the 144,000 Jewish witnesses (7:1–8)
In heaven: The multitude coming out of the Great Tribulation (7:9–17)
In heaven: The seventh seal opened; the prayers before the altar of God (8:1–6)
On earth: The first four trumpets blown bringing terror *on the earth* (8:7–13)
Bottomless Pit: The fifth trumpet; demonic creatures come out to torment those *on the earth* (9:1–12)
On earth: The sixth trumpet; a third of mankind killed (9:13–21)
On earth: John ate the little book (10:1–11)
On earth: The two witnesses killed and resurrected (11:1–14)
In heaven: The seventh trumpet; praise to Christ in heaven (11:15–19)
On earth: War against Israel (12:1–6)

In heaven: The angel Michael wages war with the Dragon (12:7–12)

On earth: The Dragon persecutes the woman (12:13–17)

On earth: The Beast and the False Prophet exercise authority (13:1–18)

In heaven: The 144,000 martyred and praising God (14:1–5)

In heaven: The angelic proclamations *to earth* (14:6–8)

Lake of fire: Prediction of the eternal torment of those who worship the
Beast and his image (14:9–13)

In heaven: Christ about to harvest the earth ripened with sin (14:14–20)

In heaven: Martyrs singing of victory with the song of Moses and the
song of the Lamb (15:1–8)

In heaven: The heavenly proclamation to begin the judgment of the seven
bowls (16:1–2)

On earth: The six bowls of judgment fall *on the earth* (16:3–17)

On earth: The prediction of the doom of Babylon, mother of harlots
(17:1–18)

On earth: Babylon the great falls (18:1–24)

In heaven: Announcement of Christ's coming victory (19:1–10)

From heaven to earth: Christ returns *to the earth* (19:11–16)

On earth: The battle of Armageddon (19:17–21)

The abyss: Satan thrown into the abyss (20:1–3)

On earth: The saints resurrected for the one-thousand-year reign of
Christ (20:4–6)

On earth: The insurrection of Satan loosed from the abyss (20:7–9)

Lake of fire: Satan is cast into the lake of fire (20:10)

In heaven: The Great White Throne judgment (20:11–15)

From heaven to earth: The New Jerusalem descends (21:1–8)

On the new earth: Description of the New Jerusalem (21:9–27)

On the new earth: Blessings of the new Jerusalem (22:1–5)

From heaven: The final message (22:6–21)

The Extent of the Tribulation in Revelation

Bible students debate how much of the seven years of the Tribulation is actually recorded in Revelation. Many commentators say that only the last three and a half years of this horrible period are in the book, beginning in chapter six. Others hold that the entire seven-year period of the Tribulation is represented in Revelation.

Two arguments are given for the first view. First, the expression "the great tribulation" is mentioned early on in Revelation 7:14. If this description is the same as "a great tribulation" in Matthew 24:21, it seems likely that the events in Revelation 6–18 are all within the last half of the Tribulation. Second, the traumatic earthly events in Revelation 6 seem to match Christ's narration of the second half of the seven years of evil.

However, those who say the entire seven-year period is depicted in Revelation question whether "the tribulation the great" (Rev. 7:14, literal Greek) and "a tribulation great" (Matt. 24:21, literal Greek), are referring to the same thing. Still others respond that the grammar and the contexts of the two passages suggest they are referring to the same period, that is, the second half of the Tribulation.

On this issue Walvoord writes:

> Many have assumed that the events of earth in chapters 6 through 19 coincide with the seven years of Israel's program culminating in the second coming of Christ. Expositors of this point of view have usually taken for granted that the book gives a panoramic view of the entire seven years even though there is no explicit proof of this in the book itself. There is some evidence, however, that the events pictured in the seals, trumpets, and vials are instead a concentrated prophecy of the latter half of this week, i.e., a period of three and one-half years, designated as a time of wrath and the great tribulation, and constituting the introduction to the second coming of Christ.[19]

More will be said about this in a later chapter.

An Outline of Revelation

The plan of the book is spelled out in 1:19, where the Lord Jesus instructed the apostle John, "Write therefore the things which you have seen, and the things which are, and the things which shall take place after these things."

Past, present, and future are represented in these instructions. As John began to receive this entire vision, what he saw first was the person of Christ in His heavenly glorified state (1:9–20). Next, through John, the Lord addressed the seven existing churches of Asia Minor, churches that were not far geographically from the island of Patmos (2:1–3:22). Then, from 4:1 through 22:17, Christ revealed what will take place in the future.

Along the journey through Revelation there are heavenly and earthly pauses or parentheses in which events are looked at and examined more closely (See 7:1–17; 10:1–11:14; 14:1–15:8; and 16:13–16 in the following outline). Yet the prophetic section of the book is chronological. As Thomas notes, "The nature of that progression, called herein the 'telescopic' arrangement, has the seventh seal consisting of seven trumpets and the seventh trumpet consisting of seven bowls."[20]

The book unfolds in this way:

I. THE SALUTATION AND INTRODUCTORY VISION (1:1–20)
   A. Introductory Remarks (1:1–3)
      1. Preface (1:1–2)
      2. The "Special Blessing" (1:3)
   B. The Addressees (1:4–8)
   C. The Exalted Christ (1:9–20): "Things Which You Have Seen"

II. THE PROBLEMS IN THE SEVEN CHURCHES OF ASIA: "THINGS WHICH ARE" (2:1–3:22)
   A. Message to Ephesus: "Left Your First Love" (2:1–7)
   B. Message to Smyrna: "I Know Your Tribulation" (2:8–11)
   C. Message to Pergamum: "You Hold Fast My Name" (2:12–17)
   D. Message to Thyatira: "I Know Your Deeds" (2:18–29)
   E. Message to Sardis: "Remember What You Have Received" (3:1–6)
   F. Message to Philadelphia: "I Have Put Before You an Open Door" (3:7–13)
   G. Message to Laodicea: "You Are Lukewarm" (3:14–22)

III. BEFORE THE HEAVENLY THRONE OF GOD (4:1–5:14)
   A. John Called into Heaven: "Come up Here" (4:1–11)
      1. God Enthroned in Glory (4:1–3)
      2. The Twenty-four Elders (4:4–5)
      3. The Anthem of Glory to God (4:6–11)
   B. The Book Taken by Christ: "A Book Written Inside and on the Back" (5:1–14)
      ☛1. The Book with Seven Seals Presented (5:1–4)
      2. Christ Takes the Book (5:5–7)
      3. Christ the Lamb Worshiped (5:8–12)
      4. God and the Lamb Receive Worship (5:13–14)

IV. THE COMING TRIBULATION: "THE THINGS WHICH SHALL TAKE PLACE" (6:1–22:5)
   A. The Six Seals Opened (6:1–17)
      1. First Seal: The Conquering of Earth (6:1–2)
      2. Second Seal: Peace Taken from the Earth (6:3–4)
      3. Third Seal: Famine and Inflation (6:5–6)
      4. Fourth Seal: Sword, Famine, Pestilence, Wild Animals (6:7–8)
      5. Fifth Seal: Martyred Remnant (6:9–11)
      6. Sixth Seal: Cosmic Cataclysms (6:12–17)
   B. Parenthesis: Saved People Coming Out of the Tribulation (7:1–17)

1. A Remnant of Servants Sealed and Protected (7:1–3)
2. 144,000 Jewish Witnesses (7:4–8)
3. A Great Multitude of the Martyred (7:9–17)

C. The Six Trumpets Sounded (8:1–9:21)
1. The Seventh Seal Opened (8:1)
2. Prayers of the Saints Before God's Altar and Throne (8:2–6)
3. First Trumpet: A Third of Earth Burned (8:7)
4. Second Trumpet: A Third of the Sea Becomes Blood (8:8–9)
5. Third Trumpet: A Third of Rivers Polluted (8:10–11)
6. Fourth Trumpet: The Heavens Darkened (8:12–13)
7. Fifth Trumpet: Creatures from the Bottomless Pit Released (9:1–12)
8. Sixth Trumpet: Four Angels "of Destruction" Released (9:13–21)

D. Parenthesis: Tribulation Horror Intensifies (10:1–11:14)
1. The Mystery of the Little Book (10:1–7)
2. The Prophecy of the Tribulation Continues (10:8–11)
3. Temple to Be Trodden Under Foot for Forty-two Months (11:1–2)
4. The Two Witnesses Seen by the World (11:3–14)

E. The Second Half of the Tribulation Grows Worse (11:15–12:17)
1. Seventh Trumpet: Christ's Future Kingdom Revealed (11:15–19)
2. Flashback: The Woman Israel Gives Birth to Christ (12:1–2)
3. Satan the Dragon Pursues Israel (12:3–4)
4. The Messiah Born: Israel Protected for Three and a Half Years (12:5–6)
5. Michael Wages War with the Dragon (12:7–12)
6. Satan Pursues the Jewish People (12:13–17)

F. The Kingdom of the Beast and the False Prophet (13:1–18)
1. The Beast (Antichrist) and His Kingdom (13:1–10)
2. The False Prophet (Religious Leader) and His Authority (13:11–18)

G. Parenthesis: Preview of the End of the Tribulation (14:1–15:8)
1. The Martyred 144,000 and the Lamb (14:1–5)
2. The "Eternal Gospel" Spreads to the Entire World (14:6–7)
3. The Doom of Babylon Foretold (14:8–12)
4. The Blessedness of Those Who Die in the Lord (14:13)
5. Armageddon: The Final Great Battle Envisioned (14:14–20)
6. The Great Chorus of Victory Before the Lord (15:1–8)

H. The Seven Bowls of Wrath (16:1–21)
1. First Bowl: Loathsome Sores on Men (16:1–2)

      2. Second Bowl: All Sea Life Dies (16:3)
      3. Third Bowl: The Waters Become Blood (16:4–7)
      4. Fourth Bowl: The Sun Scorches Men (16:8–9)
      5. Fifth Bowl: The Beast's Kingdom Becomes Darkened (16:10–11)
      6. Sixth Bowl: Euphrates Dries Up (16:12)
      7. Parenthesis: Battle of Armageddon Foreseen (16:13–16)
      8. Seventh Bowl: Earth and Cosmic Turmoil (16:17–21)

I. The Doom of Babylon (17:1–19:6)
      1. The Earth Seduced by Babylon the Harlot (17:1–6)
      2. The Beast and His Kingdom Allied with Babylon (17:7–13)
      3. The Beast and His Kingdom Turn Against Babylon (17:14–18)
      4. Babylon Destroyed (18:1–8)
      5. Babylon Mourned (18:9–19)
      6. Heaven Rejoices over Babylon's Fall (18:20–24)
      7. The Heavenly Hallelujah over Babylon's Demise (19:1–6)

J. The Coming of Christ and the One-Thousand-Year Reign (19:7–20:10)
      1. Preparation for the Marriage of the Lamb (19:7–10)
      2. Christ Returns as "King of Kings and Lord of Lords" (19:11–16)
      3. Armageddon Battle Fought (19:17–18)
      4. The Beast and the False Prophet Cast into the Lake of Fire (19:19–20)
      5. Doom of the Rest of the Unsaved (19:21)
      6. Satan Bound for One Thousand Years (20:1–3)
      7. Reign of the Resurrected Saints (20:4–6)
      8. Final Rebellion of Satan (20:7–9)
      9. Satan Cast into the Lake of Fire (20:10)

K. Preparation for the New Heavens and the New Earth: Great White Throne Judgment (20:11–15)

L. The Renovation of the Universe (21:1–22:5)
      1. The Revealing of the New Heavens, the New Earth, and the New Jerusalem (21:1–8)
      2. The New Jerusalem: The Wife of the Lamb (21:9–27)
      3. The Water of Life and the Removal of the Curse (22:1–5)

V. THE FINAL MESSAGE OF SCRIPTURE (22:6–21)
    A. The Invitation to Salvation (22:6–19)
    B. The Amen: "Come, Lord Jesus" (22:20–21)

PART 2

THE THEOLOGY OF THE
BOOK OF REVELATION

CHAPTER 6

BIBLIOLOGY IN THE BOOK OF REVELATION

MAL COUCH

BIBLIOLOGY IS A STUDY OF THE purpose and origin of the Bible itself. It deals with canonicity and inspiration of the Scriptures. It tells us not only what the Word of God is all about but also how it came to be.

Those who say Revelation should be part of New Testament Scripture certainly believe the book is inspired by the Holy Spirit—and its contents were even revealed to John by Christ Himself. Though the book was not readily accepted by several early church leaders, in time few doubted its place as the final writing of the Bible.

Those who doubt the validity of Revelation would have to prove that the author John was a liar and that Jesus did not give the prophetic messages in the book to the apostle. This is a formidable task for critics of the Bible, because there is more internal evidence for its inspired authenticity than for any other New Testament book!

The Book of Revelation Is a Book of Prophecy

Though Revelation is known as a prophetic book, it is important to understand what the book claims for itself. The words *prophecy, prophesy, prophesying, prophet,* and *prophets* are forms used twenty-one times in this writing. And the way these words are used leaves no doubt that the book is forecasting events yet to come. No other New Testament book uses this term about itself in such a clear way.

The Book Written to Be Read

Revelation is probably the least read and certainly the most puzzling book in the New Testament. And yet, ironically, it is the one book that includes a special blessing for all who will read it. John wrote, "blessed [or 'fortunate'] is he who reads . . . the words of [this] prophecy" (Rev. 1:3). He then added that those who read and hear this book are blessed if they "heed" (i.e., keep or obey) what is written. And though the entire book contains dozens of prophetic utterances, it is seen as a single unit, "the prophecy." A reminder of this blessing is repeated in the final chapter: "And behold, I am coming quickly. Blessed is he who heeds the words of the prophecy of this book" (22:7).

"Jesus Is the Spirit of Prophecy"

This remarkable statement in Revelation 19:10 was made by an angel from heaven just before the devastated earth will receive its Peace-Maker, the Lord Jesus Christ. John fell before the feet of the angel and started to worship him. But the angel said, "Do not do that; I am a fellow servant of yours and your brethren who hold the testimony of Jesus; worship God. For the testimony of Jesus is the spirit of prophecy."

What did the angel mean? Robert Thomas answers this question this way:

> The sense of the explanation is, "He who has the spirit of prophecy will convey Jesus' testimony." The message attested by Jesus is "the spirit of prophecy." . . . "The spirit of prophecy" is the Spirit of God working in and through the prophet—i.e., the divinely inspired activity of the prophet. . . . In essence, this statement means that the testimony given by Jesus is the substance of what the Spirit inspires Christian prophets to speak. . . . John and his fellow Christians who were gifted as prophets received prophetic inspiration to speak this testimony along with angels such as John's guide through 17:1–19:10. They were all merely vehicles of Jesus' words and did not merit the worship that belongs to God alone. John had mistakenly offered worship to the angel as the source of prophetic revelation.[1]

Walvoord explains the statement "the testimony of Jesus is the spirit of prophecy" by saying that "the very nature or purpose of prophecy is to testify of Jesus Christ and to bring glory to Him."[2]

The Prophets Are the Servants of God

The seventh trumpet of 11:15–19 is written like a prophetic proclamation for the end of the Tribulation. It predicts the kingdom that will soon be revealed, the coming reign of Christ, the final spurt of anger from the nations, and the nearness of the judgment to come.

But the passage also mentions the fact that God will reward His "servants the prophets" (11:18 NIV). Since this is mentioned in association with the coming glories of the kingdom, the servants are probably the prophets of the Old Testament.

Revelation 10:7 also refers to these servant-prophets. "But in the days when the seventh angel is about to sound his trumpet, the mystery of God will be accomplished, just as he announced to his servants the prophets" (NIV). Of this verse, Thomas says, "The mystery of God consists of the heretofore unrevealed details unfolded in the chapters from here to the end, chapters that tell of the institution of God's kingdom on earth and eventually in the new heavens and new earth."[3]

The fact that the kingdom is previewed here in chapter 10 would certainly make the prophets of old rejoice. The fact that this same term occurs often in the Old Testament suggests that it does refer to prophets of the Old Testament era rather than New Testament prophets. The term "My servants the prophets" occurs in the Old Testament in 2 Kings 9:7; Jeremiah 7:25; 26:5; 44:4; "His servants the prophets" occurs in Jeremiah 25:4 and Amos 3:7; and "Thy servants the prophets" is used in Ezra 9:11.

After John was told to eat a little scroll that an angel handed to him, he was told that he "must prophesy again concerning many peoples and nations and tongues and kings" (Rev. 10:11). The little scroll tasted sweet to the apostle but it was also bitter in his stomach (vv. 9–10). This seems to indicate that he was sensing that both good and bad events will occur.

Since John was instructed to "prophesy again," this would indicate that the unfolding of the message of Revelation came in stages. The old apostle was given a spiritual and even an emotional pause, perhaps even to catch his breath! Beginning to prophesy and write again, the information he was receiving was becoming increasingly intense.

Your Brothers the Prophets

Revelation 22:6 begins a kind of epilogue as it sums up the message of the book. In this verse the entire book of prophecy is called "words [that] are faithful and true." And the Lord is called "the God of the spirits of the prophets." This may be saying that God has control, or direct inspirational influence, over the prophets. And again, since the book alludes so often to the Old Testament, this may refer to those prophets of that older testament.

Hearing the angel speaking to him here, John fell at his feet, perhaps thinking he was in the presence of Jesus Christ. But the angel assured him that he was only "a fellow servant of yours and of your brethren the prophets and of those who heed the words of this book" (v. 9).

The angel was saying that all of God's special message-bearers of inspired Scripture are fellow servants and brothers in the Lord. Their common task was to communicate the prophecies God wanted revealed. Also those who obey what is revealed in the book of Revelation are also included in this faithful fraternity of fellow servants.

The Blood of the Prophets

During the Tribulation, prophets may appear and give warnings to the masses of what is coming. The third bowl of terrible wrath will pour pollution on the waters of the earth so that they will become blood (16:4). God is righteous, because He will judge evil men who will persecute the saints by pouring out their blood and the blood of prophets (v. 6).

One of the reasons God will send judgment on Babylon the harlot is that "in her was found the blood of prophets and of saints and of all who have been slain on the earth" (18:24). Again, these prophets will be messengers of the Lord in the Tribulation period.

Many martyrs in heaven will rejoice when Babylon is judged. "Rejoice over her, O heaven, and you saints and apostles and prophets, because God has pronounced judgment for you against her" (v. 20).

The Two Witnesses

Two prophets, known as the two witnesses, are described in 11:1–14. Almost in the middle of the Tribulation they will come on the scene to carry out a special mission of testifying for God to the entire world.

Chapter 11 begins by describing how the "holy city" (Jerusalem) will be trampled under the feet of the Gentiles for forty-two months, that is, three and a half years (vv. 1–2). This is the time frame often used to refer to the second half of the seven-year Tribulation.

But the Lord will send forth two witnesses who, with divine authority, will prophesy for the same period of time (1,260 days, v. 3). For the time being, these witnesses are protected by the Lord, and they are given permission to devour their enemies, those who attempt to harm them, with fire coming forth from their mouths (v. 5). Besides having this power, they will be able to cause rain to cease, to turn water into blood (pollution), and to smite the earth with plagues (v. 6).

In time they will be overcome and slain (v. 7). People everywhere will look on their dead bodies for three and a half days (v. 9). And the inhabitants of earth (referring to unbelievers) will celebrate the witnesses' death by sending gifts to each other (v. 10). These verses may indicate that these happenings are within the scope of the modern era, because, only in a technological time such as now, could the entire world take part together "electronically" with what was taking place.

The spiritual condition of the unbelieving world is evident because the message of the two witnesses will have "tormented" those who dwell on the earth (v. 10).

But the Lord will bring these two dead prophets back to life and they will be transported to heaven. This resurrection will be so shocking that "great fear" will fall on those who see it (v. 11).

What is the purpose of these two witnesses? First, they will apparently give an important and near-final testimony to Jerusalem, which by that time will be overflowing with sin and rebellion, a city called "Sodom and Egypt" (v. 8). (Probably most people in the city will be Jews.) Second, the two witnesses will demonstrate God's grace in warning the world in order to bring it to repentance. The world (perhaps through satellite television) will hear their testimony and see their dead bodies in the streets—and yet the vast majority of people will not come to the Lord!

The False Prophets

The Lord accused the church in Thyatira of tolerating the woman Jezebel, "who calls herself a prophetess," leading God's servants astray by causing them to commit "acts of immorality and eat things sacrificed to idols" (2:20). Was John simply personifying an attitude that was wreaking spiritual havoc in the church, or was there in the congregation a Jezebel-like woman who was leading people astray into immorality and idolatry?

Interestingly, Christ said He gave her time to repent (v. 21). But she refused to do so. Her children, whoever they will be, will be slain as an example to all the churches (v. 23).

The second beast in Revelation 13, "another beast" (13:11), will represent the Antichrist, the first beast, and will speak for him before the world. He will perform miracles by making "fire come down out of heaven to the earth in the presence of men" (v. 13). He will cause the world to worship the first beast (v. 12), and he will deceive those on earth with signs, even making an image of the Antichrist that will seem to come alive (v. 14). He will also convince many people to take the mark of the Beast on their right hand or forehead (v. 16).

Though not referred to as a prophet in chapter 13, he is called that in 20:10, where he is said to be cast into the lake of fire with the Beast, where both of them "will be tormented day and night forever and ever."

How the Book of Revelation Came to Be

The first few verses of Revelation are critical in understanding the source and the purpose of this book of prophecy.

"The Revelation of Jesus Christ"

Revelation 1:1–2 reads, "The Revelation of Jesus Christ, which God gave Him to show to His bond-servants, the things which must shortly take place; and He sent and communicated it by His angel to His bond-servant John, who bore witness to the word of God and to the testimony of Jesus Christ, even to all that he saw."

When John wrote that this book is a revelation of Jesus Christ, did he mean it was "from" Him or "about" Him? The Greek grammar allows both meanings.

If the genitive "of" is objective, then this message is "about" the Lord. But if it is a subjective genitive, the message is "from" Jesus. Thomas suggests that since Christ is the Revealer of truth throughout the book, the phrase should be understood as "from" Him.[4] Other scholars prefer the meaning "concerning" Jesus Christ. Since the grammar allows for both possibilities, perhaps both meanings should be accepted as viable. Walvoord accepts both. The book, he says, "is a revelation of truth about Christ Himself, a disclosure of future events, that is, His second coming when Christ will be revealed. It is as well a revelation which comes from Christ."[5]

The Greek word for *revelation* is *apokalypsis,* which combines the words *apo,* "away," and *kalypsis,* which conveys the idea of a covering. Literally, then, Revelation is a laying bare or disclosure of what has been previously hidden.[6] What is being revealed is a more complete outline of end-time events, especially as they focus on the person of Christ.

"Which God Gave Him"

God the Father gave this message to His Son to reveal it to the apostle John. The Father is the ultimate Source of what Christ reveals,[7] for God "gave them to Christ with the stipulation that He show them to God's servants."[8] This does not mean that Jesus knew nothing of what was coming to pass. Because of His deity Christ knows all things equally with the Father. But as the Son He acquiesced to the Father's timing as to when and how this message would be conveyed.

"To Show to His Bond-servants"

All the books of the Bible are written for believers. The inspired Word gives direction, comfort, and vital information to the Lord's own. Here in the first verse we are reminded of this important fact about such an important book. Revelation is meant to be studied and understood by believers in Jesus Christ.

"He Sent and Communicated It by His Angel"

An angel of God was the agent from Christ who transmitted the message to John the apostle. Some think "angel" is simply a reference to Jesus Himself. But since angels later (17:1; 21:9) speak directly to John, there is no reason to believe this is any being other than a holy messenger from the Lord. Some have suggested that this angel is Gabriel, because on other occasions Gabriel, like this angel, was active in communicating messages from God to others (Dan. 8:16; 9:2, 21–22; Luke 1:26–31).

How was this angel aiding in the transmission of the message of the book of Revelation from Christ? This we do not know, because the voice John heard is actually the voice of the Lord speaking.

"To His Bond-servant John"

John became the human recipient and recorder of this incredible last message of the Holy Scriptures. Though the message is from Christ, it has come to us through John, through his experiences, age, vocabulary, and to a degree his own thought forms. Yet the message and visions he received have been recorded accurately and preserved perfectly.

New Testament apostles were inspired to transmit the Word of God in the same way as the Old Testament prophets. The apostle Peter wrote that the prophets of old did not give us their own interpretations, for prophecy spoken from God came not by human will, but the writers were "carried along" by the Holy Spirit (2 Peter 1:20–21).

John then told how he heard the Lord speaking to him directly: "I heard behind me a loud voice . . . saying, 'Write in a book what you see, and send it to the seven churches'" (Rev. 1:10–11). He was then told: "Write . . . the things which you have seen, and the things which are, and the things which shall take place after these things" (v. 19). So far as we know, John was the only prophet or apostle who was transported to heaven in order to "see" a divine message, events that took place before his consciousness but that pertained to the distant future! "Come up here, and I will show you what must take place after these things" (4:1). This fact gives an extra dimension to the impact of Revelation.

"John, Who Bore Witness to the Word of God and to the Testimony of Jesus Christ"

More than likely this should read, "who bore witness to the Word of God, even to the testimony of Jesus Christ."[9] Earlier the apostle John wrote that Jesus is the Word of God (John 1:1–3), the ultimate expression of God's message to mankind. John lived with and walked with the Lord. Along with the other apostles, his word and testimony must be taken as true. Otherwise he must be labeled one of the greatest liars of history!

Though all the disciples who walked with Jesus testified of His life, death, and resurrection, John holds a special place in this act of witnessing of Christ. In fact, John seemed to confirm this when he wrote that he was sent to the island of Patmos for the special mission of receiving this final revelation. While John was possibly banned to Patmos because of his preaching of Christ,[10] his being there gave him opportunity to be the unique recipient of this final, powerful message. "I . . . was on the island called Patmos, because of the word of God and the testimony of Jesus" (1:9).

E. W. Bullinger writes that John was on Patmos "in order to receive this Apocalypse or Revelation, just as Paul went into Arabia to receive his revelation (Gal. i. 15–17). . . . That John was banished to Patmos on account of his witness for Christ is [but] tradition."[11]

"Even to All [I] Saw"

John saw the events of Revelation take place before his own eyes. In fact he used the verb "I saw" about seventy times! For one book of Scripture, this is an incredible number of times to describe a prophetic, future happening. Like other prophets, John sometimes saw future events as in a vision. However, most of what he wrote seems to have been revealed in a more direct manner.

This beloved apostle was told by the Lord to "write in a book what you see" (1:11). He did just that, writing down, as the Lord commanded, "the things which [he had] seen" (1:19). By this he would be shown "what must take place after these things" (4:1).

No doubt John saw unfamiliar objects and individuals doing things he never saw in his day. This may be why he often struggled to describe what he saw, writing that "the sun became black *as* sackcloth made of hair" (6:12), "the stars [Greek, *asteres*] of the sky fell to the earth, *as* a fig tree casts its unripe figs" (v. 13), and "the sky was split apart *like* a scroll" (v. 14).

And He Said to Me

At least fifty-two times John recorded the words "said unto me." Often this refers to Christ speaking directly to the prophet, as in 21:6, "He said to me, 'It is done. I am the Alpha and the Omega.'" In several instances an angel was giving John words to write down: "And he said to me, 'Write, Blessed are those who are invited to the marriage supper of the Lamb'" (19:9). One of the twenty-four elders also spoke directly with John: "And one of the elders answered, saying to me . . ." (7:13).

In addressing each of the seven churches, Jesus said, "Let him hear what the Spirit says" (2:7, 11, 17, 29; 3:6, 13, 22). The Holy Spirit spoke directly to John, stating that those who "die in the Lord" will "rest from their labors" (14:13).

In chapter 10 the apostle wrote simply of a "voice from heaven" (v. 4). This could refer to one of the escorting angels who gave him insights into the revelations he was observing, or it could be the voice of the Lord. At the end of the chapter the seven angels apparently spoke together in giving John instructions: "And they [the angels] said to me, 'You must prophecy again concerning many peoples and nations and tongues and kings'" (v. 11).

Words of This Prophecy to Be Read, Heard, and Heeded

For the believers in Christ "all Scripture is profitable" (2 Tim. 3:16). And this is equally true of the book of Revelation. This book gives us a divine timeline of yet-future, worldwide happenings. This should sober Christians and encourage them to live faithfully for the Lord.

Revelation 1:4 reads, "Blessed is he who reads and those who hear the words of the prophecy, and heed the things which are written in it."

The plural "words" suggests that each word of the Apocalypse is inspired, not simply the big ideas of the book. This is consistent with the doctrine of the Bible's verbal inspiration and inerrancy.

In fact, sixteen times in Revelation, John referred to the fact of inspiration, with the noun *logos* ("word") in its singular and plural forms. John "bore witness to the word of God" (1:2). He is on the island of Patmos "because of the word of God" (1:9). The words of this prophecy must be heard (1:3). The church of Philadelphia was reminded to keep Christ's word (3:8) and to keep the word of His perseverance (v. 10). During the Tribulation, martyrs will be slain for the word of God (6:9; 20:4). For those invited to the marriage of the Lamb, their invitations are verified by Christ's words, "These are true words of God" (19:9). In his gospel, John wrote of Jesus being the Word of God (1:1), and when he was given the visual revelation of His messianic return to earth in Revelation 19:11, the apostle again referred to Him as the Word of God (v. 13). Blessing is promised to those who "heed the words of the prophecy of this book" (22:7; see also 1:3; 20:9).

Why is this blessing given three times in this book? Because the study of prophecy can have a cleansing effect on the believer. Prophecy helps us realize that life is short and that this world as we know it will not last forever. Human mortality is made evident when we focus on certain realistic aspects of prophecy. In addition the anticipation of seeing Jesus when He comes should cause us to live and act in a godly manner.

As John wrote, we will be like Jesus when He appears (1 John 3:2), and so "every one who has this hope fixed on Him purifies himself, just as He is pure" (v. 3).

Paul also wrote of this cleansing effect of prophecy when he wrote about the new heavens and the new earth. "Beloved, since you look for these things, be diligent to be found by Him in peace, spotless and blameless" (2 Peter 3:14).

The Spirit's Work in Inspiring Revelation

John wrote that he "was in the Spirit on the Lord's day" (1:10). Some think John was speaking about Sunday. But the word "Lord" is used here as an adjective, so that the phrase could read "a Lord-like day." In other words, this day was unique for it was "controlled" by the Lord. John wrote again of the Spirit's activity in 4:2: "Immediately I was in [i.e., with or under the influence of] the Spirit." This began his heavenly tour in which he saw the throne of God in heaven. The Holy Spirit was in charge of his thoughts as he began to receive and record the message from the Lord.

Through the Holy Spirit, God revealed His truth to the apostles, including even the "depths of God" (1 Cor. 2:10). The Lord gives His Spirit so that "we might know the things freely given to us by God" (v. 12).

The greeting to the seven churches in Revelation 1:4–5 is unique in that it is from the apostle John, from God the Father, from "the seven Spirits," and from Jesus Christ.

Some think that when John wrote that he was "in the Spirit" (1:10), the apostle was saying he was dreaming. But as Thomas wrote, "This was not a revelation through a dream because, unlike Peter in Acts 10:10 and Paul in Acts 22:17, John never slept during the process. His spirit was wide awake, and its powers were exercised with exalted clarity."[12]

In Revelation the Lord Jesus personally addressed each of the seven churches in Asia Minor (Rev. 2–3). But His postscripts at the end of each message close with "He who has an ear, let him hear what the Spirit says to the churches" (2:7, 11, 17, 29; 3:6, 13, 22).

Examining these "postcards" to the churches, one can see that in the last verse to each church Jesus urged believers to "hear what the Spirit says to the churches." This points to the fact that these messages were conveyed through the Holy Spirit.

"Write in a Book"

Two Greek words for "book" in Revelation are *biblion* and *biblos*. Most scholars believe they are almost synonymous.[13] They are translated as "book" or "scroll," but more than likely a scroll is in view, since the book form we now use was unknown in that era.

Biblos is used in the phrase "the book of life," which is mentioned in Revelation 3:5; 13:8; 17:8; 20:12, 15; and 21:27.

Seven times in Revelation 22 John referred to "this book," "the words of this book," "the words of the prophecy of this book" (vv. 7, 9, 10, 18 [twice], 19 [twice]). The idea conveyed is that this work has great spiritual authority, because it is authored by God Himself and His Son.

With these references John presented an awesome and sobering warning: Do not tamper with these words! "I testify to everyone who hears the words of the prophecy of this book: if anyone adds to them, God shall add to him the plagues which are written in this book; and if anyone takes away from the words of the book of this prophecy, God shall take away his part from the tree of life and from the holy city, which are written in this book" (22:18–19).

In addition to warning against adding or taking away words from the book of Revelation, the warning may also be against adding any new "revelation" to the entire New Testament. Anyone who claims to present new "scripture" as if it were from God will be condemned. "What a solemn warning this is to critics who have tampered with this book and other portions of Scripture in arrogant self-confidence that they are equipped intellectually and spiritually to determine what is true and what is not true in the Word of God."[14]

Thomas points out that the warning in these verses verifies the close of the New Testament canon.

This is a warning not just to the would-be prophets themselves, who might try to continue prophetic ministries beyond the time of Revelation's writing, but also to "everyone who hears," i.e., those in the churches who needed to refuse any authority that challenged the divine authority, accuracy, and finality of this prophecy. The observation is true that this warning applies specifically to the book of Revelation only, but by extension it entails the termination of the gift of prophecy and the NT canon also.[15]

Conclusion

The Apocalypse, perhaps more than any other book of Scripture, is packed with numerous references to bibliology. Those who attempt to challenge the inspiration of this work must climb an enormous mountain of internal evidence. Then they must be subjective and destructive in trying to answer all this evidence. They must overlook and throw away an overwhelming amount of logical argument presented in this chapter alone. They must deny outrightly all that is said of the book's inception and genius. They must openly refute the fact that God the Father, the Lord Jesus, the Holy Spirit, the seven angels, a special and important individual angel, and the elders, all played such a miraculous part in formulating this inspired message.

Scores of allusions to the Old Testament weave a tapestry of divine revelation that make this book a summary of a vast storehouse of ancient prophetic utterances.

Though some have thought the book of Revelation would be easy to destroy, for a multitude of reasons this is certainly not the case. The Bible would be woefully incomplete without the insights and summaries of the inspired final "chapter" of Scripture, the Apocalypse.

But why would critics attempt to discredit the book of Revelation? LaHaye gives an insightful answer.

No book in the Bible has been more discredited than Revelation except for its counterpart in the Old Testament, the book of Daniel. Because Revelation deals predominantly with prophecy and the future, and because it exposes Satan as a deceptive fraud, the arch-enemy of man has tried his hardest to discredit the book. The last thing he wants is for people to become aware of Christ's majesty, Satan's treachery, and the Christian's final triumph when this old world system ultimately fails.[16]

CHAPTER 7

THEOLOGY PROPER IN THE BOOK OF REVELATION

ROBERT P. LIGHTNER

The Trinity in Revelation

THE WORD *Trinity* DOES NOT appear in the book of Revelation nor in any other book of the Bible. However, from John's description of all he saw while on the isle of Patmos, it is clear that there is one God who exists in three persons—Father, Son, and Holy Spirit.

God the Father

John described God the Father in his greetings to the churches as the One "who is and who was and who is to come" (Rev. 1:4). He is the Source of grace and peace. He is "the Absolute One, who knows no change, no dependence on time or place, but to whom the present, the past, and the future are one and the same eternal now."[1]

John continued his greeting to his readers with the words "and from the seven Spirits who are before His throne" (v. 4). "The seven Spirits might conceivably refer to a group of angelic beings. But coming between references to the Father and the Son it is more probable that this is an unusual way of designating the Holy Spirit."[2] He too is the Source of grace and peace.

Also grace and peace are from Jesus Christ (v. 5). No one can ever experience true grace and peace apart from Him. Ryrie has well said, John's salutation "is a greeting from the Trinity."[3]

God the Father is also identified as Christ's "God and Father," to whom all glory and honor were to be given (v. 6). God the Son promised to confess before God the Father the names of those who overcome (3:5). The overcomers are believers throughout the book of Revelation.

Christ also described Himself as One who overcame and who grants to all God's people the right to "sit down" with Him on His Father's throne (v. 21). John the apostle saw the 144,000 with God the Father's name and God the Son's name on their foreheads (14:1).

In addition, many references in the book refer simply to God. Many times the context points to God the Father as the One referred to or spoken of.

God the Son

Revelation includes a large number of specific references to Christ, the Son of God. In several extended passages He is the central figure. Since the next chapter of this book deals with the activities and names of Christ in Revelation, this section here stresses only John's emphasis on Christ as the Lamb of God.

But first, we need to note a few other facts about Christ in Revelation. The entire book of Revelation is the "revelation of Jesus Christ" (1:1), and "the testimony of Jesus Christ" (v. 2). He is "the first-born of the dead, and the ruler of the kings of the earth," and loved us and provided redemption for us through His blood (v. 5). He will come again just as surely as He came the first time (v. 7). As the "Alpha and the Omega . . . the Almighty" (v. 8), He is fully God.

John heard a voice telling him to write while there on the isle of Patmos (v. 9). When he turned, he saw "one like a son of man" (v. 13). This was none other than the Lord Jesus Christ, the risen and glorified Christ in all His glory. He is depicted with a number of similes. How else could John have described Him? John fell at His feet and worshiped Him (v. 17).

To the church at Thyatira, Christ spoke of Himself as the "Son of God" (Rev. 2:18). Christ the Lord will come some day and "reign forever and ever" (11:15). This was part of the message from the seventh trumpet judgment. Christ the "male child" will rule over the entire world "with a rod of iron" (12:5). The awesome authority of God the Son was recognized by John (v. 10). As he described the Second Coming of Christ to the earth, John again hailed Him as "the Lord our God, the Almighty" (19:6).

In a vision John saw Jesus Christ coming to establish His kingdom on earth (Rev. 19:11–16). When Christ, whose name is "Faithful and True," descends on a white horse, He will judge in righteousness and make war with His enemies. His appearance will be awesome (vv. 12–13), and He will have in His mouth "a sharp sword" (v. 15) as He executes divine wrath on unbelieving men and nations. The garment He will wear will display His name—"King of Kings, and Lord of Lords" (v. 16).

Jesus referred to Himself as "the root and offspring of David," (22:16). As the "root" of David, He existed before David, that is, He is eternal. And as the "offspring" or descendant of David, He is the rightful Heir to the throne of David, and the One who will fulfill the covenanted blessings promised to David. His coming will bring a new day.

As noted earlier, John emphasized the fact that Jesus Christ, God's Son, is the "Lamb" of God, a term frequently used of Christ in Revelation.

The first reference to Christ as a Lamb is in the scene in heaven in which a book (scroll) with seven seals was in the hands of God the Father (5:1–14). No one in heaven or earth was found worthy to open the sealed book. But then John saw "a Lamb standing, as if slain" (v. 6), and He alone was worthy to break the seals and open the book. Depicting Christ as a Lamb speaks of His meekness. But He was standing, ready to assume His authoritative role. He had died and had come forth from the grave triumphantly. When He took the book from God the Father, all of heaven rejoiced and praised God for Him and His ability to open it.

As a Lamb, Christ broke each of the seven seals, and divine judgment followed (Rev. 6:1, 3, 5, 7, 9, 12; 8:1). Before the seventh seal was broken (8:1), three times the Lamb was exalted because of His great saving work of all who came to Him in faith during the Great Tribulation (7:10, 14, 17).

John also saw God the Son, the Lamb, standing on Mount Zion with 144,000 individuals (Rev. 14:1). His name and the name of His Father were written on their foreheads (cf. 7:2–8). These are the Jewish evangelists who will spread the gospel of God's grace and the kingdom during the Great Tribulation. All who worship the Antichrist during that time "will be tormented with fire and brimstone in the presence of the holy angels and in the presence of the Lamb" (14:10).

In the future, war will be waged against Christ the Lamb by the Antichrist, the False Prophet, and ten kings (17:8–13). The Lamb, however, will be successful. "The Lamb will overcome them, because He is Lord of lords and King of kings" (v. 14).

Just before Christ returns to the earth with His saints, the marriage supper of the Lamb will take place (19:7, 9). In this celebration the bride is the church. After observing this, John saw heaven opened and Christ descending on a white horse (v. 11). This is the second coming of Christ, when His feet will touch the Mount of Olives (Zech. 14:4), and He will institute His kingdom on earth for one thousand years (Rev. 20:4, 6).

In the new Jerusalem in the eternal state a river will flow from the throne of God the Father and of the Lamb (22:1). The curse on the earth will be removed, and the throne of God the Father and of the Lamb will be center stage (22:3), and Christ will be worshiped and served forever.

God the Holy Spirit

What did John mean when he referred to "the seven Spirits" (1:4)? This was probably his way of calling attention to the full manifestation of God the Holy Spirit. Three facts suggest that this is a reference to the Holy Spirit. First, the phrase "the seven Spirits" comes between the references to God the

Father and God the Son. Second, the apostle may very well have had in mind the sevenfold ministry of the Spirit referred to by Isaiah the prophet (Isa. 11:2). Third, the number seven, which appears so often in Revelation (53 times), is associated with completeness and perfection.

John claimed to be "in the Spirit" (Rev. 1:10) as he saw the vision and heard God's message. This expression is used by John also in 4:2; 17:3; and 21:10. In each case it speaks of his being open to all the Spirit of God had to say. He was ready to see what God wanted to show him. The Holy Spirit spoke through John to each of the churches (2:7, 11, 17, 29; 3:6, 13, 22), emphasizing that these messages Christ gave were of divine origin.

The book of Revelation closes with a grand invitation to all who are thirsty in their souls for the water of life to come and drink or "take the water of life without cost" (22:17). This invitation is from the Spirit of God and the re-deemed "bride."

So what can be learned about the Trinity from the book of Revelation? Several things of importance stand out: (1) There is one God. (2) He exists in three persons, each of whom is either addressed as God or performs works only God could do. (3) The three members of the Trinity always work in harmony. No member stands in conflict with the other members of the Trinity. Each member of the Trinity holds a different office, but there is no subordination of essence.

The Person of God the Father in Revelation

God the Father's Personality

Many times in the book of Revelation the name "God" is used without specifically identifying which member of the Godhead is meant. But one may rightly assume that in such cases God the Father is in view.

All the works of God studied below demonstrate that He is indeed a person, not an impersonal object or a mere influence. For God to do all He does requires that He be a person, possessing intellect, emotion, and will. This is seen in the very first verse of Revelation. God the Father gave this book of Revelation to Jesus Christ, who in turn "communicated it by His angel to His bond-servant John" (1:1). An impersonal power or influence could not have communicated verbal messages such as John received concerning people, problems, judgments, and blessings.

John described God the Father in vivid terms, all of which reveal His personality. He is "the God of heaven" (11:13; 16:11) and also "the Lord of the earth" (11:4). When John referred to his God as "our God" (7:3, 10, 12; 15:6), he spoke of a personal relationship between God and believers. Seated on His throne in heaven (4:2–3; 5:1), He is the "living God" (7:2) who issues "commandments" (12:17; 14:12), and He has "priests" who serve Him (20:6).

God the Father's Sovereignty

While some Bible expositors say God's sovereignty is one of His attributes or perfections, it may be preferable to view His sovereignty as the truth about God's person which makes all His perfections possible and out of which they function as He carries out His plan. When we describe God as sovereign, we mean He is in complete control of His world. He has a plan, and He is implementing that plan. He is at the helm of the ship of all creation and life.

It is difficult to choose specific passages in Revelation that stress God's sovereignty, because there are so many. The entire book is about the sovereign Lord of all the universe working out His plan among individuals and nations as well as Satan and his demons. All the messages recorded in Revelation and all the events described there demonstrate that God is sovereign.

One of the first things John saw in his vision was the throne of God. His presence there indicated that He is sovereign and ruling. Morris addresses this fact. "John . . . is very interested in thrones, and specifically in the throne of God which he mentions in almost every chapter. . . . John's readers were familiar with earthly thrones, and they were troubled by all that Caesar's throne meant. John will not let them forget that there is a throne above every throne."[4]

Each of the references to the throne of God the Father illustrate the truth of His sovereignty. We will concentrate on the references to God's throne only in Revelation 4 and 5. These are exemplary of the other uses.

Immediately after he heard the voice from heaven inviting him to "come up here" (4:1), John saw a throne and One seated on it. The words "sitting on the throne" in verse 2 and "sitting" in verse 3 translate a present participle, which emphasizes continuous occupancy on the throne. There can be no doubt as to the identity of the One on the throne; He is "The LORD GOD, the ALMIGHTY, who was and who is and who is to come" (v. 8). Distinguished Greek authority Henry Alford said the One on the throne is "the Eternal Father . . . for He that sitteth on the throne is distinguished in ch. 6:16; 7:10 from the Son, and in ch. 4 verse 5 from the Holy Spirit."[5]

The One on the throne was "like a jasper stone and a sardius in appearance" (4:3). Walvoord discusses the significance of these stones.

> It is of interest that these same stones are used to describe the majesty of the king of Tyrus (Ezek. 28:13) where, in a list of nine precious stones, the sardius (sardine) is mentioned first and the jasper is sixth in the list. In the description of the foundation of the new Jerusalem in Revelation 21:19–20, the jasper is first and the sardius is sixth. The emerald is listed as eighth in Ezekiel and fourth in Revelation 21:19. It is evident that these stones have a peculiar significance of glory and majesty which are characteristic of God on His throne. Coupled with the brilliant reflections of

the jasper and the deep red of the sardine stone, the rainbow described as all of green like an emerald forms a rich background for the glorious scene which John beheld.[6]

A rainbow around the throne resembled an emerald in appearance and was "a vivid reminder of the faithfulness of God (Gen. 9:11–17)."[7] The fact that the rainbow encircled the entire throne highlights God's complete faithfulness. He never goes back on His word.

Everything else about this throne of the Lord God Almighty speaks of His sovereignty as well. Around God's throne were twenty-four other thrones, on which elders in white garments and with golden crowns were sitting (4:4). Flashes of lightning and peals of thunder came from the throne (v. 5). Before the throne John saw something like a sea of glass that looked like crystal (v. 6). Also closely associated with the throne were four living creatures (i.e., "living ones"). Though we cannot be certain of the identification of these "living ones,"[8] one thing is certain: They give endless praise to God. They worship Him, giving Him honor and glory and praise because of who He is— the sovereign God of all the universe (vv. 8–9).

Revelation 4 portrays God the Father on His throne in heaven worshiped by the twenty-four elders and four living ones. Chapter 5, on the other hand, focuses on God the Son, the Lamb of God, who alone is worthy to open the sealed book in the Father's hand. Chapters 4 and 5 form a unit describing the scene in heaven from earth.

Only Christ the Lamb of God is qualified to open the sealed book held by God the Father on the throne. As Sovereign, God the Father is still on the throne (just as He was in chapter 4), and He holds the book that contains the predicted events described in the rest of the book of Revelation. While chapter 5 does not state explicitly what is written in the book, it seems clear that it contains the seal, trumpet, and bowl judgments.

The world's destiny is in the hand of the sovereign God.

God the Father's Attributes and Activities

No attempt will be made here to refer to all the passages in Revelation that support the attributes or perfections discussed below. A selected sampling will be sufficient to support the claims.

Life and self-existence. The God in the book of Revelation, and in all the books of the Bible, is living. He is the One who gave the messages in Revelation to Jesus Christ, who in turn gave them to John the apostle (Rev. 1:1).

John saw "the seal of the living God" (Rev. 7:2) on the angel who was sent to bring judgment on the earth and the sea. It was also the "breath of life from God" (11:11) which brought the two witnesses back to life.

As the living God, He possesses life in and of Himself, and He depends on no one or nothing outside Himself. As the prophet Jeremiah said, "He is the living God and the everlasting King" (Jer. 10:10), and as Paul said to the Thessalonian Christians, God is the "living and true God" (1 Thess. 1:9).

Love, mercy, and grace. These three perfections of our God belong together, for mercy and grace are the expressions of God's love. God's grace is His giving of unmerited favor to the undeserving, and His mercy is His compassionate treatment of those who are in distress.

Though God the Father's love is not specifically mentioned in Revelation, twice the love of God the Son is stated. To the church of Philadelphia, Jesus said He would make those of the "synagogue of Satan . . . come and bow down at your feet, and to know that I have loved you" (3:9). "The faithful and true Witness," who is Christ, said to the church of Laodicea, "those whom I love, I reprove and discipline" (v. 19).

Though not specifically stated, God the Father's love is everywhere evident throughout the book of Revelation. The very fact that He gave this revelation to His Son to give to John shows His great love. The Father's love is seen in His deliverance of the church, the body of Christ, from the wrath of the Lamb poured out in the three great series of judgments—seal, trumpet, and bowl judgments. The church of Philadelphia, representing the true church, will be kept "from the hour of testing . . . which is about to come upon the whole world" (3:10).

John saw "a great multitude, which no one could count, from every nation and all tribes and peoples and tongues" praising God (7:9–10). They were rejoicing in their salvation. This great company of the redeemed are described as "the ones who come out of the great tribulation, and they have washed their robes and made them white in the blood of the Lamb" (v. 14). The salvation of this multitude during the time of the Great Tribulation illustrates the Father's love as well as His mercy and grace.

The scene at the Great White Throne judgment also reveals the Father's love, mercy, and grace, for all whose names were found "in the book of life" (20:15) were spared the eternal fate of those whose names were not there—"the lake of fire." Alongside the revelation of the Father's love, mercy, and grace shown at this judgment is the evidence of His justice and wrath.

Holiness, righteousness, and justice. God the Father's perfection, His awesome holiness, is clearly emphasized in Revelation by the many mighty works John saw Him perform. There is no hint that God gradually arrived at the state of perfection He now occupies. Rather, it is evident that all the judgments against those who have rejected His Son, as well as all the future blessings on those who have received His Son as Savior, rest solidly on the fact that He is altogether holy and righteous. All His activities are the outworking of His holiness.

To ascribe righteousness and justice to God is to speak of His holiness as it relates to humans. He demands holiness of His people because He Himself is absolutely holy. By the same token, He punishes sin and rejects sinners who reject His Son because He is holy.

John did not hesitate to speak of the Father's wrath. Those who worship the coming Antichrist and bow at his image in the temple "will drink . . . of the wrath of God" (14:10). The seven plagues John saw represented the final outpouring of God's wrath (15:1). The bowl judgments were "full of the wrath of God, who lives forever and ever" (v. 7). God's anger against Babylon is said to be "fierce wrath" (16:19).

All the judgments poured out on the world through the seals, trumpets, and bowls will be the outpouring of the Father's wrath because He is holy, righteous, and just. Each of the judgments is His response to the obstinate rebellion and rejection of Him by humans. These express His holiness, righteousness, and justice.

The salvation of great multitudes during the Great Tribulation (Rev. 7; 14) also shows God the Father's holiness. These will all be redeemed by the blood of the Lamb, the Son of God, who met every demand of the offended righteousness of God. They, like all others who find acceptance with God, must be clothed in God's righteousness. All others will be forever excluded from heaven.

Religious and political Babylon (Rev. 17–18) both represent the opposite of God's holiness, righteousness, and justice. Because of this, God will destroy them.

During the millennial kingdom Satan will be bound by God as His Son reigns in perfect righteousness and absolute justice (Rev. 20). In the eternal state the Father's holiness, righteousness, and justice will be displayed eternally in the new heavens and the new earth. Sin will be no more. "The tabernacle of God" will then be "among men, and He shall dwell among them, and they shall be His people, and God Himself shall be among them" (21:3).

The glory of God speaks of His presence, that is, the full manifestation of Himself. John saw "the temple of the tabernacle of testimony in heaven" (Rev. 15:5); that is, the holy place, and seven angels came out of the holy place. Each angel was given a golden bowl filled with God the Father's wrath (v. 7). Then John saw the temple "filled with smoke from the glory of God" (v. 8). Here, then, is a scene of God's awesome presence in judgment.

The New Jerusalem John saw coming down from God out of heaven also manifested "the glory of God" (21:11). Because of this, the city will have "no need of the sun or of the moon to shine upon it, for the glory of God has illumined it, and its lamp is the Lamb" (v. 23).

God the Father's Names

God is called by five specific names in the book of Revelation. Before discussing these, we need to note briefly the one instance that refers to "the name of God" (16:9) without mentioning any specific name. References to the name of God were common in the Old Testament.

> Abraham called on *the name* of the Lord (Gen. 12:8; 13:4). The Lord proclaimed His own *name* before Moses (Exod. 33:19; 34:6). Israel was warned against profaning the *name* of the Lord (Lev. 22:32). The *name* of the Lord God was not to be taken in vain (Exod. 20:7; Deut. 5:11). The priests of Israel were to minister in *the name* of the Lord (Deut. 18:5; 21:5).
>
> We learn something about the meaning and intent of the phrase, *the name of the Lord,* when we realize that to refuse to obey injunctions such as those cited above meant to refuse God and to depart from Him. In contrast, to call on the *name* of the Lord was to worship Him as God (Gen. 21:33; 26:25).
>
> We must conclude, therefore, that such phrases as "the name of the LORD" or "the name of God" referred to His whole character. These were summary statements that embodied the entire Person of God.[9]

Undoubtedly John was communicating the same meaning when he used the phrase "the name of God" (16:9). That is, when people blasphemed His name, they blasphemed *Him.*

Father. Twice John referred to God as the "Father" of Jesus Christ (1:6; 14:1). God the Father and God the Son are hereby identified as of the same essence; both possess deity as members of the Trinity. Both the Son's and the Father's names are written on the foreheads of the 144,000 (14:1).

Twice Christ Himself referred to God as His Father (Rev. 3:5, 21). In both instances He was describing the rewards for the overcomers in the churches of Sardis and Laodicea.

God. The first occurrence of this name is in the very first verse of the Bible (Gen. 1:1). Throughout the Old Testament it is used approximately twenty-five hundred times. The very first usage shows that the name "Elohim" (God) speaks of the awesome creative and eternal power of God as the Creator. He is the absolute and supreme Source of all things.

In the New Testament the name "God" is also used many times. In most of the occurrences it refers to God the Father. That is how John used it in Revelation over a dozen times. In fact, John began his book by using "God" in this way (Rev. 1:1). It is used in connection with creation (3:14), worship (7:11, 17; 11:16; 15:3), judgment (8:2, 4; 14:7; 16:19), miracle-working (11:11), a heavenly throne (12:5–6), and blasphemy (13:6; 16:21). All these instances speak of the power and authority of God the Father.

An angel from heaven cried out on behalf of the 144,000, "Do not harm the earth or the sea or the trees, until we have sealed the bond-servants of our God on their foreheads" (7:3). The multitude of redeemed during the Great Tribulation also cried out, "Salvation to our God who sits on the throne, and to the Lamb" (v. 10). All the angels standing around the throne in John's vision fell before God the Father in worship and called Him "our God" (v. 12).

Christ Himself spoke of God as "My God" (Rev. 3:2). Four times in one verse Christ referred to God as "My God" (v. 12). This parallels the many times that Jesus, while He was on earth, spoke of "My Father." He did not hesitate also to remind His own that God is also *their* heavenly Father. Only those rightly related to God through Christ can claim such intimacy with the God of all the universe.

Lord and Lord God. The name "Lord" translates Greek *kyrios* in the New Testament and parallels the name "Adonay" in the Hebrew Old Testament.

When the words *kyrios* or *adonay* are used of humans, the "lord" or master has the right to expect obedience from his subjects or servants, and the servant may expect to be provided for by his lord or master. The name "Lord" carries a similar connotation when it is used of God. As the divine Master of the universe and of humankind, He has every right to expect obedience from His servants. Likewise, the Master's servants can expect Him to meet their needs and make every provision for them.

God the Father is addressed in this way by "the souls of those who had been slain because of the word of God, and because of the testimony which they had maintained" (6:9). These cried out "with a loud voice, saying, 'How long, O Lord *[kyrios]* holy and true, until You judge and avenge our blood on those who dwell on the earth?'" (v. 10 NKJV).

Those who had been victorious over the Antichrist by not receiving his mark and, therefore, dying as martyrs sang the song of Moses. In that song they proclaimed, "Great and marvelous are Your works, Lord God Almighty!" (15:3 NKJV). And again, "Who shall not fear You, O Lord, and glorify Your name?" (v. 4 NKJV). John heard an angel also speaking to God as the "Lord God, the Almighty" (16:7).

The compound "Lord God" is used of God the Father also (1:8; 15:3; 18:8; 21:22; 22:5). With this combination of two of the common names of God, the Father's role as divine Master and His sovereign power and authority are highlighted.

Alpha and Omega. These are the first and last letters of the Greek alphabet. When applied to God, as in Revelation 1:8, they describe Him as the beginning and the ending, the first and the last, thus emphasizing His eternal existence.

Some believe the speaker in Revelation 1:8, where he says, "'I am the Alpha and the Omega,' says the Lord God, 'who is and who was and who is to come, the Almighty,'" is God the Father, but others say He is God the Son. It seems preferable to view the speaker as God the Father. This is because the word "Almighty" seems to refer to God the Father in each of the other eight times it is used in Revelation.

Almighty. Nine times in Revelation this name is given to God the Father. The first is in Revelation 1:8, where, as already noted, it is added to two other titles, "the Alpha and the Omega" and "the Lord God." The Greek word rendered "the Almighty" means "the all-powerful One," thus emphasizing His omnipotence. The four "living ones" who worship the Lord also refer to Him as the "Lord God Almighty, Who was and is and is to come!" (4:8 NKJV). The same emphasis is in 11:17, where the twenty-four elders give thanks to the "Lord God Almighty, The One who is and who was and who is to come" (NKJV). Here the awesome power of God is stressed as He begins His reign over all.

The great and marvelous works of God the Father are associated with the Almighty One, as well as His righteousness and truth (15:3). As the third bowl judgment was seen by John, he heard someone (presumably an angel) "from the altar saying, 'Even so, Lord God Almighty, true and righteous are Your judgments'" (16:7 NKJV). Likewise, as the sixth bowl judgment unfolded in John's vision, he saw demons gathering kings of the world together for "the battle of that great day of God Almighty" (16:14 NKJV).

Just before Christ returns to the earth, multitudes in heaven will praise God, saying, "Hallelujah! For the Lord our God, the Almighty, reigns" (19:6). And when Christ defeats His enemies in the battle of Armageddon, He will express "the fierce wrath of God, the Almighty" (19:15) against sin.

When John described the new Jerusalem coming down from God out of heaven, he said that "the Lord God, the Almighty, and the Lamb, are its temple" (21:22). That is, as the all-powerful sovereign God, He will be worshiped forever.[10]

God the Father and His Children

Knowing about God and knowing Him are two entirely different things. No one can really know Him personally who does not know truth about Him. However, it is possible to know about Him without really knowing Him. The question is, How can we use our knowledge *about* God so that we will come to know Him genuinely? "The rule for doing this is demanding, but simple. It is that we turn each truth that we learn about God into matter for meditation *before* God, leading to prayer and praise *to* God."[11]

Using the book of Daniel as a basis, Packer summarizes the impact that the knowledge of God should have on believers. He says they have great energy for God, have great thoughts of God, show great boldness for God, and have great contentment in God.[12]

The more and the better we come to know God personally, the more we will be submissive to Him and want to live according to Scripture, which is the expression of His will. The way we get to know God the Father is through God the Son, the living Word revealed in the written Word.

Our heavenly Father wants us, His children, to know Him as a divine Person, not an impersonal power, force, or influence. This divine, sovereign Person has a magnificent plan for humankind and the universe with a special plan for His children. The book of Revelation makes this clear by bringing to conclusion the divine drama begun in Genesis and portrayed throughout the rest of Scripture.

God revealed Himself in Revelation as a Person and as the sovereign Lord, not simply for academic reasons but so that His children may know Him and thus be moved to serve Him. John's portrayal of God the Father's attributes, activities, and names suggests certain responsibilities for believers. That is, God's perfections reveal not only wonderful things about Him but they also underscore how God's children are to live. For example, because He is self-existent, we must depend on Him for life. Because He is sovereign, we must rest in His greatness. Because He is holy, righteous, and just, we can rely on His unchanging Word. Because He is loving, merciful, and gracious, we must exercise love, patience, and a gracious spirit toward others.

CHAPTER 8

CHRISTOLOGY IN THE BOOK OF REVELATION

HAROLD D. FOOS

JOHN F. WALVOORD ADDRESSES THE great contribution of the book of Revelation to the doctrine of Christ in this way:

> Few books of the Bible provide a more complete theology than that afforded by the book of Revelation. Because of its apocalyptic character, the emphasis of the book is eschatological in the strict sense of dealing with last things (note "the word of this prophecy," Rev. 1:3). More specifically, however, it is Christological, as the material is to reveal Jesus Christ as the glorified One in contrast to the Christ of the Gospels, who was seen in humiliation and suffering. The climax of the book is the second coming of Jesus Christ. Events preceding the second coming constitute an introduction, and all events which follow constitute an epilogue. The wide range of revelation, however, deals with many subjects not specifically eschatological or Christological. In all important fields of theology, there are major contributions and, though written with the imagery and Hebraisms of the Old Testament, the revelation is definitely New Testament.[1]

This book is "the Revelation of Jesus Christ" and a "testimony of Jesus Christ" (1:1–2). These opening words in the book present two major ideas about Christ. First, this book is an unveiling *by* or from Him, that is, a revelation of the future that God gave Him to give to us through His servant. Second, the book is an unveiling *concerning* Jesus Christ, an unveiling in which

God makes known to us the future and Christ's role in it. The second of these seems more prominent. Though this book certainly is a revelation *by* Jesus Christ, it is foremost a revelation or unveiling *of* Him. "Though there is reference to both the Father and the Son, the central revelation concerns Christ, in keeping with the title of the book."[2]

This is the key to the whole book. Jesus Christ is its great subject. "Like the other Johannine writings, from a theological standpoint the focus in Revelation is Christological. . . . Unlike the gospel of John, which shows Jesus in His humiliation and tells of His return to the Father through crucifixion, death, resurrection, and exaltation, Revelation shows the exalted Christ, who has been restored to the glory He had with the Father 'before the world began' (cf. John 17:5)."[3] Another writer observes that Revelation "is not a mere prediction of divine judgments upon the wicked, and of the final triumph of righteousness, made known *by* Christ; but a book of the revelation *of* Christ, in his own person, offices, and future administration, when he shall be seen coming from heaven, as he was once seen going into heaven."[4]

The whole structure of the book reveals its Christological character. Each of John's four main visions presents some portrait of Christ. In the first vision He is seen as the Lord of the church in the midst of the golden lampstands (1:12–17). In the second vision He is the Lamb on the throne, judging and ruling over the creation with authority (5:1–14). The third vision reveals Him as the Word of God, the invincible conqueror riding in triumph (19:11–16). And though the fourth vision does not contain a separate descriptive paragraph about Him, it does place Him at the very center of the new creation in the eternal city of God.

In 1522 Martin Luther wrote of the Revelation, "My mind cannot use itself to the Book, and to me the fact that Christ is neither taught nor recognized in it, is good and sufficient cause for my low estimation."[5] Though he modified his view some years later, to the end Luther remained doubtful about the book's authenticity. One wonders what contributed to Luther's failure to see the abundant material regarding his Lord in this book. And yet today many fail to see the centrality of Jesus Christ in this volume. Some miss Him because they neglect the study of this book altogether, hesitant to explore its unusual literary style. Others miss Him because they become preoccupied with the identification of events and persons other than our Lord. Many seem to be more interested in the Antichrist than in Jesus Christ.

Tenney offers an excellent guiding principle for the study of the Revelation. "By beginning with the Person as the chief interpretive factor, fruitless debate over detail can be minimized, and the main purpose of the book can be kept constantly in sight. The thread of continuity in its thought may be followed more easily, and the initial interpretation can be noncontroversial. Whatever one's eschatological scheme may be, he must agree at the outset that the person of Christ is supremely important. All evangelical schools of interpretation would accept this concept as a point of departure."[6]

In studying Revelation we must center our gaze on Jesus Christ so that we do not miss seeing Him in the fullness of His glory. He is revealed to us in His *names* (ascriptions and titles), in His *acts,* and in *history.*

Christ Is Revealed in His Names and Titles

From the very beginning of human history names have been important. God began by naming Adam, and Adam named the animals. Names serve several purposes: to identify, to convey an attitude or a hope, to convey some meaning or information about the person either historically or prophetically (see Gen. 32:29; Exod. 3:14–15; Jer. 10:6; Matt. 1:21).

About twenty-five names and titles are given to Jesus Christ in Revelation. Varied attempts have been made at classifying them.[7] Three categories are suggested in the following pages: names and titles of power and authority, names and titles of relationships, and names and titles of character or quality.

Names and Titles of Power and Authority

Lamb. In Revelation the name "Lamb" (*arnion,* literally, "little lamb") is used more often than any other name or title of Christ. John called Him the Lamb twenty-eight times, with the first occurrence being in 5:6. There our Lord, appearing as "a lamb, looking as if it had been slain," is the only one "worthy to take the scroll and to open its seals," (v. 9 NIV) thus initiating the extensive series of judgments on the earth and its inhabitants. The combination of His death and power (cf. "Lion," 5:5) suggests both His suffering (as a Lamb) and His reigning as Messiah (as a Lion). Two other references to the "Lamb who was slain" are in 5:12 and 13:8; and 7:14 and 12:11 refer to "the blood of the Lamb."

The power and authority of the Lamb are also seen in the fact that He opened the seals (6:1, 3, 5, 7, 9, 12; 8:1). His power is evident in the phrase "the wrath of the Lamb" (6:16) and in the overpowering of His enemies (17:14) who will suffer torment in His presence (14:10). "The Lamb will overcome them, because He is Lord of lords and King of kings" (17:14).

Additional examples of the use of the name "Lamb" to depict His power and authority are these: The Lamb is worthy of worship (5:8, 13; 7:9–10), and His throne is associated with the throne of God the Father (22:1, 3). "The song of the Lamb" (15:3–4) is a victory song to praise the "Lord God . . . Almighty."

In the eternal city the Lamb will be the center of worship. "I did not see a temple in the city, because the Lord God Almighty and the Lamb are its temple" (21:22 NIV). Nor will the city need the light of sun or moon, "for the glory of God gives it light, and the Lamb is its lamp" (21:23 NIV).

Lord (and Lord of Lords). When used in a religious context, even in the case of deified Roman emperors, "Lord" *(kyrios)* means that the bearer was worthy of divine recognition and honor. The apostolic writers and early believers were well aware of this meaning. Polycarp, for example, died as a martyr rather than call Caesar *kyrios*.

In Revelation *kyrios* is generally applied to God (1:8; 4:8, 11; 11:15, 17; 15:4; 16:7; 18:8; 19:6; 22:5–6), but it is clearly used of Jesus Christ on three occasions. In 11:8 the death of the two witnesses will take place "where also their Lord was crucified." In 17:14 and 19:16, "the full expression 'Lord of lords' is applied to the conquering Lamb (an expression which occurs in Deut. 10:17 applied to Yahweh). At the consummation there is no doubt that Jesus Christ is entitled to the same ascriptive of sovereignty as God himself. In the New Jerusalem the throne is described as the throne of God and of the Lamb (22:1, 3)."[8]

King of Kings. Whereas "Lord" emphasizes authority and position, this title adds the element of sovereignty. As "King of kings" (17:14; 19:16) He is the supreme ruler. There is none greater nor more powerful. In a similar title He is "the ruler [Greek, *archon*] of the kings of the earth," the supreme Ruler over all.

Christ. This is more a title than a name. *Christos* is the Greek equivalent for the Hebrew *mĕšîaḥ* which means "anointed One." "Christ" is used seven times in Revelation. In its first three occurrences, it is combined with "Jesus." This book is the authoritative "revelation of Jesus Christ' (1:1 NIV), "the testimony of Jesus Christ" (1:2 NIV), and is "from Jesus Christ, who is the faithful witness" (1:5 NIV). His power and authority are also seen in that "the kingdom of the world has become the kingdom of our Lord and of his Christ, and he will reign for ever and ever" (11:15 NIV). This rule of God is under 'the authority of his Christ" (12:10 NIV), and those who are faithful will reign "with Christ a thousand years" (20:4, 6 NIV).

Other Names or Titles of Power and Authority. He is "the Son of God" (2:18; surprisingly only one such reference occurs in Revelation); He is the One "who searches the hearts and minds" (2:23), "who has the key of David" (3:7), and is "the Beginning [or better, Ruler] of the creation of God" (3:14). He is "the Lion that is from the tribe of Judah" (5:5), the conquering Rider on the white horse (19:11), and "the Word of God" (19:13). "Though the Apocalypse contains no defense of the deity of Christ, no book of the Bible is more plain in its implication, for here indeed is the eternal God who became man. This is, of course, confirmed by His relationship to God the Father described in 4:2–3 and 5:1, 7."[9]

Names and Titles of Relationships

Alpha and Omega, the First and the Last, the Beginning and the End. In Revelation 22:12–13, the One who is "coming soon" to judge and reward declares, "I am the Alpha and the Omega, the First and the Last, the Beginning and the End" (NIV). Some Bible students say "the Alpha and Omega, the Beginning and the End" in 21:6 and "the Alpha and Omega" in 1:8 refer to God the Father. But there is little doubt that in 22:12 these titles refer to Christ. This is further buttressed by 1:17–18, in which Christ said to John, "I am the first and the last . . . the living One; and I was dead, and behold, I am alive forevermore." The words in 2:8 also speak of Christ, the One who is "the first and the last, who was dead, and has come to life."

As Creator and Sustainer the existence and sustenance of all things is totally dependent on Him (cf. Col. 1:16–17). "The meaning is clear. The claim is to all-inclusiveness, not in a pantheistic sense, but as embracing all human history."[10] Just as Alpha and Omega are the first and last letters of the Greek alphabet, so Jesus Christ is the beginning and culmination of history, the One who has existed from all eternity.

Lamb. As noted earlier, this name for Christ speaks of His power and authority. It also speaks of His relationship to believers, as seen in Revelation 7. Those who have had their garments made white "in the blood of the Lamb" (7:14) are told that "the Lamb at the center of the throne will be their shepherd; he will lead them to springs of living water" (v. 17 NIV). How striking a truth that the Lamb will be the Shepherd, a fact that recalls Psalm 23.

The Lamb will stand on Mount Zion with the 144,000 (14:1) who belong to Him and who "follow the Lamb wherever He goes" (v. 4). On the foundation stones of the new Jerusalem will be inscribed the "names of the twelve apostles of the Lamb" (21:14).

Another relationship is seen in the presentation of "the bride," the church who is called "the wife of the Lamb" (21:9), who takes part in "the wedding of the Lamb" (19:7 NIV), and in "the wedding supper of the Lamb" (v. 9 NIV). And finally only "those whose names are written in the Lamb's book of life" will have access to the new Jerusalem (21:27).

Jesus. In the first three of fourteen occurrences of this name it is combined with the title "Christ" (1:1–2, 5). In the last two occurrences the name "Jesus" is joined with "Lord" in an expression of a desire for His return and in the book's benediction (22:20–21).

The name Jesus speaks of His humanity (Phil. 2:5–8), the One who in His incarnation came to reveal God to us. On seven occasions the name is related to His testimony or witness as the One who reveals God's purposes (again see 1:1–2, 5). Three verses refer to "the testimony of Jesus" (1:9; 12:17; 19:10), and at the end of the book we read, "I, Jesus, have sent my angel to give you this testimony for the churches" (22:16 NIV). With respect to this affirmation Seiss writes, "Thus the very God of all inspiration, and of all inspired men, reiterates and affirms the highest authority for all that is herein written. Either, then, this Book is nothing but a base and blasphemous forgery, unworthy of the slightest respect of men, and specially unworthy of a place in the Sacred Canon; or it is one of the most directly inspired and authoritative writings ever given."[11]

In addition, the believers' relationship to Christ is seen in how the name Jesus is used in relation to those who are faithful to Him in their testimony. John wrote of that which is "ours in Jesus" (1:9 NIV), and he spoke of "those who obey God's commandments and hold to the testimony of Jesus" (12:17 NIV). John also wrote of those who "remain faithful to Jesus" (14:12 NIV), and of "brethren who hold to the testimony of Jesus" (19:10 NIV). Among them are "those who bore testimony to Jesus" to the point of martyrdom (17:6 NIV; cf. 6:9; 11:7; 12:11), "who had been beheaded because of their testimony for Jesus and because of the word of God" (20:4 NIV).

This intimacy of this relationship between Jesus and believers is seen in the book's climactic appeal, "Come, Lord Jesus," in response to His saying, "Yes, I am coming soon" (22:20 NIV).

Other Names and Titles of Relationships. Jesus Christ's identity with our humanity is seen in His appearing as One "like a son of man" (1:13; 14:14). When the New Jerusalem will descend from heaven, it will be "prepared as a bride beautifully dressed for her husband" (21:2 NIV), one of the most intimate of relationships. And Jesus' relationship to God the Father is clearly stated in the title the "Son of God" (2:18).

Names and Titles of Character or Quality

Obviously the names already considered suggest strength, gentleness, faithfulness, compassion, and truthfulness. However, some additional ascriptives point to yet other qualities of Christ. When He speaks, His words are the words of "the Amen [or True One], the faithful and true Witness" (3:14). As the rider on the white horse, who will come with justice to judge and make war, Jesus is called "Faithful and True" (19:11; cf. 1:5; 3:7). Justice will be executed in truthfulness. Dependency and trustworthiness are found in the One whose "name is called The Word of God" (19:13). The unspecified "name written upon Him which no one knows except Himself" (v. 12) manifests His character in keeping with its immediate context (vv. 11–13), which depicts His faithfulness, truth, and justice.

Some additional names of Jesus Christ will be noted in the following discussion on His acts and His place in history.

Christ Is Revealed in His Acts

Jesus came to fulfill three offices in His service to God and humanity. As Prophet He reveals God to man. As Priest He represents man to God in both sacrifice and intercession. As King He rules as God's Sovereign over all the creation. Revelation clearly emphasizes the last of these as the One who comes to judge and rule over the millennial earth and the eternal kingdom.

Prophet

Attention has already been given to Jesus' work of revealing truth as we considered the name "Jesus" and the frequent references to "the testimony of Jesus." In addition, two ascriptions speak of His work as Revealer. One is the fact that His name is "the Word of God" (19:13). As the Word (Greek, *logos*), He is the ultimate revelation of God to man (John 1:1, 14, 18; 1 John 1:1; cf. Heb. 1:1–2).

The second ascriptive is "the bright morning star" (22:16). Like a bright star or planet in the early morning hours before dawn, so Jesus in His brilliant character will usher in a new day, the eternal state.

Priest

Just as a priest must offer sacrifices, so Jesus provided a sacrifice—Himself. He is the Lamb that was slain (5:6, 12; 13:8), and as a Lamb His blood was shed (7:14; 12:11). The twenty-four elders said to Him, "with your blood you purchased men for God" (5:9 NIV). The names of the redeemed are written "in the Lamb's book of life" (21:27). And so, purchased and cleansed, they became "a kingdom and priests to [serve] our God" (5:10).

English offers the following comments on Jesus' apparel in 1:13:

> No description of the garment is given other than its length. It might be the noble robe of a king or the august gown of a priest. Christ is, after all, both King and Priest. I am inclined to the opinion that in this case the reference is to a priestly robe. For the apostle had this vision during the present age, the church age in which the ascended Lord is acting as a priest on behalf of His own people making intercession for us. . . . Furthermore, it is to be observed that He was wearing a golden girdle. The girdle of the Old Testament priest was intertwined with gold. However, whereas the Aaronic priests wore their girdles around their waists, the exalted Christ is said to have had His about His breast. His ministry of humble service, in the pursuance of which He girded Himself with a towel and washed His disciples' feet, ended with His supreme service at Calvary. Now the golden girdle is placed around the breast, speaking even more strongly of His divine devotion to and constant concern for the members of His body who are still on earth.[12]

King

As noted earlier under the discussion of Jesus' names and titles, His title of King speaks of His sovereign authority, His supreme right to rule and judge. This concerns both earthly and heavenly realms, over all principalities and powers, for He is "the ruler of God's creation" (3:14 NIV).

His glory and authority are unmatched (1:13–18; cf. 2:26). The four living creatures and twenty-four elders will sing to Christ, a song that acknowledges His authority: "Worthy is the Lamb, who was slain, to receive power and wealth and wisdom and strength and honor and glory and praise" (5:12 NIV). They will be accompanied by "every created thing which is in heaven and on earth and under the earth and on the sea, and all things in them," and they will say, "To Him who sits on the throne, and to the Lamb, be blessing and honor and glory and dominion forever and ever" (5:13). The "throne of God and of the Lamb" will be the center of the eternal city with all its glory (22:1–5).

Jesus' authority is evidenced through His omnipotence and omniscience (1:8; 2–3). In addressing the seven churches He repeatedly said, "I know" (2:2, 9, 13, 19; 3:1, 8, 15). And in His authority He rebuked five of the churches (2:4–5, 14–16, 20–23; 3:3, 15–18).

The ability of Jesus ("the Lion that is from the tribe of Judah, the Root of David") to open the scroll and its seven seals will manifest His authority and power to initiate the judgments (5:5). Those who have rejected the truth should know that He "searches the minds and hearts" and "will give to each one of you according to your deeds" (2:23), for He holds "the keys of death and of Hades" (1:18).

When Satan and his forces are overcome "by the blood of the Lamb" (12:11), the promised kingdom of God will be ushered in with "the authority of His Christ" (v. 10), and He will fulfill the covenant promises to God's people, Israel. In 5:5 the title "the Root of David" "is linked with the title 'Lion of the tribe of Judah.' Since in this case the conquering aspect is stressed, the Davidic kingship is unmistakable. In the message to one of the seven churches Jesus is introduced as 'the true one, who has the key of David' (Rev. 3:7), which must be understood as expressing his royal authority."[13]

When He reigns as King, "the kingdom of the world [will have] become the kingdom of our Lord, and of His Christ; and He will reign forever and ever" (11:15). Those who have been promised a share in God's kingdom (1:6, 9) and who have been faithful will reign with Him (20:4, 6; 22:5; cf. 3:21). When He comes, He will reward everyone according to what he has done (22:12). Rewards will be apportioned "to him who overcomes." These include "the right to eat from the tree of life" (2:7 NIV); "authority over the nations" (2:26); being made "a pillar in the temple of [Christ's] God" (3:12); and "the right to sit" with Christ on His throne (3:21 NIV). Those who are faithful to the point of death will receive "the crown of life" (2:10).

Christ Is Revealed in History

As "the Alpha and Omega, the Beginning and the End" (Rev. 21:6 NIV), the second person of the Godhead transcends all space, time, and history. The One who existed from all eternity (John 1:1–2) was active in creation and is now active in providence (John 1:3, 10; Col. 1:16–17). But by His incarnation He entered history in a unique fashion. As the God-Man, He has made God known in the fullest possible way (John 1:18; 14:9–11; Phil. 2:5–11; Heb. 1:1–3). Though this book focuses on the revelation of the Son in His end-time glory and activity, the book includes numerous references to His revelation in past history.

His Birth and Incarnation

Since Revelation centers on the heavenly vision, there is little stress on His humanity. His name "Jesus" (the human name), His description as "one like a son of man" (1:13; 14:14), and allusions to His suffering and death (1:7; 11:8) point to His genuine humanity.

The reference to the woman who gives birth to "a son, a male child, who will rule all nations with an iron scepter" (12:5 NIV; cf. vv. 2, 4, 13) clearly points to Jesus' human birth. Some suggest that these verses imply His virgin birth, since reference is made to only His mother. In human lineage He is from the tribe of Judah and is a descendant of David (5:5; 22:16).

His Earthly Life, Ministry, and Death

Revelation makes no mention of His life on earth between His birth and death. But several verses refer to His death. In addition to the references to the slain Lamb (5:6, 12; 13:8) and the "blood of the Lamb" (7:14; 12:11), His death is mentioned in 1:7 (He was "pierced") and 11:8, which speaks of the city where "their Lord was crucified." Furthermore He was "slain" (5:9) and He "died" (2:8). In His own words He declared, "I was dead" (1:18).

His Resurrection and Ascension

Revelation clearly centers on the risen and ascended Christ. The One who was slain is active in the present age because of His resurrection from the dead. He is "the firstborn from the dead" (1:5 NIV), and in reassuring words to His servant John He declared, "I am the Living One; I was dead, and behold I am alive for ever and ever!" (1:18 NIV). To the suffering church in Smyrna He spoke as the One "who died and came to life again" (2:8 NIV). His victory and authority over death is seen in that He holds "the keys of death and of Hades" (1:18; cf. 20:2, 10, 14).

Reference to His ascension may be indicated in 12:5, which mentions that the child of the woman "was caught up to God and to His throne."

His Present Activity

The Son is presently in heaven at the Father's throne (3:21; 7:9; 12:5), where He will remain until His return for the living saints at the Rapture. However, by His Spirit, He is presently ministering to His church in instruction, rebuke, comfort, encouragement, correction, guidance, and judgment (Rev. 2–3).

His Return

When He ascended, our Lord promised His followers that His return will be seen, just as His departure was seen. From the opening words of this book this fact is declared. "Behold, He is coming with the clouds, and every eye will see Him" (1:7). And throughout this book that coming and its attendant features are said to occur soon. The opening words of the book state that what God gave "to show to His bond-servants . . . must shortly take place" (1:1). Four times our Lord declared, "I am coming quickly" (3:11; 22:7, 12, 20). And other references are made to the "soon" occurrence of related events (cf. 11:14; 22:6).[14] Chafer has made this striking observation: "The general theme concerning the return of Christ has the unique distinction of being the first prophecy uttered by man (Jude 14–15) and the last message from the ascended Christ as well as being the last word of the Bible (Rev. 22:20–21)."[15]

Surely our salvation is nearer than when we believed (cf. Rom. 13:11; 1 Peter 1:5). The "bright morning star"—Jesus Christ—is heralding the dawn of that new day (Rev. 22:16)! The concluding word of our Lord, who has testified of all these things to His servants, is that awesome and encouraging declaration, "Yes, I am coming soon!" (22:20 NIV) With John may we eagerly respond, "Amen. Come, Lord Jesus!"

CHAPTER 9

PNEUMATOLOGY IN THE BOOK OF REVELATION

RUSSELL L. PENNEY

WE CAN DO NOTHING IN THIS WORLD without the work of the Holy Spirit. Though the Lord Jesus and God the Father are ever present, in a unique way the Spirit is the functional presence of the Lord God throughout the generations.

In the present dispensation of the church age, the Spirit of God has specific ministries that are different from ages past and even from the ages beyond the period of the church. The book of Revelation records His work in the future, but also chapters 1–3 clearly show His activities during this church age.

The Word *Pneuma* in Revelation

Pneuma, the Greek word for "Spirit," is used twenty-four times in Revelation. In 13:15 it probably should be translated "life," and three times it clearly refers to the spirits of demons (16:13–14; 18:2). Nineteen times the word refers to the Holy Spirit, though in several of these references some scholars say *pneuma* points to the human spirit of John the apostle.

Interestingly, the word *pneuma* is used more than 350 times in the rest of the New Testament, with many references referring to the human spirit or the spirits of demons. More than two hundred of these references may speak of the Holy Spirit. However, the number varies among scholars because they differ on how to interpret some passages.

The "Seven Spirits" of Revelation

One of the most controversial references to *pneuma* in the book of Revelation is in 1:4. This verse records a greeting from John the apostle, God the Father, and then "from the seven spirits who are before His throne." The same expression is mentioned in 3:1; 4:5; 5:6. The seven spirits are positioned before the Lord's throne in chapters 4 and 5, and in chapter 3, in the message to the church at Sardis, Jesus "holds the seven spirits of God" (NIV).

Some writers say these verses are speaking of the seven angels who are before the throne of God (8:2). Charles writes, "Whether these seven spirits are to be identified with the seven archangels cannot be inferred with certainty, but this identification may be regarded as highly probable; since ... Christ's sovereignty is asserted over the highest order of the angels."[1] Others hold that the term refers to the perfect fullness of God, represented by the word "seven."

To help us understand the expression "seven Spirits," it is important to look at the other references. In 3:1, it is said of Christ that He "has the seven Spirits of God, and the seven stars." "Has" *(eko)* is a present participle and can read, "The One who is possessing the seven Spirits." Jesus also was seen as possessing or holding the seven stars (1:16), which are interpreted as the seven angels (or messengers) of the seven churches (v. 20).

In 4:5, John wrote that "there were seven lamps of fire burning before the throne, which are the seven Spirits of God."

In 5:6, Christ, the Lamb of God, is said to have "seven horns and seven eyes, which are the seven Spirits of God, sent out into all the earth." In Scripture horns generally represent power and authority, and eyes picture intelligence and omniscience. These characteristics are an integral part of the seven Spirits.

Part of the answer to this symbolic mystery seems to be found in Zechariah 3:8–9, in which the Lord's servant, called the Branch and Stone, has seven eyes. This clearly seems to refer to the Messiah who will be ruling in His millennial, kingly authority through the power and assistance of the all-seeing Holy Spirit. And when He is finally revealed, the Lord says He "will remove the iniquity of that land in one day" (v. 9). Unger concurs and writes that this is speaking of "infinite intelligence either directed by God on it in loving care (Ezek. 1:18; 10:12) or omniscience, if the eyes are pictured on the Stone itself (cf. Zech. 4:10), as the 'Lamb' of the Apocalypse that had been slain had 'seven horns and seven eyes' which are said to be the 'seven spirits of God, sent forth into all the earth' (Rev. 5:6)."[2]

Many evangelical scholars agree that "the seven Spirits" is a reference to *the* Spirit of God. Morris writes, this is necessarily a "reference to the Holy Spirit, rather than to seven great angelic spirits, as might otherwise be thought."[3] LaHaye says, "The number seven denotes perfection or completeness; the term 'seven spirits' does not mean seven Holy Spirits but the seven ministries of the Holy Spirit."[4] According to Scott, the Holy Spirit's "plenitude of ... power and diversified activity are expressed in the term 'seven Spirits,' the fullness of spiritual activity."[5] And Seiss notes that this is the Spirit "in the full completeness of his office and powers, as sent forth for the illumination, comfort and edification of all the subjects of God's redeeming grace."[6]

The most obvious Old Testament reference to the seven Spirits is found in Isaiah 11:1–2. This prophecy describes the coming of the "shoot" and "stem" of Jesse, David's father. This coming One, like a stem, grows to be called the Branch, and fruit will blossom from His roots. He is the Son of God who will reign by the power and influence of the Spirit of the Lord. Verse 2 reads, "And the Spirit of the Lord will rest on Him, the spirit of wisdom and understanding, the spirit of counsel and strength, the spirit of knowledge and the fear of the LORD."

The Holy Spirit is described in seven ways, showing that He has a sevenfold ministry.[7] This does not destroy the idea of the unity of the Spirit. "The Holy Spirit, in all His sevenfold fullness and blessing (Matt. 3:16; John 1:16; 3:34; Col. 1:19; cf. Rev. 1:4), because seven is the number of fullness and perfection, would rest upon [the Messiah] permanently, not merely come upon Him for temporary ministry."[8]

"I Was in the Spirit"

This expression is used twice in Revelation by John the apostle to describe how he received the vision given him by the Lord. The clause could read, "I became in the Spirit." The preposition "in" might better be translated "with" the Spirit. Then, suddenly he heard the loud, commanding voice from Jesus saying, "Write in a book what you see" (1:10–11). In Jude 20 the same preposition *en* is used in the phrase, "praying in the Holy Spirit." Certainly this means "with" or "by means of."

The same expression, "I became in the Spirit," is used in Revelation 4:2, with the result that John suddenly and dramatically saw the Lord seated on a throne in heaven. In both instances (1:10 and 4:2) new revelation was presented dramatically to John. "In a word, he was . . . *in Spirit*—in a condition wholly loosened from the earth—transported by means of the Spirit, . . . stationed as a spectator amid the very scenes of the great judgment itself."[9]

A similar idea is stated in 17:3 and 21:10. In 17:3, John was carried away by one of the seven escorting angels "in the Spirit into a wilderness." The Greek preposition *en* is used here too, giving the idea again that he was "with" the Spirit while receiving this vision.

In 21:10, one of the seven angels again swept John away and carried him "in the Spirit to a great and high mountain." There he was shown the new Jerusalem coming down out of heaven from the Lord!

Some writers believe the word *pneuma* in 17:3 and 21:10 is referring simply to John's human spirit. But Greek grammarian A. T. Robertson believes the reference could be to the Holy Spirit.[10]

Alan Johnson also holds that both verses are referring to God's Holy Spirit.

On 21:10 he writes, "John was taken to the desert, but now he is elevated by the Spirit to the highest pinnacle of the earth to witness the exalted New Jerusalem (cf. 1:10; 4:2; 17:3)."[11]

The thought in these verses is that the Holy Spirit is the Revealer, Processor, and Interpreter of the visions and scenes presented to John. One cannot escape the dynamic work of the Spirit in giving us the book of Revelation.

The Direct Speaking of the Holy Spirit in Revelation

The New Testament gives ample evidence that the Spirit of God occasionally spoke directly to certain individuals for specific purposes. Jesus said that when He departed He would send the Holy Spirit to the disciples. The Lord then gave a wealth of information on how the Spirit would operate in this dispensation.

> But when He, the Spirit of truth, comes, He will guide you into all the truth; for He will not speak on His own initiative, but whatever He hears, He will speak; and He will disclose to you what is to come. He shall glorify Me; for He shall take of Mine, and shall disclose it to you. All things that the Father has are Mine; therefore I said, that He [the Spirit] takes of Mine, and will disclose it to you. (John 16:13–15)

Jesus said the Spirit will guide, speak, disclose, and glorify the Lord. Not that the Spirit speaks audibly, but in His communication to believers there is "directness" and intimacy.

We learn from Peter, with reference to the Old Testament, that the Holy Spirit "foretold [prophesied] by the mouth of David concerning Judas" (Acts 1:16). At Pentecost the Spirit "was giving [the disciples] utterance" as they spoke in tongues (2:4). "The Spirit said to Philip" (8:29), "the Spirit said to [Peter]" (10:19), and a message was "indicated by the Spirit" to Agabus (11:28).

To the church at Antioch, "the Holy Spirit said, 'Set apart for Me Barnabas and Saul for the work to which I have called them'" (13:2). Then they were "sent out by the Holy Spirit" (v. 4). The Spirit witnessed (20:23), spoke through others to Paul (21:4), had spoken through Isaiah (28:25), speaks expressly (1 Tim. 4:1), signifies (Heb. 9:8), and bears witness (1 John 5:6).

As in the book of Acts, the book of Revelation refers several times to the Spirit's "speaking." In a final salvation appeal, the Holy Spirit and the bride, the people of God, say, "'Come.' And let the one who hears say, 'Come.' And let the one who is thirsty come; let the one who wishes take the water of life without cost" (Rev. 22:17).

When the prophecy was given in 14:9–11 about the final demise of the Beast, the Antichrist, a voice from heaven said, "Write, 'Blessed are the dead who die in the Lord from now on!'" (v. 13a). Since Jesus commanded John to write down what he saw (1:11) and to record the letters to the seven churches (2:1, 8, 12, 18; 3:1, 7, 14), perhaps He is the One who also told John to write these words of encouragement. Interestingly, the Spirit responded, "'Yes,' says the Spirit, 'that they may rest from their labors, for their deeds follow with them'" (v. 13b).

Christ also placed a direct, verbal salutation at the end of each of His addresses to the seven churches. This is in the form of an appeal that reads, "He who has an ear, let him hear what the Spirit says to the churches" (2:7, 11, 17, 29; 3:6, 13, 22).

These dramatic instances of the Holy Spirit's speaking directly point up the importance of Revelation and its message. "The use of the plural *tais ekklesiais* [to the churches] indicates the universal character of the invitation each time it occurs in these two chapters. . . . By means of this call the message to a single congregation is extended to all the churches of Asia and through them, . . . to the churches throughout the world."[12]

The New Covenant and the Spirit in the Tribulation

How will the Holy Spirit's work in the Tribulation differ from His work in the present dispensation of the church? This question has puzzled Bible scholars for some time because the book of Revelation does not give us much information on that subject. Walvoord feels we have to work from inference, though he suggests that the work of the Spirit in believers in the Tribulation will be somewhat restricted. On the basis of 2 Thessalonians 2:7, he says the Spirit of God will be taken out of the way during the Tribulation and will not be indwelling believers during that time.[13]

To find the answer one must understand the difference between the new covenant and the church dispensation. Though these two entities work together during this age of grace, they are also different and unique.

The New Covenant

This covenant has to do with the blessings promised in the Abrahamic covenant (Gen. 12:3), promises to be given to Abraham's children but also to the Gentiles. As Jeremiah prophesied, the new covenant will contrast with the Mosaic covenant (Jer. 31:32) and will take its place.

By giving His body and shedding His blood for our sins, Jesus was ratifying this new covenant. "This cup which is poured out for you is the new covenant in My blood" (Luke 22:20). This covenant, then, is what actually provides salvation for believers. It also includes God's giving believers "a law within," a closer relationship with the Lord, a personal knowledge of God, and permanent forgiveness of sins (Jer. 31:33–34).

Also, the new covenant includes the promise that the Holy Spirit will reside with each believer (Ezek. 36:27; 37:14; John 7:38–39). So it seems preferable to say that though the Holy Spirit "[will be] taken out of the way" (2 Thess. 2:7) in the Tribulation, this has to do with His work of restraining sin and not with His indwelling and empowering believers.

The Dispensation of the Church

As noted, church-age believers receive numerous spiritual benefits from the new covenant. But people who come to Christ in the Tribulation will differ from believers who are now part of the church.

Church-age saints are technically called "those in Christ." The believer in the dispensation of the church is placed in the body of Christ by the Holy Spirit (1 Cor. 12:13). Those in Christ will be raptured to glory by the sudden appearance of Christ at the Rapture (1 Thess. 4:16–18). Believers who have died "in Christ" will be resurrected at the Rapture, and those believers who are alive will then be caught up with them (1 Thess. 4:13–18). "Those who are Christ's at His coming" (1 Cor. 15:23) will be given new resurrection bodies.

The Tribulation Believers

The new covenant was ratified by the death of the Lord and is eternal. So it will benefit Jews and Gentiles not only during the age of the church but also during the Tribulation period. However, those who will be saved in the Tribulation cannot technically be called church saints or "those in Christ," although they will be saved by His death. In the Tribulation people will be saved on the basis of the finished work of Christ just as they are today. That means they receive the spiritual blessings of the new covenant.

However, Tribulation believers are not placed into the spiritual body of Christ, the church, for the "Christians" will have gone home to heaven at the moment of the Rapture. Those who will be saved during the seven-year period of God's wrath should be called Tribulation saints; they will have put their faith in Jesus for their salvation (Rev. 14:12).

During the Tribulation the "eternal gospel" will be preached by the influence of an angel flying in midheaven "to those who live on the earth, and to every nation and tribe and tongue and people" (v. 6). This gospel, then as now, has to do with the message of the death of Christ whereby He ratified the new covenant.

A Return to Old Testament Law?

Many dispensationalists teach that during the Tribulation there will be a return to conditions as they were under the Old Testament Law. This is partly based on the fact that, as Jesus presented Himself to Israel as their King, He expounded the Law to them in what is called "the Sermon on the Mount" (Matt. 5–7).

Without discussing this issue in detail, it is enough to say that Christ's purpose in the Sermon on the Mount may not have been to indicate that the Law would return in the Tribulation and kingdom period. More likely, the Lord was building His case against the sins of that present generation by referring often to the Law. He was not necessarily saying that the Law is to be the guiding force during those two future periods; instead, He was using the Law to convict the Jews and to lead them to repent. Though Glasscock also hints that the Law may be part of the rule of the kingdom, he writes, "Disciples [in the early Gospels] were indeed chosen members of the kingdom and needed to understand at the beginning of their walk with Christ that His standards were higher than the oral traditions being propagated by the scribes and Pharisees. Though the millennial kingdom is not as yet being experienced in this world, the standards of the King are to be realized in the lives of His servants."[14]

Another reason some believe the Law will be restored during the Tribulation and kingdom periods is that Christ spoke of those who will see the abomination of desolation set by the Antichrist in the temple, as written by the prophet Daniel (Dan. 9:27; Matt. 24:15–21). Concerning the Tribulation, Jesus said "Pray that your flight [from Jerusalem] may not be in the winter, or on a Sabbath" (v. 20). But the fact that Jews would be offended to travel on the Sabbath does not mean that they will be under the dispensation of the Law.

During the Tribulation a new temple will be standing, with sacrifices being offered again. This comes from the longing of the Jews who are back in the land. But this Tribulation temple is the "impostor" temple, not the one sanctioned by God Himself. The Tribulation temple will not be the same as the millennial temple.

The Holy Spirit, the New Covenant, and the Millennial Temple

The millennial temple in Jerusalem is described in detail in Ezekiel 40–48. New temple guidelines, laws, and rules are given for the construction and function of this structure. Nowhere is it indicated that this is a return to the Old Testament law system in its entirety, though there is what is called the new "law of the house" (43:12). New moon festivals and Sabbaths (45:17), the Passover (v. 21), and the Sabbath day (46:1) will be reestablished, but many other Old Testament feasts and regulations will not be. So temple worship is not a return to the Mosaic Law.

"If these great festivals of Passover and Tabernacles are to be observed during the Millennium, there is no reason why sacrifices would not also be offered. Then, of course, they will be memorials of the finished sacrifice of Christ."[15]

On Ezekiel's temple vision, Fruchtenbaum writes: "To summarize, there will be a sacrificial system instituted in the Millennium that will have some features similar to the Mosaic system, along with some new laws. For that very reason, the sacrificial system of the Millennium must not be viewed as a reinstitution of the Mosaic system, because it is not. It will be a new system that will contain some things old and some things new and will be instituted for an entirely different purpose."[16]

Surprisingly, the only reference to the Holy Spirit in Ezekiel 40–48 is in 43:5: "And the Spirit lifted me up and brought me into the inner court; and behold, the glory of the LORD filled the house." It would only make sense to assume that the Holy Spirit continued this work of showing Ezekiel the prophetic layout of the entire temple, not simply the inner court. God's Spirit is certainly important in the manifestation of God's glory in this new temple. As Feinberg remarks, "Thus Ezekiel was expressly given the privilege by the Spirit Himself of viewing the glorious return of the Lord to His abode and His people. God's glory may always be depended upon to fill His house; it has been so in the past and will be in the millennial era."[17]

Conclusion

Many believers will be empowered during the Tribulation to witness for Christ. This is true since He spoke of worldwide preaching of the gospel of the kingdom during this terrible period on earth (Matt. 24:14). This ability to bear witness has always come from the ministry of the Holy Spirit. The victories experienced by the martyrs to the faith in the Tribulation could hardly be accomplished without the spiritual work of the Spirit.

It is important to note that no reference is ever made in Scripture to the baptism of believers into the body of Christ in the Tribulation period or in the Millennium. Being baptized by the Spirit into the body of Christ applies only to church-age saints.

Thus in the Tribulation the Holy Spirit will continue to minister in the world, but the corporate body of believers knit into one living organism as the body of Christ will not be present.

The Holy Spirit is an active personality in the book of Revelation. He joined Christ in giving this important message of prophecy. As part of the Godhead He played a vital part in the inspiration and revelation of this last book of Scripture.

CHAPTER 10

ECCLESIOLOGY IN THE BOOK OF REVELATION

MAL COUCH

THE BOOK OF REVELATION IS NOT about the church. The church plays an important role in the first three chapters, but after that it is certainly not seen again on the earth. However, Revelation mentions multitudes of people in heaven glorifying God. These are probably church saints gathered into the Lord's presence by death or by the Rapture. But again it is important to note that the bulk of the book of Revelation is not about the church.

Defining the Church

In the Septuagint, the Greek translation of the Old Testament, *ekklesia* (the "called out") is sometimes used to describe an assembly or congregation. But in the New Testament the word usually refers to the church, the spiritual body of Christ, the redeemed "in Christ."

The church age is a new and unique dispensation. The church is not simply an extension of Israel.

Paul made it clear that the church is God's "workmanship, created in Christ Jesus" (Eph. 2:10). Believing Jews and Gentiles in the church age have been made into "one new man," having been reconciled "in one body to God through the cross" (vv. 15–16). Together they are "fellow-partakers of the promise in Christ Jesus through the gospel" (3:6). In Revelation Jesus addressed seven churches in Asia Minor. These assemblies were part of the "new" thing, the body of Christ.

Though the Lord addressed seven local churches in Revelation 2–3, the bulk of the book of Revelation is about the coming Tribulation and the kingdom that will follow it.

Revelation: A Summary of Bible Prophecy

With scores of allusions to the Old Testament, Revelation can be thought of as a synopsis of Old Testament prophecies that describe the terrors of the Tribulation and the coming Messiah who will establish His earthly kingdom. But Revelation is a fulfillment of predictions made in the New Testament as well.

> The book of Revelation is in many respects the capstone of futuristic prophecy of the entire Bible and gathers in its prophetic scheme the major themes of prophecy which thread their way through the whole volume of Scripture. The scope and plan of the book as contained in the opening phrase "to show unto his servants things which must shortly come to pass" (1:1) indicate that the primary intent of the book was to prepare the way for the second coming of Christ.[1]

The Church in Chapter 1: "Kingdom, Priests"

In Revelation 1 the apostle John clearly addressed the entire body of Christ (His bond-servants) as well as the seven churches in this chapter (vv. 1, 4, 11). The bond-servants are those who are now serving Christ in this present church dispensation. John also wrote that Jesus loves us and released us from our sins (v. 5).

John also recorded a dramatic picture of Christ standing in the middle of seven lampstands, holding seven stars in His right hand (vv. 13, 16). The stars are the angels or messengers of the churches, and the lampstands represent the congregations or assemblies (v. 20).

There is no doubt this prophecy was given to the churches in order to remind the believers in this dispensation of the ultimate victory of our Savior. Perhaps Revelation will also be a guidebook for Tribulation saints as they attempt to survive that horrible seven-year period.

Two other important verses in chapter 1 pertain to the church, verses that are sometimes misunderstood. In verse 6 the church is called "a kingdom," and church-age saints are called "priests." Amillennialists try to argue from these terms that the church is an extension of Old Testament Israel. But even nondispensationalist Lange notes that there is no relationship between the Old Testament and the church. "Christians are spiritually possessed of kingly dignity . . . The term [kingdom] then, denotes neither, on the one hand, a people of kings, nor, on the other: the subjects of the kingdom."[2] What makes some think there is a connection is Exodus 19:6, in which the Lord said to Israel, "You shall be to Me a kingdom of priests and a holy nation."

But how did Peter handle this issue? Addressing Jewish believers in his first epistle, he spoke of them as "aliens, scattered throughout Pontus" and elsewhere (1 Peter 1:1). They are the *diaspora,* the dispersion, Jews scattered "among the Gentiles" (2:12) as "aliens and strangers" (v. 11). Peter saw these Israelite believers as "completed" Jews. He reminded them that by their having trusted Jesus as their Messiah they had become what God intended for their nation in the Old Testament.

Peter then wrote that these Christian Jews were "a chosen race, a royal priesthood, a holy nation, a people for God's own possession, that you may proclaim the excellencies of Him who has called you out of darkness into His marvelous light; for you once were not a people, but now you are the people of God; you had not received mercy, but now you have received mercy" (2:9–10). In these verses Peter quoted portions of verses from the prophets to make his point (Exod. 19:6; Deut. 19:15; Isa. 43:20; 61:6; 66:21; Hos. 2:23; 11:10).

In these verses Peter did not even come close to saying that the church is an extension or fulfillment of Old Testament Israel. Neither did he associate the "kingdom" nature of the church with the messianic, Davidic, earthly rule promised by the prophets.

Peter referred to all believers in this present age as "a royal priesthood," and John wrote that all Christians are "priests." This doctrine of the priesthood of all Christians is a far different teaching from the Old Testament Aaronic priesthood under the Law.

A second verse in Revelation that is often misunderstood is 1:9, in which John wrote to the churches that he was their "brother and fellow-partaker in the tribulation and kingdom and perseverance which are in Jesus." Though an apostle of the church age, some think John was indicating that the church is the promised messianic kingdom and that the church was entering the Tribulation.

However, John may have simply picked up the central thought of this verse from Paul's statement in Acts 14:22: "Through many tribulations we must enter the kingdom of God." Interestingly Paul made clear that they had not arrived at that kingdom, even though the church age was well established!

By using the word "tribulation" in the singular in Revelation 1:9 (whereas Paul used the same word in Acts 14:22 in the plural), John, like Paul, was referring to tribulation as a way of life, the ongoing experience of believers. Grammatically the Greek joins the three nouns of the tribulation, the kingdom, and perseverance together as a package. That is, though all Christians have tribulation or distress in this life, they have the hope of taking part in the millennial kingdom, and they are all to persevere in those sufferings.

> General tribulation of the Christian life, although it may foreshadow that of the end-time, is not identical with it. John was drinking of the cup of suffering that Jesus had predicted according to Matt. 20:22–23. . . . Little difference of opinion exists over the meaning of *basileia* in 1:9. It is the millennial kingdom described more fully

in Revelation 20. It is the future kingdom spoken of by Christ (e.g., Luke 12:32; 22:29). . . . Anticipation of this kingdom is an integral part of present Christian experience. This conclusion is confirmed further by the virtue of "endurance," which is next in the series of three. This is a quality that has as its motivation an expectation of coming deliverance (cf. 1 Thess. 1:3).[3]

The Seven Churches of Revelation

Theories About the Seven Churches

Bible scholars hold three different views about the seven churches of chapters 2 and 3.

The Historical View. In this view the churches are seen as influential historic congregations, addressed by the Lord because of their importance in the development and growth of the church at large. Though each assembly had different spiritual and moral problems to face, other congregations may have been struggling with additional issues not mentioned among the seven.

The Typological View. This theory says the churches, which were actual existing congregations, are like seven types of churches that one may find at any given time in the history of the church. The historicity of these assemblies is not denied, but this views holds that the Lord chose to single them out because they represent seven kinds of problems that typify various congregations of believers. For example:

1. Ephesus (2:1–7). This church is like other orthodox churches that have departed from their love for Christ.
2. Smyrna (2:8–11). This church represents churches that are suffering under persecution.
3. Pergamum (2:12–17). Pergamum is like churches that face satanic opposition and finally succumb to the immorality of the culture.
4. Thyatira (2:18–29). This congregation represents churches that tolerate an idolatrous system.
5. Sardis (3:1–6). The Sardis church is typical of churches that are "asleep" and have not completed the work God gave them to do.
6. Philadelphia (3:7–13). This church, like some churches today, had not denied the name of the Lord (v. 8) and had remained faithful to Christ.
7. Laodicea (3:14–22). The Laodicean church typifies churches that think they are rich but are actually lukewarm spiritually.

Representing the typological view, Morris writes, "Seven churches—the perfect number representing all churches—and all are most unpromising churches. . . . They were real churches, but they are also chosen as representative churches and they still represent our churches today. There is some of Ephesus and Smyrna and all of the others in each of our own churches today."[4]

The Church-Age View. This view holds that the seven churches represent seven periods of church history. Morris continues:

> Although it is by no means the dominant theme, there is a sense also in which the seven churches seem to depict the respective stages of development and change of Christ's churches during the ensuing centuries. History has, indeed, shown such a general development through the years, and it is reasonable that the sequential development of the respective exhortations in these messages should be arranged by the Lord in the same sequence. . . . The Book of Revelation—all of it—is said to be prophecy, and if there is any prophecy in it concerning the Church Age, it must be here in these two chapters.[5]

Larkin holds to the historical nature of these churches but also imposes the church-age theory on the verses. He outlines the churches like this:

1. Ephesus (A.D. 70–170): With the Nicolaitans (2:6) begins "the origin of the dogma of 'Apostolic Succession,' and the separation of the Clergy from the Laity."[6]
2. Smyrna: The "ten days" are "doubtless a prophetic reference to the 'Ten Great Persecutions' under the Roman Emperors, beginning with Nero, A.D. 64, and ending with Diocletian in A.D. 310."[7]
3. Pergamum (A.D. 312–606): The stormy council of Nicaea (A.D. 325) was full of intrigue and political methods with the supremacy of the clergy overtaking the laity. The doctrine of the Nicolaitans had finally secured a foothold in the church. "Now the word 'Pergamum' means 'Marriage,' and when the Church entered into a union with the State it was guilty of 'Spiritual Fornication' or 'Balaamism.'"[8] The paganism of the world had overrun the church! Also the bishop system triumphed when Boniface III was crowned "universal bishop" in Rome.
4. Thyatira (A.D. 606–1520): Jezebel the harlot dominated this church with immorality and idolatry, which caused the Lord's servants to be led astray. This represents Roman Catholicism, with all its idolatry and new doctrines.
5. Sardis (A.D. 1520–1750): This was a formalistic, dead church that had a form of godliness without the power. "The meaning of the word 'Sardis' is the 'escaping one,' or those who 'come out' and so it is an excellent type of the Church of the Reformation Period."[9]
6. Philadelphia (A.D. 1750–1900): This church of "brotherly love" had

an open door that could not be closed. This church with its missionary opportunities typifies the evangelical period.

7. Laodicea (A.D. 1900 to the Rapture): This represents the liberal church that is "lukewarm" with very little warmhearted spirituality. This is the church that will lead to apostasy.

This view, however, faces several problems. First, to make the seven churches representative of church history, one has to force the specific problems of each congregation into a certain period of church history. And those issues do not fit as easily as one may wish. Church history is far more complex.

Second, the Scriptures give no indication that the churches are to be understood in this way. We should not impose on the Scriptures a theory without some evidence that it stems from the Bible.

Third, one can readily observe that all seven kinds of congregations exist now and have probably existed simultaneously throughout much of church history.

However, in opposition to this Walvoord writes:

> What is claimed is that there does seem to be a remarkable progression in the message. It would seem almost incredible that such a progression should be a pure accident, and the order of the messages to the churches seems to be divinely selected to give prophetically the main movement of church history. . . . instead of progressive improvement and a trend toward righteousness and peace in the church age, it may be expected that the age will end in failure as symbolized in the church of Laodicea.[10]

Messengers of the Seven Churches

The Lord Jesus spoke to these churches directly through the instrumentality of the prophet John. And each letter begins with the words "To the angel of the church in . . ." Were these actually angels, or were they human messengers (as the Greek word *angellos* means)? It does not make sense to believe that the Lord was addressing an angel sent from God. We have no record of a church guardian angel, though that idea is not an impossibility.

But the idea conveyed is that this person would share with the congregation the message given to him by Christ. Thus *angellos* should be understood as human messengers. As Thomas writes, "The word *[angellos]* referred to an envoy sent to carry a message. . . . the same were men who represented their churches, but not in the sense of being sole leaders of the individual churches. These were moral representatives, so to speak, who as individuals epitomized the conditions of the churches they represented. Hence, each letter is addressed to the church's representative, not directly to the church itself."[11]

Some think these men journeyed to Patmos to receive the finished book of Revelation from the hands of John, and that they then returned to their respective cities and shared the message.

The Church in Heaven

After chapter 3 in Revelation the word *church* is not mentioned again. And as the book unfolds, no group or body is seen on earth that could be called the church. However, several times John saw *in heaven* a great company of saints that had been martyred on earth.

Saints

The Tribulation begins in chapter 6. But just before this, the apostle John saw the four living creatures holding golden bowls of incense, "which are the prayers of the saints" (5:8). Most likely these are church saints worshiping the Lamb in heaven. Christ purchased these with His blood (v. 9) who are "from every tribe and tongue and people and nation" and who are now residing with Him. They are not martyrs, as are other groups seen in heaven who will be killed during the Tribulation (e.g. 7:12–17; 16:6; 18:24). The church-age saints, to be raptured before the Tribulation, have been made "a kingdom and priests to our God; and they will reign upon the earth" (5:10).

These saints, the church in glory, will return with Christ and reign with Him on the earth. Walvoord observes:

> The church is a priesthood rather than having a priesthood, and is a royal family rather than merely being ruled by a king. The members will not be so much subjects of the kingdom as they will be reigning with Christ on the earth. Here again is intimated the purpose of God to consummate and fulfill the prophecies of an earthly kingdom in which Christ will reign as King of kings and Lord of lords. The phrase "on the earth" is significant as referring to the earthly millennial reign of Christ in which the church will participate.[12]

When Babylon the harlot is destroyed (Rev. 18), church "saints and apostles and prophets" will rejoice at the judgment that will fall on her (18:20). Could the "saints" here be church saints who are now residing in heaven? Probably so. Babylon in Revelation is described as a geographical place, a city. But she may also represent the false religious system that has deceived humanity throughout history, including the present dispensation of the church. As John wrote, "And in her was found the blood of prophets and of saints and of all who have been slain on the earth" (v. 24). If verse 20 represents the church, verse 24 would also, because the context and subject are the same.

Since the religious philosophy of Babylon is embedded deeply in Roman

Catholicism, this view makes sense. Though this view is sometimes controversial, most evangelical scholars hold to this position. Many also believe that the system of Roman Catholicism may not be the only visible religious entity at that time, but it may form the core of or the catalyst around which other religions become a part. (For more on the connection of Roman Catholicism and the harlot see the excellent statement by Harry Ironside on pages 148–49.)

On this subject Walvoord also writes:

> The chief priests of the Babylonian cult wore crowns, in the form of the head of a fish, in recognition of Dagon the fish god, with the title "Keeper of the Bridge," that is, the "bridge" between man and Satan, imprinted on the crowns. The Roman equivalent of the title, *Pontifex Maximus,* was used by the Caesars and later Roman emperors, and was also adopted as the title for the bishop of Rome. In the early centuries of the church in Rome, incredible confusion arose; and attempts were made to combine some of the features of the mystery religion of Babylon with the Christian faith, a confusion which has continued down to the present day. . . . Apostasy, which is seen in its latent form today, will flower in its ultimate form in this future superchurch which will apparently engulf all Christendom in the period after the rapture of the church.[13]

Millions of true saints in Christ have died through the centuries through the torment of that system. And now in heaven the saints in Christ will have their moment to rejoice at her destruction.

As the marriage of the Lamb is about to get underway in Revelation 19, "a great multitude in heaven" shout, "Hallelujah! Salvation and glory and power belong to our God" (19:1). This multitude are the Lord's bond-servants, small and great (v. 5). They will shout in joy that the harlot Babylon is slain (v. 2). Who are the people in this great multitude?

Some say they are Tribulation martyrs, whereas others think the group is the church. Still others have suggested that this is the larger body of the redeemed from all past generations, including, of course, church saints. The passage seems to say that everyone in heaven is anticipating the return of Jesus the Messiah to the earth, as described in the verses that follow (vv. 7–16).

This makes sense because people in every dispensation are redeemed by Christ's blood and are aware that someday He will return to earth as the triumphant King! Their shout is awesome and as loud "as the sound of many [rushing] waters and as the sound of mighty peals of thunder, saying, 'Hallelujah! For the Lord our God, the Almighty, reigns'" (19:6)

The Twelve Apostolic Foundation Stones

After all the pain and sorrow of earth's history, the book of Revelation closes with the glorious appearing of the eternal New Jerusalem coming down from the Lord above (Rev. 21). Tears will be wiped away, and pain, crying, and death will cease (v. 4).

With the New Jerusalem, memorials and monuments are established, recalling two of the three most important dispensations in human history. For example, twelve gates hanging from a great high wall will memorialize the twelve tribes of the sons of Israel (v. 12). Though imperfect as shown in their failure to keep the Law, the Jews were God's earthly people chosen to reveal His grace to the nations surrounding Palestine.

But the wall of the New Jerusalem also will have twelve foundation stones, "and on them were the twelve names of the twelve apostles of the Lamb" (v. 14). As the twelve tribes represent Israel, so the twelve apostles represent the church.

Some assume John was saying that Israel and the church somehow merge in the Lord's eternal program. This is not so. In fact, the opposite seems to be the case. The two peoples, Israel and the church, have their different roles even as eternity begins.

> Continuity from the twelve sons of Israel to the twelve apostles is not the teaching of this passage. . . . The words clearly show that God has an eschatological role for both peoples. Beyond dispute, this description of the bride-city separates believers among Israel from believers of the church, and in a symbolic way assigns the two groups separate roles in the new creation. If the two were one merged group of believers, there would have been twenty-four gates instead of twelve or twenty-four foundations instead of twelve.[14]

CHAPTER 11

ANTHROPOLOGY IN THE BOOK OF REVELATION

MAL COUCH

REVELATION USES A VARIETY OF descriptions in speaking of humanity during the Tribulation. John went from collective descriptions of the entire world to classifying and drawing profiles of both saved and lost individuals. But since human beings are connected to the planet, it is worth noting first how John described the earth.

The Whole World

John used the Greek word *gēs* ("earth") some twelve times in his gospel. But in Revelation he used the same word seventy-three times! He used the word *kosmos* fifty-nine times in his other writings, but the same word occurs only three times in Revelation.

Though the two words are sometimes interchangeable, *gēs* means "land, ground, earth, or dirt," whereas *kosmos* more often means the world system, humanity, and/or its moral or religious nature. In terms of the scope of Revelation, this is remarkable. For John, then, was stating that the Tribulation will be a universal phenomenon, affecting all the territories, land masses, continents, and countries where people dwell.

Some interpreters theorize that the book is covering events that will take place only in Palestine or in the past Roman Empire. But with the apostle using *gēs* some seventy-three times, these localized and limited views do not seem to make sense.

Gēs clearly means the whole earth in, for example, 6:8 ("over a fourth of the earth"), 6:15 ("the kings of the earth"), 13:8 ("all who dwell on the earth"), and 14:15 ("the harvest of the earth is ripe"). Thus it is difficult to see these

131

events as having taken place in the past, as amillenarians contend. So even the word *gēs* lends support to the premillennial view of Revelation.

Terror on the Land

In most verses where *gēs* is used, the apostle John was describing something evil happening to the earth. Of course, there are exceptions, as in, for example, 1:5, where Christ is called "the ruler of the kings of the earth *[gēs]*, and in 1:7, which states that "all the tribes of the earth *[gēs]*" will see Christ when He returns. Also, when the seven-year Tribulation begins, peace will be taken "from the earth *[gēs]*" (6:4), and when the kingdom begins, the redeemed will form a kingdom and will be "priests to [their] God; and they will reign upon the earth *[gēs]*" (5:10). Following the kingdom, this physical earth and the heavens will flee away (20:11), and new heavens and a new earth *[gēs]* will appear (21:1).

But more often in the Tribulation, destruction and terror will take place on the earth. Near the beginning of the Tribulation the stars will fall on the earth, causing kings and other leaders to hide in caves (v. 15).

Four angels will harm the earth and sea (7:2). Fire from the heavenly altar will be thrown on the earth (8:5), with hail and fire following and consuming a third of the trees and all the green grass on the earth (v. 7). The earth will be smitten with plagues (11:6), and those dwelling on the earth will be tormented (v. 10) and destroyed (v. 18). Things will be so bad that the inhabitants of the earth will scream a great cry of "Woe" (12:12).

Kings, Commanders, and Great Men

John used three terms in reference to the earth's leaders, ones to whom people look for safety and protection. But with all that will be coming on the earth, even the strongest leaders can do nothing to stop the onslaught of horror that will overwhelm humankind.

Kings

Jesus is said to be "the ruler *[archon]* of the kings of the earth" (1:5). A king generally rules over a territory or land with a group of people under his rule. As the *archon*, the Lord Jesus is the preeminent authority who will control all earthly governors. He is aptly described as "the King of kings and Lord of lords" (17:14; 19:16).

In 10:11 the word *kings* is used of government heads who are listed along with "many peoples and nations and tongues." John referred to the kings of the earth (6:15; 17:18; 18:9), kings of the east (16:12), kings of the earth who commit immorality with Babylon the harlot (18:3), kings who will be destroyed and eaten by the birds at the Battle of Armageddon (19:18). But prior to that battle, the kings of earth will assemble with the Beast and the False

Prophet to make war against the Messiah, but they and the armies assembled with them will be quickly defeated (vv. 19–20).

Church-age saints are said to be made kings and priests to the Lord (1:6; 5:10). Describing the glories of the eternal New Jerusalem, John noted that "the nations shall walk by its light, and the kings of the earth shall bring their glory into it" (21:24). By describing the redeemed in the eternal state by the terms "nations" and "kings," the prophet may simply have used common language similar to what we might now use to depict a great company of millions of souls. Or he may have been stating that there will be structure and order even among the saints of eternity. The redeemed may well be scattered throughout the world in nations, with leaders over each area. He added that "the glory and honor of the nations" will be brought into the New Jerusalem (v. 26).

It must also be remembered that there will be a new earth, though there will be no sea (21:1) and no more night (v. 25).

Commanders

The word for commander is *kīliarchos,* literally, "leader of a thousand," possibly referring, as we would say today, to the general of the army. These are the men who make war, but who will be overwhelmed as the Tribulation begins. They will join millions of others who flee and hide in the mountains from the wrath of God on the throne and the Lamb (6:15).

Commanders will lead in the final effort to take Jerusalem, but they will be defeated by Christ at Armageddon and their bodies eaten by birds (19:18).

Great Men

This term (Greek, *megistanes*) may refer to sub-rulers, that is, political leaders or business leaders during the Tribulation. With the military commanders, they too will flee what is coming on the earth as the Tribulation begins (6:15). Toward the end of the Tribulation, they will be among those who are deceived by the sorcery of Babylon the great. Witnessing her destruction, they will apparently join the leaders and merchants of the earth in mourning her death (18:23).

These leaders—kings, commanders, and great men—will be part of the world system that will defy the Lord and rebel against Him. They will deceive the peoples of the earth and will resist the message of redemption.

Rich and Strong, Slave and Free

These words (in three passages in Revelation) seem to describe the general population of the earth. The descriptions—along with three other words: the small, the great, and the poor—and the contrasts seem obvious. Some are wealthy and influential ("strong"). And the common people are either in bondage or free. Whatever their station in life, people in all levels of society will suffer God's wrath in the Tribulation.

In the sixth seal judgment "the rich and the strong and every slave and free man [will hide] themselves in the caves" (6:15). Half way through the Tribulation, as the world grows darker in its terror, the False Prophet "causes all, the small and the great, and the rich and the poor, and the free men and the slaves, to be given a mark on their right hand, or on their forehead" (13:16). With this, every kind of person will be locked into the evil system of the Beast, for they will not be able to buy or sell anything without this mark (v. 17).

Gathering at Armageddon, all classes of people on earth, apparently in some state of desperation, will fight against the regathered Jews and against the Lord, being led by the Beast and the kings of the earth (19:19). They are "all men, both free men and slaves, and small and great" (v. 18).

But in this final great rebellion in the Tribulation; no one who joins forces against Christ will be spared.

> The victims of Harmagedon will be food for the birds of prey. The groups listed include all classes of mankind and every status of life. . . . The sweeping reference of ['all'] clearly refers to those who have accepted the mark of the beast and yielded allegiance to the false Christ. . . . The only survivors of this awful confrontation will be those loyal to Christ who have not died or suffered martyrdom.[1]

Tribe and Tongue, and People and Nation

These words describe the distribution, characteristics, and relationships of human beings. "Tongue" refers to the division of people by languages. "Tribe" probably refers to smaller groups such as clans, or how people are identified in a limited territory. "People" may refer to a larger grouping, and a "nation" may suggest a larger territory with large and small groups speaking various languages.

On these words Thomas writes:

> This is the totality of humanity among which the Jews have been scattered. . . . Behind *phylēs* ("tribe") is the idea of the same descent. It is a group belonging to the same clan and united by family lineage. . . . People speaking the same language are intended in *glōssēs* ("tongue") (cf. Acts 2:4, 6, 8, 11). . . . *Laou* ("people") unites a people of the same race or stock . . . or possibly of the same interests. . . . The group indicated by *ethnous* ("nation") is one bound together by political unity . . . or perhaps, more broadly, by habits, customs, and peculiarities.[2]

Using these four descriptions, twice John pictured a great company of saints in heaven who have been redeemed from the earth (5:9; 10:11). But more often he used these descriptions in a negative light to portray almost the entire world in rebellion against God.

"Peoples and tribes and tongues and nations" will rejoice as they look at the dead bodies of the two witnesses in Jerusalem (11:9). The Beast is said to have authority "over every tribe and people and tongue and nation" (13:7). Yet God in His mercy will command an angel to preach the gospel "to every nation and tribe and tongue and people" (14:6).

All the world is pictured as a sea of humanity that will be dominated by Babylon the harlot in the latter part of the Tribulation. "The waters which you saw where the harlot sits, are peoples and multitudes and nations and tongues" (17:15).

Eight times John used only the "nation(s)" to describe the people of earth. "All nations" will have drunk the wine of the harlot (18:3), and the nations will be deceived by her sorceries (v. 23). When Christ returns, He will smite the nations (19:15) for their rebellion, and they will be deceived no more (20:3) until Satan is released from confinement. Then after the Millennium Satan will lead a final insurrection of the nations against the King, His saints, and Jerusalem (20:8–9).

The final three references to nations are positive. "And the nations shall walk by [Jersualem's] light, and the kings of the earth shall bring their glory into it" (21:24), and the nations' glory and honor will be seen in the city (v. 26). And at last, with sin completely purged from the universe, the tree of life will bear fruit "for the healing of the nations" (22:2).

The Horns and the Kings

In the New Testament the word "horn" *(keras)* is mentioned only ten times, with nine of these references in the book of Revelation. Six of these have to do with the revived Roman Empire. The first reference occurs in the context of the satanic war against the Jewish people (12:1–17).

John described Satan as the "great red dragon having seven heads and ten horns, and on his heads were seven diadems" (12:3). What is the meaning of the heads and horns in this vision? To answer this, we need to go back to the prophecy in Daniel 7, in which Daniel saw four great beasts in a vision. The first beast was a lion, the powerful nation of Babylon (v. 4). "There is, therefore, no uncertainty that in this chapter, the first kingdom is either the reign of Nebuchadnezzar or the Neo-Babylonian empire which he represents."[3]

The second great world power Daniel saw was the Medo-Persian Empire, pictured as a fierce bear (v. 5). Its terrible teeth would devour and swallow other nations. "The overall stress for this beast is on conquest; and Medo-Persia did take over far more land than any prior kingdom, reaching finally all the way from the Indus River on the east of Egypt and the Aegean on the west."[4]

Daniel 7:6 describes Greece and its powerful leader, Alexander the Great. That nation is pictured as a leopard, with four wings and four heads, which portray his sudden and swift conquest of the Middle East. Alexander died prematurely on the battlefield, and his quickly acquired empire was divided between his four leading officers. The leopard "is known as swift, cunning, cruel, and with an insatiable appetite for blood. History records the fact that the Persians were defeated by Greece, under the leadership of Alexander the Great, who was the progenitor of the military strategy called the blitzkrieg. The lightning character of his conquest is without precedent in the ancient world."[5]

The fourth kingdom in Daniel 7 is most important because of its role in the past, but also because it will be revived for the future. In the Tribulation the Beast will head up this revived kingdom. Daniel wrote that it is dreadful and terrible, extremely strong with iron teeth, and different from the other three beasts (v. 7). This indescribable beast represents the powerful Roman Empire that overwhelmed Greece. "The outstanding feature of this beast, however, is strength, with all described aspects serving to amplify this quality. . . . Rome also reduplicated within itself many of the characteristics which had been especially true earlier of Babylonia, Medo-Persia, and Greece. More description is given of this beast than of the first three, which means that its significance in the vision is greater."[6]

This beast will have ten horns (v. 7) with another little horn coming up among the ten (v. 8). This little horn represents a person, who will wage war against "the saints of the Highest One" (v. 22), the followers of Christ in the Tribulation. His "overpowering them" (v. 21) refers to their becoming martyrs because of their faith in Christ.

This little horn is the Antichrist, the Beast of Revelation 13:1–10. The ten horns are ten nations that will make up the final form of the Roman Empire. The horns are the nations or powers led by ten kings (Dan. 7:24). The little horn, who will utter great boasts (v. 20), "will speak out against the Most High and wear down the saints of the Highest One, and he will intend to make alterations in times and in law; and they will be given into his hand for a time, times, and half a time" (v. 25).

Unger comments as follows on this verse:

> The beast, Antichrist, will think . . . to change the times and the laws of religious ordinances and the worship laid down by God in His Word, setting himself up "above all that is called God" (2 Thess. 2:4) and arrogating his own will above God's times and laws (Dan. 11:36–37; cf. Rev. 13:1–18).
> The saints (the Jewish remnant) shall be given into his hand (13:7)

to be persecuted for a limited time. The days of his willfulness are to be limited "for the elect's [of Israel] sake" (Matt. 24:22); so there will be a remnant of Israel saved and delivered through the Tribulation to form the nucleus of the Kingdom over Israel (Acts 1:6–7).[7]

The words "time, times, and half a time" in Daniel 7:25 refer to the last three and a half years of the seven-year Tribulation period. This begins in Revelation 13. More will be said about these seven years and Daniel's "Seventieth Week" in chapter 15.

In the Tribulation Daniel's far-off predictions about the Antichrist, the little horn of the fourth beast, will be fulfilled.

John saw Satan, the red Dragon, supporting and carrying the seven heads (the nations) and ten horns (the leaders) (Rev. 12:3). Though this is Satan's kingdom, it is also the kingdom of the Beast, who will come out of the sea (the world), also supporting or holding up the seven heads and ten horns (13:1). The Dragon, Satan, will give the Beast "his power and his throne and great authority" (v. 2). The core of this power is the revived Roman Empire centered in the nations of Europe.

At some point also in the Tribulation, Babylon the harlot will sit on, that is, influence or control, the Beast (17:3). She will also rule over seven kings: "the seven heads are seven mountains on which the woman sits, and they are seven kings" (v. 9–10). John then wrote that "five [kings] have fallen, one is, the other has not yet come; and when he comes, he must remain a little while" (v. 10). The apostle added, "And the beast which was and is not, is himself also an eighth, and is one of the seven, and he goes to destruction. And the ten horns which you saw are ten kings, who have not yet received a kingdom, but they receive authority as kings with the beast for one hour. These have one purpose and they give their power and authority to the beast" (vv. 11–13).

On these difficult verses Walvoord writes: "The explanation of the beast introduced by the unusual phrase 'here is the mind which hath wisdom' [v. 9a] anticipates the difficulty and complexity of the revelation to follow."[8] The five kings may be the five rulers of the Roman Empire just before John's lifetime. Domitian, who was reigning in John's day, may be the sixth king. And the seventh king, who "has not yet come" is the Antichrist in the time of the Tribulation.[9] Verse 11 reads, "the beast which was and is not, is himself also an eighth, and is one of the seven, and he goes to destruction." But how can the Antichrist be the seventh ruler and also the eighth? Constable explains it this way: "Evidently the beast is one of the seven in the sense that his initial kingdom is on a par with the seven major empires just mentioned. He is the eighth in that he will establish an eighth major empire with a worldwide government after he revives a formerly defunct nation."[10]

In the Tribulation the Beast will die and will then mimic the resurrection of

Christ by coming back to life. However, at the end of the Tribulation he will be destroyed forever (19:20).

The ten horns who are on the fourth beast of Daniel 7, ten kings, coincide with the ten toes of Nebuchadnezzar's dream (Dan. 2) and the ten horns of the nondescript Beast of Daniel 7 and Revelation 13. The ten kings form the Antichrist's confederacy of nations. He will appoint them as leaders of various world nations in the revived Roman Empire.

> With the revival of the Beast to the wonderment of the world comes a confederation of kings who are associated with the Beast in the end time persecution and closing days of the "Times of the Gentiles." We cannot speculate as to these kings, but this one thing is evident, they have "one mind and give their power and strength to the Beast." This will be the most colossal and gigantic confederation and alliance the world has ever seen.[11]

Individual Names Mentioned in Revelation

Antipas

Antipas is mentioned in 2:13 as a faithful witness and martyr of the church at Pergamum. Why was he singled out among the many early-church martyrs and mentioned by name? According to tradition he was burned to death in a bronze bull. Little else is known of him, but his testimony must have been dramatic and the knowledge of his sacrifice widespread.

Balaam and Balak

With all that was commendable in the church at Pergamum (2:13), it still had a problem similar to the teachings of Balaam, a Moabite prophet mentioned in Numbers 22–24. Thomas explains the Old Testament story.

> In Numbers 24 Balaam persistently refused the request of Balak, king of Moab, to curse Israel. In the account of Israel's seduction to worship Baal in Num. 25 no mention is made of Balaam's agency in causing this defection. Nevertheless, according to Num. 31:16, he had apparently advised Balak that Israel would forfeit God's protection if he could induce them to worship idols, which he did. This tragic incident at Baal-Peor made a deep impression on subsequent generations of Israelites. The doctrine relevant to the downfall resulting from Balaam's counsel advocates that the people of God commit sexual immorality or intermarry with the heathen and compromise in the matter of idolatrous worship. Balaam bears more guilt than even antagonistic King Balak.[12]

Similar to Balaam's influence, some people in the Pergamum church were eating things sacrificed to idols and practicing sexual immorality (Rev. 2:14). In response the Lord told the people to repent lest He come quickly and "make war against them" (2:16).

Nicolaitans

The teaching of the Nicolaitans was active in both the Ephesus and Pergamum churches (2:6, 15). The name means "conquering the people." No one can be certain of what this cult was all about. But Jesus, as well as the congregation at Ephesus, hated this group and their deeds (v. 6). In Pergamum, only a few in the assembly were following this group and teaching its doctrines. But they, like those in the church who were following the teaching of Balaam and involved in immorality, were to repent (v. 14).

What were the Nicolaitans teaching? Though no one can be sure, the church father Irenaeus, who lived in the latter part of the second century, says the heretical sect was started by Nicholas of Antioch, one of the seven original deacons (Acts 6:5). Many of the early church fathers support this view. It is said that Nicholas apostatized, with the cult turning into a licentious, lawless religion. It sought also to link Christianity and paganism with a form of Gnosticism. Some say the sins of the Balaam cult and the Nicolaitans joined to break down the doctrines of Christianity. These arguments for the Nicolaitan cult seem to have some historical basis, as Thomas summarizes.

> Added to Irenaeus are the testimonies of Tertullian, Hippolytus, Dorotheus of Tyre, Jerome, Augustine, Eusebius and others. . . . They all say this was a sect of licentious antinomian Gnostics who lapsed into their antinomian license because of an overstrained asceticism. Hippolytus adds that Nicholaus was the forerunner of Hymenaeus and Philetus who are condemned in 2 Tim. 2:17. . . . Eusebius adds that after the group was censured by John in the Apocalypse, the sect disappeared in a very short time.[13]

Holding a more tenuous position on the subject, Lenski writes, "The most one can say in regard to the minor question as to who the Nicolaitans were, is that they were an early Gnostic sect. All else is uncertain."[14]

Jezebel

The church at Thyatira is said to have tolerated the woman Jezebel (2:20). Is the name Jezebel a symbolic reference to immorality in that assembly, or was she a woman in the congregation who influenced believers to sin in the same way Jezebel did in the Old Testament? Jesus said she "calls herself a prophetess, and she teaches and leads My bond-servants astray, so that they commit acts of immorality and eat things sacrificed to idols" (v. 20).

Jezebel was the evil wife of King Ahab of the northern kingdom of Israel (874–853 B.C.). She became active in killing the Lord's prophets (1 Kings 18:4), and she caused even Elijah the prophet to run in fear from her wrath (19:2–3). She continually intimidated her husband and provoked and incited him to do the evil she wanted done (21:25). "Do you now reign in Israel?" she taunted (21:7). Because of her influence he erected an altar for Baal worship (16:31–32). Her harlotries and witchcraft were well known throughout the kingdom. Her end came when King Jehu had her thrown from a window and had her body trampled by horses (2 Kings 9:33). As prophesied, her remains were eaten by scavenger dogs (1 Kings 21:23).

Possibly Revelation 2:20 is speaking of an actual woman who was infecting the Thyatira congregation with Jezebel-like sins of idolatry and immorality. The Lord said he would give her time to repent of her immorality (2:21) but, if not, she would be cast into a bed of sickness (v. 22) and her children slain with pestilence (v. 23). About her career, Morris writes the following.

> Thyatira had actually entrusted a position of teaching leadership to an immoral woman calling herself a prophetess. . . . Whether Jezebel was the actual or assumed name of this false prophetess or merely a graphic appellation given her by Christ, the spiritual kinship with the Jezebel of old is clearly recognized.
>
> The Thyatiran "prophetess" had in some way not stated, actually been made aware of the serious nature of her sin; it was not merely a case of a misguided but sincere woman who thought she was divinely inspired and sharing God's revelations with the church. Rather, she knew she was in the wrong, but had deliberately rejected God's Word and refused to change her mind. Evidently this was also true of those who had become her followers in the church. The only remedy was judgment.[15]

David

King David is referred to three times in Revelation (3:7; 5:5; 22:16). Speaking to the church at Philadelphia, and quoting Isaiah 22:22, the Lord said, "He who is holy, who is true, who has the key of David, who opens and no one will shut, and who shuts and no one opens, says this: 'I know your deeds, Behold, I have put before you an open door which no one can shut, because you have a little power, and have kept My word, and have not denied My name'" (Rev. 3:7–8).

As recorded in Isaiah 22, the Lord God replaced wicked and unfaithful Shebna, a foremost leader in Jerusalem (vv. 15–19), with Eliakim. The people were discouraged with threats from Egypt and needed a strong, godly voice of assurance. Through Isaiah the Lord said that Eliakim, a faithful palace administrator, would be to the people like a father with authority (v. 21). And He added, "I will set the key of the house of David on his shoulder [and] he will become a throne of glory to his father's house" (vv. 22–23).

As the Son of David, Jesus picked up these comforting words from Isaiah and repeated them to the Philadelphia church. In this way the church could sense Jesus' own power and authority! As Walvoord states, "Christ, the great antitype of Eliakim, has the key to truth and holiness as well as opportunity, service, and testimony. To the church at Philadelphia surrounded by heathendom and wickedness, Christ gives assurance that He has power to open and close according to His sovereign will."[16]

In John's vision of the scroll that no human could open (Rev. 5:1–5) an angel showed John that only One had the right and the authority to break open its seals and reveal its awesome message. The prophet was told, "Stop weeping; behold, the Lion that is from the tribe of Judah, the Root of David, has overcome so as to open the book and its seven seals" (v. 5).

"The Lion that is from the tribe of Judah" is a prophetic messianic allusion to Genesis 49:9. Here Jacob's son Judah is called a lion's whelp. This is a cryptic, far-off prediction, a kind of foreshadowing of a future son of Jacob who would be Jesus the Messiah! The apostle John was reminded that He is this One, the Lord Jesus, who holds the right to open the scroll and launch the judgments of the Tribulation. When the first seal is broken, the Tribulation will start (6:1).

In the final verses of Revelation reference is made again to Jesus in relation to David. Speaking directly to the readers, the Lord said, "I, Jesus, have sent My angel to testify to you these things for the churches. I am the root and the offspring of David, the bright morning star" (22:16). Scott concludes, "His connection with Israel in royalty is here asserted. As divine He is the Root of David's house. As man He is the Offspring of David. . . . The crown of Israel is His in virtue of who He is, and His, too, by promise and prophecy. He was born King of the Jews (Matt. 2. 2). He died as King of the Jews (Matt. 27. 37). He shall reign as King of the Jews (Zech. 9. 9)."[17]

CHAPTER 12

HAMARTIOLOGY IN THE BOOK OF REVELATION

MAL COUCH

A MAJOR THEME OF REVELATION is the subject of sin. The Apocalypse is teeming with sin and all its ramifications for the universe. The sins of the local churches are seen in chapters 2–3, and throughout the book we see in vivid detail the evil nature and deeds of Satan, the fallen angels, the demons from the pit, the Beast, and the False Prophet. In the end, however, sin will be judged. There will be no more sorrow or evil in the eternal state. This fact makes Revelation one of the most important books of Scripture. Sin and evil will finally and completely be judged and done away with. The universe will never again be dominated by the scourge of wicked rebellion against God.

The doctrine of sin (called hamartiology) is no small subject in the Word of God. Sin manifests itself in the positive acts of wrongdoing, but also it can be measured by its negative aspects. Bancroft shows how sin is not simply a chance happening; it is an act of responsible disobedience, not an accident.[1]

Paul's words in Romans 5:12, that sin entered into the world by one man and thereby was passed on to all humanity, fly in the face of those who claim sin is accidental. Sin is also innate and not merely creaturely weakness.[2] Nor is sin an infirmity "because of which we are very unfortunate, but in no wise culpable or guilty."[3] Nor is sin the mere "absence of good."[4]

Also sin, Bancroft points out, is not simply a step backward. "Sin cannot be defined as immaturity, lack of development, or the remnant of primitive characteristics."[5] Instead, sin is a conscious rebellion against God that produces individual acts that challenge His will and laws of morality. Sinful acts generally produce harm and pain in others, who become the victims of human waywardness. Walvoord writes that "few books of the Bible [like Revelation] describe man in greater depravity and as the object of more severe divine judgment. The acme of human blasphemy and wickedness is portrayed in the beast and the false prophet who are the supreme demonstration of Satan's handiwork in the human race."[6]

The Sins of the Seven Churches

Generally speaking, the seven churches of Asia represent the second generation of believers in the various cities mentioned. Therefore, the letters point out that evil in various forms had infiltrated the churches and was damaging the effectiveness of their witness to the world.

In the assembly at Ephesus were evil men who were liars and who were apparently teaching false doctrine (2:2). But the congregation itself had departed from its initial love for Christ (v. 3), fallen from its high and respected spiritual position (v. 5), and needed to repent of its sins.

Little criticism is aimed at the church of Smyrna. But the people there were suffering from "tribulation," probably persecution from their neighbors and Jews in the synagogue (v. 9). The church would suffer horribly from the hands of unbelievers (v. 10).

A strong evil influence permeated the city of Pergamum (v. 13). Thus the local assembly there suffered much martyrdom, with one such victim mentioned by name, Antipas (v. 13). But worse, there were those who followed the teachings of Balaam, performed acts of immorality (v. 14), and followed the doctrines of the Nicolaitans (v. 15).

The church at Thyatira was tolerating the woman Jezebel, practicing immoral acts, and eating things sacrificed to idols (v. 20). John warned those in the church who may have fallen into such sins that they would suffer the consequences of such practices (v. 23). Not all in this congregation, however, had succumbed to these evils.

The church at Sardis was dead but also asleep spiritually (3:1–2). Their works were incomplete (v. 2), and they were ungrateful and needed to repent (v. 3). Many had soiled their garments (spiritually) and needed to be clothed in robes clean and white, that is, purified from sin (v. 4).

Like the church of Smyrna, Philadelphia had few internal sin problems. The congregation was persecuted, however, by the local synagogue that belonged to Satan (v. 9).

Laodicea was lukewarm in its spiritual condition (v. 15). It thought of itself as spiritually wealthy, but it really was "wretched and miserable and poor and blind and naked" (v. 17). The church needed to buy from the Lord valuable gold "refined by fire," and it needed white garments (righteous deeds) to compensate for its past shame, nakedness, and (spiritual) eyes that were full of sores (v. 18). Jesus invited those who heard him to repent (v. 19) and to open the door for fellowship with Him personally (v. 20).

Though Jesus was walking among these suffering churches (1:13), their apostate condition could not be ignored. And while sin is always carried out individually, there is also often a corporate nature about its manifestation that becomes a blight on the name of Christ and is infectious to others. The sins of these churches could not be left to fester.

Repentance could bring restoration, but without it the Lord would not hesitate to bring judgment. He spoke of coming to "remove your lampstand out of its place—unless you repent" (2:5), of making war against those who hold the teachings of the Nicolaitans (v. 16), of slaying the children of Jezebel as a witness to all the churches of their deeds (v. 23), of coming in judgment like a thief on those sinning and not repenting at Sardis (3:3), and of reproving and disciplining (v. 19) those in Laodicea who are wretched, miserable, poor, blind, and naked in their sinfulness (v. 17).

The Wickedness of the Lost

Unabated murder and killing will be horrible features in the Tribulation. The fifth seal judgment depicts a host of those who will become believers in the early days of the Tribulation but who will soon be martyred for their testimony and the Word of God (6:9–11). They will plead for the Lord to avenge their blood shed on earth (v. 10). Those slain will know that more of their brothers will be slaughtered later. So they are told to "rest for a little while longer, until the number of their fellow servants and their brethren who were to be killed even as they had been, should be completed also" (v. 11).

This seems to be partly fulfilled in 7:14, for more martyrs entering heaven will "come out of the great tribulation, and [will] have washed their robes and made them white in the blood of the Lamb." This wording suggests that they too will have died martyrs' deaths.

As the torment of the demonic hordes begins (9:13–19), the lost will have opportunity to fall on their knees and to beg God for relief and salvation. But even with a third of mankind slain before their eyes (v. 15), they will harden their hearts, refusing to repent of their sins. They will refuse to stop worshiping demons and idols (v. 20), and they will not repent of their murders, acts of sorcery, immorality, and thievery (v. 21).

Sorcery

Sorcery (Greek, *pharmakeia*) is especially interesting in this list in that it probably means hallucinogenic drugs, by which people placed themselves in trances and engaged in incantations and burned incense to their idols. This practice will be especially evident in the Tribulation, for, John wrote, "all the nations [will be] deceived by your [Babylon's] sorcery *[pharmakeia]*" (18:23).

Though clearly related to idolatry, sorcery goes beyond idol worship, as

Paul showed in Galatians 5:20, where he wrote of sorcery as distinct from idolatry.

Toward the end of the Tribulation, in the fourth bowl judgments, the sun will scorch people with intense heat (16:9). And in the fifth bowl judgment the kingdom of the Antichrist will grow darker, and people will gnaw "their tongues because of pain" (16:10). Does this wrath of God poured out on humanity cause people to turn to Him and repent? No. In fact, they will blaspheme "the name of God who has the power over these plagues; and they [will] not repent, so as to give Him glory" (v. 9). In addition, they will blaspheme "the God of heaven because of their pains and their sores" (v. 11), and because of the huge hailstones that plummet the earth in the seventh bowl judgment (v. 21).

In many other places in Revelation John described how people will become terribly evil in the Tribulation. Jerusalem, where Jesus was crucified, is called Sodom and Egypt (11:8), suggestive of the corrupt, idolatrous lives of Jerusalem's inhabitants. This is where the Beast will kill the two witnesses sent by the Lord for a testimony to Him. Their bodies lie in the streets of Jerusalem, but they will be seen by the entire world, who in their wickedness will "rejoice over them and make merry" (v. 10).

The Beast

When the Beast will have been revived after sustaining a deadly wound, "the whole world" will be amazed and will follow him (13:3). In fact, because of this, people will worship Satan and the Beast (vv. 4, 8). The Beast will have control and "authority over every tribe and people and tongue and nation" (v. 7). Adding to the Antichrist's deception, the False Prophet will cause people everywhere to worship the image of the Beast (v. 12). The inhabitants of the earth will willingly take the mark of the Beast on their right hand or forehead (v. 16), because without it they will be unable to buy or sell (v. 17). This will seal their fate because everyone who takes the mark will be under the power of the Beast.

Besides the Antichrist having authority over people, Babylon the harlot will also cause "those who dwell on the earth [to be] made drunk with the wine of her immorality" (17:2). Also the kings and merchants of the earth will be seduced by her (18:9, 15), but her end is certain (v. 21).

Even the millennial kingdom, with its nearly perfect environment, will not be immune to sin. Toward the end of this one-thousand-year period, Satan will be released from his prison "and will come out to deceive the nations which are in the four corners of the earth" (20:8). But destruction will come swiftly on those who follow him (v. 9).

Unbelievers in the Tribulation period will not be simply manipulated into sinning by Satan, the Beast, or the False Prophet. The people will already be sinners by nature (Eph. 2:3), but they will be directed into certain sins by the seduction and trickery of these evil forces. Even in the Tribulation people will be responsible for their actions and will have an opportunity to know good from evil. In fact, the entire world will hear the gospel by the testimony of the 144,000 Jewish bond-servants (7:1–8), the two prophesying witnesses (called "lampstands," 11:4–12), and the angel who will preach "to those who live on the earth, and to every nation and tribe and tongue and people" (14:6).

The willful sins of the people who will worship the Beast and his image explains why God's wrath will be so fierce. "If anyone worships the beast and his image . . . he also will drink of the wine of the wrath of God . . . he will be tormented with fire and brimstone in the presence of the holy angels and in the presence of the Lamb" (vv. 9–10).

The Great White Throne Judgment

The final judgment of humankind will take place at the Great White Throne (20:11–15). In this judgment, all unbelievers of all generations will be given resurrected bodies and will be brought before the Judge for a just hearing. Who is this Judge? The Bible speaks often of God being the Judge of sinful humanity. But it seems as if God the Son will be the Judge in this final judgment. Talking about eternal destiny, Jesus said, "the Son also gives life to whom He wishes" (John 5:21). And when Christ gives eternal life to the person who believes in Him, that one will "not come into judgment, but has passed out of death into life" (v. 24). Thus God gave His Son "authority to execute judgment, because He is the Son of Man" (v. 27).

Speaking with Cornelius, Peter added more light on this subject when he said that Jesus "is the One who has been appointed by God as Judge of the living and the dead" (Acts 10:42). This idea is strengthened when, at the end of the book of Revelation, Christ added, "Behold, I am coming quickly, and My reward is with Me, to render to every man according to what he has done" (22:12).

The Great White Throne judgment has to do with the deeds or works of the lost. If a person does not accept Christ as his or her Savior, that person must face Him as Judge. And the only criterion by which He can judge is the unbeliever's works or actions. Since the Book of Life (20:12) has the names of those who have trusted in Jesus, the "books" opened at the Great White Throne judgment must contain lists of the works of the unbelieving dead.

Some have mistakenly assumed that the Great White Throne judgment is like a second chance of salvation for the lost. Nothing could be further from the truth. The judgment takes place not to give people another opportunity to be saved, but so that Christ may give the lost a fair hearing. But the sentence is absolute as expressed in verse 15, "And if anyone's name was not found written in the book of life, he was thrown into the lake of fire."

As unpleasant as this judgment is, the Lord will thereby complete His punishment for sin.

Speaking of the New Jerusalem John wrote, "Outside are the dogs and the sorcerers and the immoral persons and the murderers and the idolaters, and everyone who loves and practices lying" (22:15).

Is this verse teaching that a group of sinful people will be loitering outside the New Jerusalem? No. Instead, the passage is a literary device that is simply describing the moral purity of the new city. As Thomas notes, "Jesus continues His proclamation regarding eternal destiny by focusing on those who fail to qualify because they have never washed their robes. The adverb *exō* refers to the position of those who are 'outside' the wall of the city mentioned at the end of v. 14. To be outside the Holy City means a final destiny in the lake of fire (20:15; 21:8). . . . Such people could never have gained access to the city in the first place, because they are totally distinct from the new heaven and the new earth."[7]

It is difficult for mortals to imagine that sin will someday be wiped away and that peace will permanently rule in the new heavens and the new earth. But God will accomplish this—a fact that should bring tremendous comfort to those who belong to Christ.

Babylon the Harlot

Ancient Babylon

Ancient Babylon cast a long and dark shadow over the Middle East, and it also greatly influenced the affairs of the Jewish people. The story of Babylon begins with the waters that nourished the Garden of Eden. Four rivers flowed out of the Garden with two of them being the Tigris and Euphrates (Gen. 2:10–14). This was the area where in later years Nimrod first settled "his kingdom Babel" (an early name for Babylon), which means "confusion" (10:10). In this area in the plain of Shinar the great tower of Babel was constructed to "reach into heaven" (11:4). And from there God scattered humankind "over the face of the whole earth" (v. 9).

From this region polytheism quickly began to flourish and mature. People began to worship the stars of heaven, and soon an entire religious system was developed with a pantheon of gods.

Babylon the Mystery Religion

Though the nation Babylon with its dominating territorial powers exists no longer, the religion it spawned is still with us, as presented in Revelation 17. However, a number of Bible scholars believe Revelation 17–18 addresses the revival of the literal city of Babylon, not its religious system. Still others feel that Revelation 17 is discussing Babylon's system, but one that has developed in another geographical region, namely Rome, and that the system exists in the religion of Roman Catholicism. Many older Protestant scholars held that the Babylon of Revelation was Catholicism, following the arguments of Hislop in his classic work, *The Two Babylons.*[8]

Hislop traces the relationship between ancient Babylon and the religious practice of the harlot system called mystery Babylon. Following this argument, Ironside makes an excellent case for Roman Catholicism being the religious power of Revelation 17–18.

> Ancient lore now comes to our assistance, and tells us that the wife of Nimrod-bar-Cush was the infamous Semiramis the First. She is reputed to have been the foundress of the Babylonian mysteries and the first high-priestess of idolatry. Thus Babylon became the fountainhead of idolatry, and the mother of every heathen and pagan system in the world. . . .
>
> Within 1,000 years Babylonianism had become the religion of the world, which has rejected the Divine revelation. . . .
>
> Linked with the central mystery were countless lesser mysteries. . . . Among these were the doctrines of purgatorial purification after death, salvation by countless sacraments such as priestly absolution, sprinkling with holy water, the offering of round cakes to the queen of heaven as mentioned in the book of Jeremiah, [and] dedication of virgins to the gods, which was literally sanctified prostitution. . . .
>
> When Julius Caesar (who, like all young Romans of good family, was an initiate) had become the head of the State, he was elected Pontifex Maximus, and this title was held henceforth by all the Roman emperors down to Constantine the Great, who was, at one and the same time, head of the church and high priest of the heathen! The title was afterward conferred upon the bishops of Rome, and is borne by the pope today, who is thus declared to be, not the successor of the fisherman-apostle Peter, but the direct successor of the high priest of the Babylonian mysteries, and the servant of the fish-god Dagon, for whom he wears, like his adulterous predecessors, the fisherman's ring.
>
> During the early centuries of the church's history, the mystery of iniquity had wrought with such astounding effect, and the Babylonian practices and teachings had been so largely absorbed by that which bore the name of the church of Christ, that the truth of the Holy Scriptures on many points had been wholly obscured, while idolatrous practices had been foisted upon the people as Christian sacraments, and heathen philosophies took the place of gospel

instruction. Thus was developed that amazing system which for a thousand years dominated Europe and trafficked in the bodies and souls of men, until the great Reformation of the 16th century brought in a measure of deliverance.[9]

Pentecost sums these observations this way: "It is not too much to say that the false doctrines and practices found within Romanism are directly attributable to the union of this paganism with Christianity when Constantine declared Rome to be a Christian empire. It is thus concluded that the harlot represents all professing Christendom united in a single system under one head."[10]

Though many Bible students separate commercial Babylon (Rev. 18) from religious Babylon (Rev. 17), the two chapters probably represent different phases of the same entity. Thus this false religion will have both religious and commercial influence on the powers of the world. And Babylon will be responsible for killing many Tribulation saints. This is stated in both chapters. "And I saw the woman drunk with the blood of the saints" (17:6). "And in her was found the blood of prophets and of saints and of all who have been slain on the earth" (18:24). Because of this, to make too much of a division between Revelation 17 and 18 may detract from the main point.

Will Roman Catholicism be Babylon the harlot in the Tribulation? No one can be dogmatic, but many evangelical scholars certainly point in this direction. A question may help reveal the answer: "If the Rapture took place tomorrow, what great religious power is dominant to influence events in the Tribulation?" One can certainly mention Roman Catholicism, though many resist this argument. In the opinion of this writer, Romanism would be the best option as Babylon the harlot. Only those living in the Tribulation will know for certain.

CHAPTER 13

ANGELOLOGY IN THE BOOK OF REVELATION

MAL COUCH

OVER A FOURTH OF THE REFERENCES TO angels in the Bible are found in the book of Revelation. If the references to the demons, who are the fallen angels, and Satan, who is described as an angel, are counted, the number is even higher. This is what one would expect in a book that scans the heavenlies and describes the events that will take place on the earth and even under the earth in the days to come.

Both the Hebrew word *målak* and the Greek word *angelos* mean "messenger," with the emphasis on the fact that they are the messengers and servants who carry out the Lord's bidding. Though angels reside in a realm other than the physical world that humans know, they are allowed from time to time to take on physical form in order to communicate with humans.

Angels are pictured as powerful and swift beings who, in coming from the presence of God, protect human beings and deliver messages to them. Also angels worship the Lord, continually giving Him praise and adoration. In Revelation a number of angels communicated information to John for him to record. When John fell in worship (Rev. 19:10; 22:9), they reminded him that they, too, were fellow servants with him and were simply carrying out the wishes of the Lord.

Angels are spirit beings but occasionally seemed to appear in human bodies to communicate with humans. All angels were no doubt created long before the physical universe came into existence.

The Angels of God

In Revelation the following angels of God are mentioned.

- The special angels who make dramatic appearances and give special messages.
- The seven special angels.
- The warring angels, who are seen in conflict with the fallen angels.
- The adoring angels, who stand before the presence of God giving Him glory and honor.
- The four angelic "living creatures."

The Special Angels

These seem to dominate in Revelation. They are given unique assignments and are marked out for unusual appearances before John.

The first of these special angels is the one the Lord used to communicate the message of Revelation to the apostle (1:1). Though Jesus Himself often spoke in Revelation, this angel is the Lord's angel and communicated directly with the prophet. This may be the same angel who closed the Revelation message (22:6). John was so overwhelmed by this angel's appearance that he fell at his feet to worship him (v. 8). The angel instructed the prophet that he should worship God instead (v. 9).

Another angel, called the "strong angel" asked, "Who is worthy to open the [special] book [scroll] and to break its seals?" (5:2). Another angel with a powerful voice gave instructions to four angels not to harm the earth, sea, or the trees "until we have sealed the bond-servants of our God on their foreheads" (7:2–3).

Other special angels in Revelation include *(a)* the angel who will minister before the heavenly altar, holding up the prayers of the saints before God (8:4), and who also will fill the censer with fires of judgment for the earth below (v. 5); *(b)* the angel described as an eagle who will pronounce judgments of woe on the land (v. 13); *(c)* the angel who will spread the gospel worldwide (14:6); and *(d)* the angel who will pronounce judgment on Babylon (v. 8).

One angel given a most unusual task is the one sent from heaven to open the bottomless pit, which causes the release of the demonic horde described as locusts (9:2–3). This angel is called a star (v. 1).

Other angels performing special tasks for the Lord are mentioned in 14:15, 17–19; 16:5; 18:1; 19:17; 20:1; and 21:17.

The Seven Special Angels

Each of seven angels will sound one of the seven trumpet judgments (8:2–9:21; 11:15–19), and seven angels will pour out the seven bowls of wrath on the earth (16:1–21). These two groups of seven may be the same angels. Thomas writes:

Because of the article with *angelous* ("angels") [in 8:2] and because of an alleged correspondence with seven archangels in Jewish tradition, some have identified these angels as a special group consisting of Uriel, Raphael, Raguel, Michael, Saraqael, Gabriel, and Remiel. The perfect participle *hestekasin* ("stand") indicates that they were in position before God and had been there some time as a special class of angels would be.

What makes them special is their commission to sound the trumpets. Their position before God marks their readiness for service, in this case the service of symbolically initiating the trumpet afflictions. This is the natural sense of the words, and no reason has arisen to point to another understanding.[1]

The Warring Angels

Many Bible students believe the reference to the "third of the stars of heaven" being swept away by the tail of the Dragon, Satan, speaks of the fall of the angels of God from their coveted position in glory (12:4). This happened in the ancient past, when Satan and this part of the host of angels rebelled against God. But in the Tribulation, as Constable points out, God will expel the Dragon, Satan, from heaven. The angel Michael and other angels with him will fight with the Dragon and his angels, and they will be expelled from God's presence.[2] Lenski notes:

Gone is "their place in the heaven" to bring accusation against the brethren before God; the Accuser [will be] "thrown to the earth" as the song states it: "he came down to you," to the earth and the sea, there now to vent his fury since he is able now to reach no farther and to do no more.

"Michael and his angels" is to be understood literally; so also is "the dragon and his angels" except that the term "the dragon" is retained from v. 2, etc. Yet since he has "angels" (Matt. 25:41) as his army he, too, must be an angel.[3]

Some have said Michael is Jesus, but no evidence points in that direction. According to Daniel 12:1, Michael "stands" for Daniel's people, Israel, perhaps in a defensive posture. In Jude 9, he is called the archangel, and he contended with the Devil over the body of Moses. The struggle was great and Satan is powerful, because Michael did not bring a railing accusation against him! All Michael could utter was, "The Lord rebuke you." When Christ returns for His church in the Rapture, believers will hear "the voice of the archangel" (1 Thess. 4:16), probably Michael.

Then when Christ will return to the earth with His church-age saints "the armies which are in heaven, clothed in fine linen, white and clean," will accompany Him (Rev. 19:14). These angelic "armies" are most likely the "hosts" referred to in the Old Testament in the term "the Lord of hosts" (e.g., Ps. 103:21). Some argue that only redeemed human beings will be clothed in fine linen in heaven, but as with humans, the clothing of these angels will represent their holiness before God. When Christ returns from heaven, angels will accompany Him and will "gather together His elect from the four winds" (Matt. 24:31).

The Adoring Angels

Many angels are said to praise God continually. If the "living creatures" of Revelation 4:6–9 are angels, then they are involved in worshiping the Lord by exclaiming His holiness, as did the seraphim (a special category of angels) in Isaiah 6:3. The living creatures, John wrote, praise God forever, giving Him "glory and honor and thanks to Him who sits on the throne" (Rev. 4:9). Daniel too may have been describing this worshiping host of angels, when he wrote of the "thousands upon thousands [who] were attending [God], and myriads upon myriads [who] were standing before Him" (Dan. 7:10).

The Living Creatures

These living beings, though giving God adoration, as noted above, have other tasks to perform as recorded in the book of Revelation. These "living creatures" are "full of eyes in front and behind" (Rev. 4:6); that is, they have unusual intelligence. The one that is like a lion may suggest his strength (v. 7), the one that is like a calf may suggest his seeming holiness or innocence (v. 7), the one with a human face may suggest wisdom (v. 7), and the one that could fly like an eagle (v. 7) and had six wings might refer to its swiftness in fulfilling tasks assigned by the Lord (v. 8).

The four "living creatures" are referred to in Revelation seventeen times—more often than any other angelic group.

Interestingly, these beings will fall down before God with the redeemed of humanity and will give Him great shouts of praise for His greatness (19:4). With the saved, they will cry, "Hallelujah! For the Lord our God, the Almighty, reigns" (v. 6).

The Fall of Satan, His Person and Works, and His Angelic Hosts

Some of the fallen angels are demons who now serve Satan. Two Old Testament passages—Isaiah 14:12–21 and Ezekiel 28:11–19—describe their fall and their being banished from the presence of God. It is important to understand these passages in order to comprehend what Revelation says will happen to the demonic angels. These verses also reveal the ancient account of the fall of Satan from the domain of God.

Isaiah 14:12–21

After a poetic taunt against the king of Babylon and that nation's evil system (Isa. 14:4–11), Isaiah suddenly changed and spoke of another being, a creature that is other-worldly and beyond the historic events in Babylon.

A heavenly creature called "the star of the morning" and "son of the dawn" fell from grace and came down to the earth and "weakened the nations" (v. 12). In five proud "I will" statements this angelic personality sought to put himself above other angels in an effort to make himself "like the Most High" (v. 14).

For these egotistical efforts to replace God, he was cast from heaven and fell to the earth. That fall made the earth tremble and shook kingdoms (v. 16). In time, he would be judged and slain.

On his title "star of the morning" (literally, Lucifer) Archer writes that Lucifer is "the Roman name for the morning star (Heb. *hêlēl,* 'the bright one'), which speedily disappears before the far greater splendor of the sun. This title is addressed to the king of Babylon . . . as a representative or embodiment of Satan, who is regarded as the power behind the king's throne. The titanic pride and ambition expressed in verses 13, 14 are out of place on any lips but Satan's."[4]

Ezekiel 28:11–19

This passage is similar in ways to the passage in Isaiah. Ezekiel's words in 28:1–10 address a human leader, the king of Tyre, but verses 11–19 go beyond the worldly ruler to one who was "full of wisdom and perfect in beauty . . . in Eden, the garden of God" (v. 13). He was "the anointed cherub" (v. 14), who was "blameless in your ways from the day you were created, until unrighteousness was found in you . . . and you sinned" (vv. 15–16). He was cast from the presence of God (v. 16), and someday he will be judged and will be no more (vv. 18–19). Unger comments as follows on Satan in verses 11–19.

> Such terminology is most inappropriate from the lips of the Lord concerning a fallen man, who at best was but a pagan monarch. The expression, however, is filled with meaningful truth when applied to the greatest angelic being in his original unfallen state. This great passage is of tremendous import, recording the origin of sin and Satan and the character and panoramic career of the greatest of the angels. . . . This revelation is made under the king of Tyre because of the very close connection between human government of the fallen world system and Satan and the powers of darkness as the superhuman agencies, who are the real actors behind the scenes.[5]

Revelation 12:1–17

Revelation 12–15 give the reader a reprieve from the ongoing hammering of the judgments falling on the earth. It is as if the writer John paused in his prophetic chronology to describe other important events that parallel his main narration. Chapter 12 tells of the fall of Satan from heaven and his pursuit of the woman, Israel, and her male child, the Messiah (vv. 5–6).

Verse 4, as already noted, speaks of the fall of Satan ("the star of the morning") in eternity past. Then verse 9 addresses his future fall from the presence of God to the earth at the midpoint of the Tribulation. As Morris writes, "the remarkable vision seen by John in this chapter looks back first of all to the very beginning of earth history, then races forward to the time of Christ and finally to the events still to be consummated in this final period. This review was necessary for John (and for us) to comprehend the full significance of the great sign about to be unveiled."[6]

In the Tribulation God will prepare a place of protection in a wilderness for 1,260 days, or three and a half years, the last half of the Tribulation (vv. 6, 14). The Dragon will attempt to destroy the Jewish people; becoming enraged, he will make war with "the rest of her offspring, who keep the commandments of God and hold to the testimony of Jesus" (v. 17).

This chapter sets up the great satanic conflict between Christ and the Devil that so dominates heaven and earth history, climaxing in the Tribulation. Satan now accuses believers before God, but the time will come in the Tribulation when he will be "thrown down" (v. 10). Thrown to the earth, he will persecute believers in an attitude of "great wrath, knowing that he has only a short time" (v. 12).

The Names of Satan in Revelation

Revelation 12 includes five names of Satan and implies a sixth name or description. Studying these names helps us understand his person and work.

Red Dragon

The adjective "red" depicts the Devil's sinister and evil nature (v. 3), and perhaps even his anger and fierceness against the Lord and His people. In the New Testament the word "Dragon" is used only in Revelation, where it occurs thirteen times (12:3–4, 7 [twice], 9, 13, 16–17; 13:2, 4, 11; 16:13; 20:2). Though not a serpent, Satan is certainly a serpent-like creature, fierce, powerful, wild, and dangerous.

The reference to Satan being a Dragon seems to come from Isaiah 27:1: "In that day the LORD will punish Leviathan the fleeing serpent, with His fierce and great and mighty sword, even Leviathan the twisted serpent; and He will kill the dragon who lives in the sea."

Written in vivid poetic form, Isaiah 27:1 is the Old Testament equivalent of Revelation 20:10, in describing Satan's final demise at God's hands.

When the Dragon is first mentioned in Revelation, he is seen with seven heads and ten horns, which depict the revived Roman Empire (Rev. 12:3; cf. Dan. 7:7, 24–25). He will pursue the woman, that is, the Jewish people who gave birth to the Messiah (Rev. 12:1–3, 5, 12). In the end he will be cast into the lake of fire and brimstone "where the beast and the false prophet are also; and they [all three] will be tormented day and night forever and ever" (20:10).

The Serpent

To make certain the reader understands who is meant by this term, John wrote in 12:9 that the "serpent of old" is "the devil and Satan, who deceives the whole world." As the "serpent of old," Satan is identified as the one in the Garden of Eden who tempted Eve and thereby caused the entire human race to fall into sin (Gen. 3:1–19; Rom. 5:12). The apostle Paul also mentioned that Satan, as the serpent, beguiled Eve (2 Cor. 11:3).

Though *herpeton,* the more common Greek word for serpent, is used four times in the New Testament (Acts 10:12; 11:6; Rom. 1:23; James 3:7), the word used in Revelation is *ophis,* and four of those five references refer to Satan (12:9, 14–15; 20:2).

The Devil

The Greek word for the Devil is *diabolos,* which comes from a verb meaning "to throw" or "throw against." It may also be translated "to slander." Thirty-four times in the New Testament the word *diabolos* is used of the Devil, and three times it refers to people and is translated "slanderers" (1 Tim. 3:11) and "false accusers" (2 Tim. 3:3; Titus 2:3). The book of Revelation uses the word five times to refer to the Devil (2:10; 12:9, 12; 20:2, 10).

Satan

This name, used thirty-six times in the New Testament, stems from a verb meaning "to show enmity," "to accuse." It is virtually a synonym with *diabolos,* but in Greek it is almost always used with the word "the" ("the Satan," as in 12:9). In the New Testament, the demonic spirits of disease are subordinated to him (Luke 13:16; 2 Cor. 12:7), and his realm is that of darkness (Acts 26:18) and death (1 Cor. 5:5). The chief spirit or demon, Satan, leads people to worship idols and to accept false teachings (Rev. 2:24).

The Accuser

The word in Greek is *katēgōr* and is used only one time (12:10) to describe Satan as an accuser. The word means one who speaks against another in an accusatory fashion.

Satan cannot come before the Lord in fellowship or worship, but apparently he has access into His presence in which he accuses believers of wrongdoing. Here in Revelation he is called "the accuser of our brethren [who] has been thrown down, who accuses them before our God day and night." He also accused Job (Job 1:11; 2:5) and Joshua the high priest (Zech. 3:1). He sought permission to accuse and sift Peter, but Christ stated that He intervened and prayed that he would be spared and that his faith would not fail (Luke 22:31–32).

Though Satan accuses, God defends His own and Jesus Christ stands as our Advocate or Defense Attorney (1 John 2:1). As with Job, the Lord may allow His children to feel the pain of satanic persecution. But after lessons of trust are experienced, "the God of all grace, who called you to His eternal glory in Christ, will Himself perfect, confirm, strengthen and establish you" (1 Peter 5:10–11). God has the final word, not the accuser!

Satan, an Angel

There are several hints in Revelation 12 that Satan is an angelic being. For example, when he fell from heaven, he "swept away a third of the stars of heaven," which may refer to that part of the angelic host that rebelled and fell from God's presence (v. 4). Referring to Satan and the fallen angels, John the apostle said there "was no longer a place found for *them* in heaven" (v. 8, italics added). Also verses 7 and 9 speak of the fallen angels as "his" angels.

The apostle Paul reminded his Corinthian readers that Satan is an angel, in fact a deceptive angel of light (2 Cor. 11:14). He is also a spirit *(pneuma)* who is presently "working in the sons of disobedience," that is, unbelievers, to keep them in spiritual bondage and blinded from receiving the truth of the gospel (Eph. 2:2).

After the one-thousand-year millennial kingdom, Satan will be released from his prison, and he will attempt once again to defeat Christ (Rev. 20:7), but he will be defeated. He will be cast into the lake of fire (v. 10), and his angels (demons) will be there also (Matt. 25:41).

Satan and the Seven Churches

Satan has tremendous influence during the present dispensation of the church. This is demonstrated by the number of references about him and his activities in the seven churches of Asia (Rev. 2–3). Presumably he is equally active today in the assemblies of believers worldwide. Satan also has influence on groups and peoples other than the seven churches, influence that brought about persecution and pain.

For example, Satan controlled the synagogue in Smyrna that brought tribulation, poverty, and blasphemy on the congregation (2:9). At Pergamum his activities were so strong it was as if he dwelt in that city and occupied his throne there (2:13). In the city of Philadelphia he also controlled the synagogue. But the Lord said that Satan's activities would fail and that the Jews would come to the Christians and bow down at their feet (3:9). John did not explain, however, what would cause them to reverse their actions and withdraw their persecution of the believers in Philadelphia.

As Peter wrote, Satan is the believer's adversary, prowling about as a roaring lion seeking someone to devour (1 Peter 5:8).

It is no surprise to see Satan so active in the Tribulation. In that seven-year period of God's wrath Satan will attempt to thwart God's plans. The Devil knows his hour is short and that his career of rebellion will soon come to an end. Though his end has already been set forth in the prophetic Scriptures, Satan still makes a conscious effort to subvert God's plans and purposes. He believes his own lie and thinks that he is more powerful than the Lord Himself. This is part of his evil mind that moves him forward in such hatred of God.

Chafer makes these summarizing statements about Satan:

> This mighty angel appears in the Bible with prominence, importance, and power second only to the Godhead Three. He is as often mentioned in the text of the Scriptures as all of the angels together. He is drawn into the story of human history from its first page to its last and always presented as a most vital factor in the ongoings of men, of angels, and of the universe itself. It is of great significance that the Scriptures trace with detail and care this archfiend from his creation, through all his career, and on to his final judgment.[7]

The Demons in Revelation

The fallen angels are demons that torment people on earth. Before Satan's fall he was described as the anointed cherub (Ezek. 28:14), the blameless, covering, and beautiful cherub (vv. 15–17). But with his expulsion from the throne room of God, he brought down to earth with him "a third of the stars of heaven" (Rev. 12:4); that is, many angels who rebelled with him became devils. Other evidence confirms this fact. For example, these fallen beings know of their future judgment by Christ when they cried out through the voices of the two demon-possessed men, "What do we have to do with You, Son of God? Have You come here to torment us before the time?" (Matt. 8:29). These creatures know there is a place of judgment already prepared for their future eternal confinement along with the Devil (Matt. 25:41).

Demons

In Revelation demons are mentioned only three times (9:20; 16:14; 18:2). They can be worshiped (9:20), and they are as spirits who are powerful beings, able to perform signs that cause the kings or rulers of the earth to come together for the great and final war of Armageddon (16:14).

Also these demonic personalities will find a home in the revived Babylon, "a dwelling place of demons and a prison of every unclean spirit" (18:2). These beings will congregate in Babylon to intensify the sin that will flow from this city of rebellion and evil. As a result the nations will drink of Babylon's immorality and sensuality (v. 3), more than likely prompted and tempted by the work of the spirits.

Spirits

The Greek word *pneuma* may refer to spirit beings, such as angels or demons. But it can also refer to the breath or life in a living being. Since the third person of the Trinity is the Holy Spirit, the word *pneuma* points to His spiritual or nonphysical nature.

In Revelation *pneuma* is used three times to describe the demonic world (16:13, 14; 18:2). As spirit beings, the fallen angels do not have bodies like that of humans, though they occupy space.

Revelation 16:13 says the demons are "unclean spirits like frogs" (16:13) and are "unclean" (18:2). *Akathartos* has the idea of "dirty," "filthy," or "impure." The word encompasses the concept of moral and spiritual uncleanness. Since frogs are slimy and may dwell in an unclean, slimy pond, this helps describe the impure nature of these demon spirits.

In 9:1–12 the demons are portrayed as locusts with a powerful sting in their tails like that of scorpions (v. 3). God will not allow them to hurt the grass or trees of earth, though they will torment the unsaved, those who do not have the seal of God on their foreheads (v. 4).

The torment they inflict may be physical, spiritual, or psychological, or all of them. But whatever it is, people will seek death but will be unable to die (v. 6).

The description of these locust-like beings is extreme, to say the least. They appear as horses ready for battle, with gold crowns on their heads and with faces like men (v. 7). They have hair like women, teeth like lions, breastplates of iron, and their wings will sound like swift chariots and horses (vv. 8–9).

Some of these descriptions may speak for themselves. For example, war horses were the most fearsome of animals, trained to run over enemy infantrymen in the field of combat. Though the demons are the servants of Satan, gold crowns may speak of some aspects of authority and independence of action. Their human-like faces suggest that they are intelligent. Their teeth of lions portray fierceness and power to destroy and subdue. Breastplates of iron indicate they will be protected and resistant to destruction. Wings and chariots represent speed of action. But why are they said to have "hair like women?" Johnson suggests, "The comparison of their 'hair' with that of women may refer (as in other ancient texts) to the locusts' long antennae."[8]

These demons will come from the bottomless pit, which the angel of the abyss will open (v. 11), so these creatures can bring their torture on the lost.

Verses 13–21 speak of a different set of fallen creatures, who will be released from somewhere around the Euphrates River by four angels. Two hundred million demonic creatures will be released. Some suggest that these will be a human army. The problem with this is the description of the troops and horses in verse 17. The riders will have breastplates the color of fire, hyacinth, and brimstone. The horses' heads will be like lions, and the creatures will spew forth fire, smoke, and brimstone. This army sounds very much like the demonic troops in verses 1–12. The difference in the two lists is that people are only tormented in verses 1–12, whereby there is actual death of one-third of humanity in verses 13–21.

Nowhere else in Scripture are holy angels kept bound as are the four angels confined at the great Euphrates River (v. 14). "It may be concluded that the four angels bound in the Euphrates River are evil angels who are loosed on the occasion of the sounding of the sixth trumpet in order to execute this judgment. It is another instance of the loosing of wicked angels similar to the release of the demonic locusts earlier in the fifth trumpet."[9]

What is the significance of the river Euphrates? This river runs through Babylon, and Babylon is the great source of evil, idolatry, and false religion, as is graphically illustrated in chapters 17–18. In these final days of spiritual conflict, the demons will pour forth into the world from this region to inflict their torment. Thomas adds that the river "separated Israel from her two chief enemies, Assyria and Babylon. The name refers not to just the river itself, but to the whole region drained by the river. This was also the frontier between Rome and her enemy to the east, the Parthian Empire. The area beyond the Euphrates to the east is traditionally the source from which enemy attacks came against Israel."[10]

The Angel of the Abyss

"The angel of the abyss" (9:11) is the leader of the locust-like creatures who will be released from the "bottomless pit" or "shaft of the abyss" (9:2). This place of confinement, so vividly and horribly described, retains a certain number of the fallen angels until they will be released in the Tribulation to torment men on the earth (v. 5). While the locust creatures are clearly fallen angelic demons, there is some debate over the identity of their "king," the angel of the abyss.

Some say this is Satan, and others claim he is an elect unfallen angel serving as a guard over the pit. But more likely he is a demon, since he will serve as ruler over this host who will be released from the abyss. Obviously, God must give him permission to carry out his role as chief tormentor over the people of earth.

This angel carries two titles: the Hebrew *Abaddōn*, "Destruction," and the Greek *Apollyōn*, "Destroyer" (9:11). The word *Abaddōn* is used in Job 26:6;

28:22; 31:12; and Proverbs 15:11 as a synonym of death. In Revelation 9:11 this title is appropriate for this demonic king because he will be the cause of intense pain for many unbelievers, those who will "not have the seal of God on their foreheads" (9:4). "To propose that the king is a figure of speech for death takes the OT usage of the Hebrew name into account, but it fails to acknowledge that the angel is a real being and not merely a personification. . . . The name is simply an appropriate designation given to the fallen angel who rules the locusts from the abyss."[11]

Idols and Idolatry

The Word of God makes it clear that sacrificing to idols is actually a practice of worshiping demons (Deut. 32:17; 1 Cor. 10:19–21). They are active in influencing people to serve idols rather than to honor God. Idolatry seems to be revived in the book of Revelation, and this makes sense because of Satan's intense and renewed activity.

Apparently the people in the Pergamum church had returned to some form of eating sacrificial meals offered to idols (2:14). And in Thyatira the Lord's "bond-servants" were "led astray" and were caught up in eating "things sacrificed to idols" (v. 20). For people living in such an idolatrous world, the temptations were strong to return to old habits.

When the four angels (demons) will release the two hundred million horsemen, who will bring on plagues of fire and brimstone that will kill a third of humankind, "the rest of mankind, who were not killed by these plagues, did not repent of the works of their hands, so as not to worship demons, and the idols of gold and of silver and of brass" (9:20). A great number of people will go back to the old gods of the pagan world, and their hearts will become extremely hardened.

Idolatry keeps people from coming to God (1 Cor. 6:9–10). Because of this, those given over totally to idol worship in the Tribulation will refuse to accept Christ. They will be doomed to the lake of fire and eternal separation from God. John the apostle writes that idolaters have "their part . . . in the lake that burns with fire and brimstone, which is the second death" (Rev. 21:8). John also stated that those who practice idolatry will be kept forever outside the walls of the New Jerusalem (22:15).

The Final Demonic Struggle and Revelation

The One who will end Satan's evil global system is Jesus Christ, who, at His death on the cross, "spoiled principalities and powers" and "made a show of them openly, triumphing over them" (Col. 2:15 KJV). He purchased man's redemption and also redeemed the world from Satan's usurpation.

Christ alone was worthy to open the seven-sealed scroll because of His sacrifice (5:1–7). He will bring about the judgments on the earth, and then at His return to the earth He will defeat His enemies—the Antichrist, the False Prophet, and kings and their soldiers—at the Battle of Armageddon (16:13–14; 19:19–21).

As Unger writes:

> At the end of the Great Tribulation the confederated armies under the Antichrist, Satan's tool, will be assembled in the plain of Megiddo, in preparation for moving against Jerusalem (Zech. 14:2) to annihilate the Jew. Pouring the "spirit of grace and supplications" upon "the house of David" (Israel) and the inhabitants of Jerusalem (Zech. 12:10), the glorious Christ, leading the "armies of heaven," will come to their rescue (Rev. 19:11–16), clashing with the Antichrist and the wicked kings and their demonized armies of earth, assembled by unparalleled demon activity (Rev. 16:13–16) to make war against the Lord. . . . In the terrible carnage "all the fowls will be filled with their flesh" (Rev. 19:21).
>
> With the Satanic system destroyed and Satan and demons locked up, the time will have at last come for the restoration of the kingdom to Israel (Acts 1:6), that glorious era of peace and blessing so magnificently predicted by the seers of the Old Testament.[12]

CHAPTER 14

SOTERIOLOGY IN THE BOOK OF REVELATION

MAL COUCH

THE WORD *soteriology* COMES from two Greek words, *sotēria,* "salvation, deliverance, rescue," and *logos,* "word" or "the study of." Thus it is the study of the biblical teaching of salvation. Lightner writes, "God solved the problem man's sin presented to Him. He is the only One who could. After man's fall God the Father began in time the plan of salvation He ordained in eternity past. This divine plan centered in His divine Son: 'He gave His only begotten Son' because He 'so loved the world' (John 3:16). 'He laid down His life for us' (1 John 3:16)."[1]

The Blood of the Lamb

One of the first references in Revelation to salvation is found in 1:5, where John spoke of the Lord, "who loves us, and released us from our sins by His blood." He demonstrated His love by pouring out His blood on the cross. In 1:7 John referred to "those who pierced Him" (an allusion to Zech. 12:10), which suggests that He shed His blood. The giving of His blood was proof that He went all the way to death (see Phil. 2:8) for those He loved.

Following the Rapture, the saints of the church are seen in heaven in Revelation 5. They are brought before the presence of their Savior, the Lamb of God, a title that speaks of Himself as a sacrifice for sin. The church saints will sing to Him a new song: "You were slain, and with your blood you purchased men for God from every tribe and language and people and nation" (v. 9 NIV).

In another scene in heaven John saw Tribulation saints who, having been martyred, will be before the throne of God and the Lamb in heaven (7:15, 17).

Their salvation will have been accomplished by His blood: "These are the ones who come out of the great tribulation, and they have washed their robes and made them white in the blood of the Lamb" (v. 14).

These martyrs will have given up their lives as a testimony for Christ in their struggle against Satan. "And they overcame him because of the blood of the Lamb and because of . . . their testimony" unto death (12:11). When Christ descends to the earth to reign as King, His "robe dipped in blood" (19:13), suggestive of His sacrificial death, will be a sign of His authority. He is called "The Word of God," and on that same bloody robe will be written His name, "King of Kings, and Lord of Lords" (v. 16).

The blood of the Lamb is the blood of the new covenant that makes possible salvation for all, no matter what dispensation they are in (Luke 22:20). Writing about the Last Supper, Paul referred to the new covenant in relation to the church: "This cup is the new covenant in My blood; do this, as often as you drink it, in remembrance of Me" (1 Cor. 11:25).

The Overcomers

The Greek word translated "overcome" (nikaō) means "to be victorious" or "to conquer." What did John the apostle mean when he used this verb in Revelation? Was he describing a special class of Christians, those who are victorious against sin? Or using the word of all Christians in referring to their victory against the opposition of disbelief? The latter seems more likely, in view of what the apostle wrote in 1 John 5:4–5. "For whatever is born of God overcomes the world; and this is the victory that has overcome the world— our faith. And who is the one who overcomes the world, but he who believes that Jesus is the Son of God?" On these verses Barker writes:

> Our being born of God is God's act on our behalf, the event through which he moves to overcome the world. The supernatural act by which human beings are being translated . . . out of the kingdom of death into the kingdom of life through the Son—all this is in view.
>
> The victory that overcomes the world is now identified with "our faith." The Greek literally says, "The victory that is victorious over the world." The participial form (nikēsasa, "that has overcome") is in the aorist tense. It may be taken as a simple statement of fact . . . or more likely as a reference to a past event [our salvation].[2]

Though John wrote of the Lamb's victory over the ten kings and the Beast (17:14), the apostle's references to overcoming in chapters 2–3 seem to refer to salvation. Almost all the references to overcoming mention a promise for all believers, promises that accompany salvation.

"To him who overcomes, I will grant to eat of the tree of life, which is in the Paradise of God" (2:7). "He who overcomes, shall not be hurt by the second death" (v. 11). "To him who overcomes to him I will give some of the hidden manna" (v. 17). "He who overcomes shall thus be clothed in white garments; and I will not erase his name from the book of life, and I will confess his name before My Father, and before His angels" (3:5). "He who overcomes, I will make him a pillar in the temple of My God" (v. 12). "He who overcomes, I will grant to him to sit down with Me on My throne" (v. 21). It would seem strange to think of only some believers eating of the tree of life, or not being hurt by the second death, or not being clothed in white garments.

Though obviously many believers attended these seven church assemblies, no doubt not everyone in them was born again. Is it correct to assume that every individual in those churches in Asia Minor—or that every individual in any church since then—was saved? It seems as if the Lord was simply pleading for unsaved people who may have been in those assemblies to "overcome" the tug of sin that was against them and to become victorious by accepting Christ as their Savior and departing from their sinful practices.

Repentance and Salvation

In the word "repentance" *(metanoia),* which means "to change one's mind," the preposition *meta* can be translated "with" or "against." That is, when a person repents, he goes against what he had believed and reverses his opinions, accepting a new belief. The word may be used of believers who have sinned and then were "made sorrowful to the point of repentance" (2 Cor. 7:9), or it can refer to Christians "who have sinned in the past and [have] not repented" (12:21).

However, the word "repentance" more often refers to salvation. "Repent therefore and return, that your sins may be wiped away" (Acts 3:19). "God is now declaring to men that all everywhere should repent" (17:30). The word is used eight times in Revelation 2–3, and almost each time it may refer to salvation. One exception may be 2:5, where the Lord urged some in the church at Ephesus to "remember . . . from where you have fallen, and repent and do the deeds you did at first." This admonition addressed Christians who had fallen into sin and needed to turn away from it. Another exception may be 3:19: "Those whom I love, I reprove and discipline; be zealous therefore, and repent."

All the other references seem to be speaking of a repentance unto salvation. For example, the woman Jezebel was given an opportunity to repent but refused (2:21), and those who were guilty of adultery with her would be punished with her unless they repented (2:22).

During the Tribulation, with God's wrath intensifying, people will continue to worship demons, refusing to repent (9:21). Scorched with terrible heat, they will refuse to give God the glory and will continue blaspheming His name and will not repent (16:9, 11).

Is repentance a separate act in salvation, or is it part of the process of believing? Chafer gives a cogent and clear scriptural answer to this question.

> Repentance, which is a change of mind, is included in believing. No individual can turn to Christ from some other confidence without a change of mind, and that, it should be noted, is all the repentance a spiritually dead individual can ever effect. That change of mind is the work of the Spirit (Eph. 2:8).
>
> To turn to Christ is a solitary act, also, and the joining of these two separate acts corresponds to the notion that two acts, repentance and faith—are required for salvation. On the other hand, turning to Christ from all other confidences is one act, and in that one act repentance, which is a change of mind, is included.
>
> Upwards of 150 texts—including all of the greatest gospel invitations—limit the human responsibility in salvation to believing or to faith. To this simple requirement nothing could be added if the glories of grace are to be preserved.[3]

The Words "Holy" and "Saint"

The Greek objective *hagios* ("holy") means "special or unique" and conveys the idea of separation from sin. Holiness is one of the attributes of God (4:8; 6:10). Jerusalem is called holy (11:2; 21:2, 10; 22:19), the prophets and apostles are holy (18:20), and so are the angels (14:10). Most of the occurrences of the noun *hagios,* however, refer to believers who will trust Christ in the Tribulation. There are the prayers of the martyred saints (8:3–4); the Antichrist, the Beast, will make war against the saints (13:7); Babylon will be responsible for the martyrdom of many saints (17:6; 18:20, 24), but they will persist in their faithfulness to the Lord (14:12), and they will be rewarded when Christ returns to the earth (11:18).

An unusual usage of the word "holy" is near the end of the book in 22:11: "Let the one who does wrong, still do wrong; and let the one who is filthy, still be filthy; and let the one who is righteous, still practice righteousness; and let the one who is holy, still keep himself holy."

John could be saying that, even though they will hear the plan of salvation in the Tribulation, many unsaved people will go on as they are, refusing to heed the call to salvation. Sinners will go on in their sin, whereas the holy ("saints," believers) will stay in that blessed condition. As Thomas explains, "The time is short [22:10] so let people go their own way [22:11]." This is another way of expressing the hopelessness of the final state of the wicked. "Throughout the career of the book after publication, however long that may be until its fulfillment, a persistence in evil or in good is all that is expected from the recipients. . . . The other side of the picture is that the righteous one will be marked by a continued practice of righteousness and the holy one by a continuation of being made holy."[4]

The Gospel

Though the word "gospel" *(euangelion)* is only used once in Revelation (14:6), the concept of salvation in Christ permeates the book. That verse refers to "another angel flying in midheaven, having an eternal gospel to preach to those who live on the earth, and to every nation and tribe and tongue and people."

How the angel will proclaim this eternal gospel in the Tribulation is not explained, but the entire world will hear the truth—people of every nation, tribe, language, and people group.

In the Tribulation people will be saved the same way as in any other period of history—by faith in the Lord (14:12). Because of this, the saved are called "the faithful" (17:14). Though not often mentioned in Revelation, this fact of individual faith or belief undergirds the entire book. As the Beast rages against believers, they will be known for their steadfastness and their faith in Christ (13:10).

Just as in the church age, so in the Tribulation people will be saved by faith in Christ. This will make them participants of the New Covenant just as it does for believers in this present age of grace.

Eternal Life in Revelation

The apostle Paul often wrote of eternal life (Gal. 6:8), which comes only through Christ (Rom. 6:23). *Zoē,* the Greek word for life, refers to spiritual life as well as physical life. Eternal life comes by the regenerating power of the Holy Spirit (Titus 3:5), who is called "the Spirit of life" (Rom. 8:2).

John wrote of the believer's crown of life (Rev. 10:1), the breath of life from God (11:11), and the water of life (21:6; 22:1, 17). Though Paul mentioned the Book of Life only once (Phil. 4:3), John mentioned it five times (13:8; 17:8; 20:12, 15). This is probably the same book (or scroll) that he called the Lamb's Book of Life (21:27).

The Book of Life

Is there a connection between John's reference to the Book of Life and what Moses said in Exodus 32:32 about being blotted "out of the book you have written" (NIV)? The Lord answered that He blots out from His book only those who have sinned (v. 33). Unger explains that this expression "comes from the practice of keeping registers of citizens and removing the names of those who die in a time of judgment."[5] And Hannah observes that this was not a list of believers' names but of the census of the people, so that Moses meant he was willing to die a premature death rather than be associated with a sinful, unforgiven people.[6] In other words God's words to Moses referred to physical death, not spiritual death.

Jesus said to the church at Sardis, "He who overcomes shall thus be clothed in white garments; and I will not erase his name from the book of life" (Rev. 3:5). Does this mean that a believer, whose name is in God's Book of Life, can be removed from that book thereby losing his salvation? If so, then this would contradict many other Bible verses that affirm that a believer in Christ cannot lose his salvation. Various answers to this question have been suggested. At least three possible solutions seem to make sense of this passage.

First, Lange suggests that Revelation 3:5 does not assert that the names of any who will finally perish were ever entered in the Book of Life in the first place, "nor is it necessarily implied."[7] Second, Thomas suggests that John used a figure of speech known as a litotes. "Interpreters," he says, "could take the 'blotting out' as an example of litotes, a figure of speech in which an affirmative is expressed by the negative of a contrary statement. Coming by way of denial of the opposite, this is an understatement to express emphatically the assurance that the overcomer's name will be retained in the book of life. . . . The emphasis of this viewpoint is certainly valid in the context of the message to Sardis."[8] Also, Walvoord holds this view.[9]

Third, some say that God placed everyone's name in the Book of Life in eternity past, but that an individual's name is removed when he or she dies without having received Christ as his or her Savior. "Christ must in some sense have died for all men because at the beginning the names of all men were in the book. In the words of Johannine theology outside the Apocalypse, He died for 'the world,' no one excluded (cf. John 1:29; 3:16; 4:42; 1 John 2:2; 4:14)."[10]

Though any one of these three views may be valid, John's words in Revelation 13:8 and 17:8 would seem to rule out the third option.

As John focused on the coming Beast, he was given a vision of a mass of humanity trusting, worshiping, and following the Antichrist. Their names had "not been written from the foundation of the world in the book of life of the Lamb who has been slain" (13:8). The Antichrist's worldwide followers will "wonder," or marvel at him, and John again wrote that their names were not "written in the book of life from the foundation of the world" (17:8).

At the final Great White Throne judgment, the unsaved will be resurrected for a final sentencing before Christ the Judge. The terrible scene pictures a multitude resurrected, great and small, with no place to hide from God (20:11–12). A set of books will be opened along with the Book of Life. The deeds of the unsaved will have all been duly recorded in these many record books. Based on their deeds and the fact that their names will not be found in the Book of Life, they will be thrown into the lake of fire (v. 15). This is the "second death" (v. 14), which heralds a permanent separation from the Lord.

The Tree of Life

The drama of this tree begins in Genesis 2–3 and ends in Revelation 22, so that these references to it are like bookends in the Bible. In the Garden of Eden God placed Adam and his wife along with the Tree of Life and the Tree of the Knowledge of Good and Evil (Gen. 2:9). They were told by the Lord that they could eat of the fruit of any tree except from the Tree of the Knowledge of Good and Evil (v. 17).

After their fall from their position of innocence and protection by the Lord, Adam and Eve were expelled from the Garden lest they eat of the Tree of Life and live forever (3:22–24). By some means not explained in Scripture, this tree held some life-giving properties that would have sustained them with physical life.

Morris writes that "it would have been calamitous had [Adam and Eve] continued in a perfect environment as sinful people, especially eating of the life-tree fruit and living on indefinitely in such a condition. They and their descendants to many generations must be taught the true nature and effects of sin, and of living out of fellowship with God."[11]

The last chapter of the Bible returns to this tree. The New Jerusalem has a river "clear as crystal, coming from the throne of God and of the Lamb" (Rev. 22:1). There by the river will be the "tree of life, bearing twelve kinds of fruit, yielding its fruit every month; and the leaves of the tree were for the healing of the nations" (v. 2).

Because the Lord does not need a tree to sustain the lives of the redeemed, no doubt the actual tree pictures a certain truth to be grasped. Some have suggested this is simply a "spiritualized" illustration and not actually a tree with such preserving powers. But Thomas notes, "Though eating the fruit of the Tree of Life is unmentioned here, the implication is that this is what brings immortality, the same as was true for Adam and Eve originally (Gen. 3:22). Conditions of future bliss will mean a return to the original glory and privileges of God's presence with man, before sin raised a barrier that prevented that direct contact."[12]

Near the very end of Revelation, John wrote, "if anyone takes away from the words of the book of this prophecy, God shall take away his part from the tree of life and from the holy city, which are written in this book" (22:19). With these words the old prophet, the apostle John, was warning everyone of the danger of claiming any additional revelation or of removing what has been written. With the book of Revelation the canon of God's Word was closed. God will give no more recorded, authoritative messages. So anyone claiming to have received such messages shows that he is denying the inspired Word of

God. Therefore as an unbeliever he or she will not be allowed to have access to the Tree of Life or the New Jerusalem itself. Such individuals will be in hell.

Though evangelical scholars believe verses 18 and 19 are first referring to the book of Revelation, most believe this can include the fact that the entire New Testament canon is closed, and we can expect no more revelation from the Lord. What John writes certainly has to do with the close of the Apocalypse, but because of the nature and the scope of the writing, it seems to imply that the canon of New Testament revelation is complete. This is because the book picks up with the close of the church age and tells us what comes after—the Tribulation, the kingdom, the judgment of the lost, and eternity.

If we argue that more revelation is coming about the Christian life, the church, the Tribulation, and the kingdom, we are admitting that the New Testament is incomplete about these doctrines.

Though this can be challenged, especially by the cults who claim they have been given additional revelation, church history confirms no one has written anything that the majority would admit is truly revelation from God. One can certainly ask, "If new revelation has come to us over the last two thousand years, where is it?"

On the full message of 22:18–19, Walvoord writes,

> Frequently in the Bible there are other warnings against tampering with the Word of God, this is among the most solemn (cf. Deut. 4:2; 12:32; Prov. 30:6; Rev. 1:3). No one can dare add to the Word of God except in blatant unbelief and denial that the Word is indeed God's own message to man. Likewise, no one should dare take away from the words of the Book (the Bible), since to do so is to do despite to the inspired Word of God.[13]

Lenski adds,

> We hold . . . all [the books of Scripture] inviolate. This word of Jesus' uttered by him in regard to this prophetic and last New Testament book will ever move us the more to do so with all the inspired books, in all of which the same truth, doctrine, gospel are given us to keep . . . inviolate.[14]

Chafer well concludes,

> The formal closing of the New Testament canon is at least intimated in Revelation 22:18. The dissimilarity in the manner in which the two Testaments end is significant. All the unfulfilled expectation

of the Old Testament is articulate as that testament closes and the last verse give assurance of the coming of another prophet. But no continued revelation is impending as the New Testament is terminated; rather the announcement is made that the Lord Himself will soon return and the natural conclusion is that there would be no further voice speaking from heaven before the trumpet heralds the second advent of Christ.

Of no small moment is the fact that since the canon of the Bible was divinely closed no attempts have been made to add to it.[15]

With sobering words about these verses, Seiss writes:

And when we consider how unbelief despises this Book and its philosophy of things . . . how a presumptuous criticism disables [the revelation] with wild and stilted theories of poetry and symbolization,—and how even Christian men fight against the admission of its clear teachings when allowed to speak for themselves,—what are we to conclude, but that in these very things we have the sowing for the whole harvest of plagues written in this Book?

. . . it is a fearful thing to suppress or stultify the word of God, and above all "the words of the prophecy of this Book." To put forth for truth what is not the truth,—to denounce as error, condemn, repudiate, or emasculate what God himself hath set his seal to as his mind and purpose, is one of those high crimes, not only against God, but against the souls of men, which cannot go unpunished.[16]

See further comments on 22:18–19 on pages 308–9.

CHAPTER 15

ISRAELOLOGY IN THE BOOK OF REVELATION

MAL COUCH

ISRAELOLOGY IS THE STUDY OF the Jewish people and their purpose and significance in the Bible from Genesis to Revelation. The study focuses on God's call of the Israelites, beginning with Abraham, and examines the plans and purposes the sovereign God has for this people.

A study of the book of Revelation would be incomplete without examining what the prophet John foresaw concerning the nation Israel. It must be noted, however, that, since Revelation concludes the entire Word of God, much of what is said in Revelation about Israel needs to be understood in the light of other Old and New Testament prophecies.

As noted earlier, John alluded to the Old Testament more than three hundred times, though he never quoted it directly.

Revelation, then, is a "Jewish" book, alluding more often to the Old Testament than does any other New Testament book. It capstones prophetic history as it concludes the message of the entire Bible. This chapter examines certain facts about Israel that Revelation assumes from Old Testament prophecies, and it examines direct references to God's future for His "earthly" people, the nation Israel.

Daniel's Seventy Weeks and the Book of Revelation

Premillennialists maintain that the Tribulation, as seen in Revelation 6–18, is the last seven years of what is called Daniel's seventy weeks (Dan. 9:20–27). Of all the arguments for Daniel's seventy weeks, this is the only one that is true to a consistent and normal system of interpretation. As well, it is the only view that holds up under careful scrutiny.

While living in the Babylonian captivity, Daniel realized that the seventy-year period of the Jews' exile, as prophesied by Jeremiah (Jer. 25:11–12; 29:10), was coming to an end. The reason the southern kingdom of Judah was in captivity was that the people had refused to obey the Word of the Lord (29:17–19) and to give their land a sabbatical rest every seven years (2 Chron. 36:21). God had told the people they would go into captivity among the nations until the land had enjoyed its seventy years of Sabbaths. Daniel realized that if the seventy years were about over, the people needed to repent of their sin of disobedience before the Lord (Lev. 26:40–46).

As Daniel was praying, the angel Gabriel came to him and told him he was highly esteemed and would be given unusual insight and understanding (Dan. 9:20–23). Then Gabriel added:

> Seventy weeks have been decreed for your people and your holy city, to finish the transgression, to make an end of sin, to make atonement for iniquity, to bring in everlasting righteousness, to seal up vision and prophecy, and to anoint the most holy place. So you are to know and discern that from the issuing of a decree to restore and rebuild Jerusalem until Messiah the Prince there will be seven weeks and sixty-two weeks; it will be built again, with plaza and moat, even in times of distress. Then after the sixty-two weeks the Messiah will be cut off and have nothing, and the people of the prince who is to come will destroy the city and the sanctuary. And its end will come with a flood; even to the end there will be war; desolations are determined. And he will make a firm covenant with the many for one week, but in the middle of the week he will put a stop to sacrifice and grain offering; and on the wing of abominations will come one who makes desolate, even until a complete destruction, one that is decreed, is poured out on the one who makes desolate. (9:24–27)

Some scholars have said this passage was fulfilled in the Maccabean period of the Jewish revolt against the Greeks. Others say the numbers simply represent periods of time that are not defined as to the length. Yet Daniel seemed to be specific with a distinct time frame in view.

A key to understanding this passage is the word "weeks," which is literally "sevens." Each "week" is a heptad of seven years.[1] The seven "weeks," plus sixty-two "weeks" and one "week," totals seventy, and seventy years multiplied by seven years totals 490 years.

The decreed seventy weeks (490 years, v. 24) began with the issuing of a decree to restore and rebuild Jerusalem. That decree, based on a 360-day calendar, was made by Artaxerxes Longimanus, who on Nisan 1, 444 B.C. (March 4), gave the commandment to restore and rebuild Jerusalem. Based on 483 years (sixty-nine "weeks" times seven "weeks"), this comes down to March 30 (of A.D. 33), or Nisan 10, and the exact date of Jesus' triumphal entry into Jerusalem.[2]

> The final decree is that of Artaxerxes to Nehemiah in 444 B.C. to rebuild the city of Jerusalem (Neh. 2:1–8). Several factors commend this decree as the one prophesied by Daniel (9:25) for the commencement of the seventy weeks. First, there is a direct reference to the restoration of the city (2:3, 5) and of the city gates and walls (2:3, 8). Second, Artaxerxes wrote a letter to Asaph to give materials to be used specifically for the walls (2:8). Third, the Book of Nehemiah and Ezra 4:7–23 indicate that certainly the restoration of the walls was done in the most distressing circumstances, as predicted by Daniel (Dan. 9:25). Fourth, no later decrees were given by the Persian kings pertaining to the rebuilding of Jerusalem.[3]

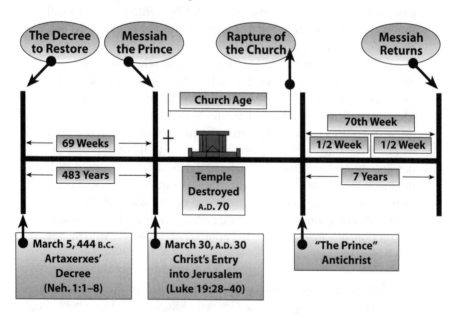

Figure 12: Daniel's Seventy Weeks

If sixty-nine weeks (483 years) comes up to the final week of the life of Christ, when did the last week (of seven years) take place? Amillenarians, as Walvoord explains, answer this by saying that the seventieth period of seven years occurred in Christ's first-advent ministry on earth. However, this ignores the fact that Jesus' ministry on earth was only three and a half years in length, not seven.[4] This seven-year period is yet to be fulfilled, and since it pertains to Israel, it is natural to see this as the seven-year Tribulation, which

Jeremiah called "the time of Judah's distress" (Jer. 30:7). When this terrible period of seven years begins, God will start Israel's clock again.

John wrote of this period in halves. The two witnesses will have authority to testify "for twelve hundred and sixty days" (Rev. 11:3; cf. 12:6). This is three and a half years or forty-two months of thirty days each (13:5).

Though some scholars believe that Revelation covers only the last half of the Tribulation, the view that seems most consistent with what is happening in the book is that John's prophecy covers the entire seven years of Daniel's final week. The book seems to make better sense when it is understood this way.

The 144,000 Witnesses

As the Tribulation intensifies, 144,000 Jewish witnesses (7:4), called God's "bond-servants" (v. 3), will have a special mark on their foreheads (v. 3; 14:1). In ancient times a mark on a soldier's forehead meant that he was consecrated to his god. Or if the soldier was a slave, the conspicuous forehead mark would leave no doubt as to the identity of the master to whom he belonged.

These witnesses will be men who will not have defiled themselves with women, that is, who will remain sexually chaste (14:4). After witnessing for the Lord, they will apparently be martyred, for they will be "purchased from the earth" (v. 3), "purchased from among men as first fruits to God and to the Lamb" (v. 4). Though others will have been martyred in the Tribulation before they come on the scene, as "first fruits" they will be like a unique or special "crop" of those who have been serving the Lord.

Will these Jewish witnesses testify only in Israel or will they be scattered around the world? Since the earth, sea, and trees are not to be harmed until these witnesses are sealed and protected (7:3), this may suggest that they will be planted throughout the earth to proclaim the way of salvation and the coming threat of more intense judgments.

Because of their testimony and faithfulness, the 144,000 will be in glory with the Lamb (v. 1), singing as a chorus with a sound like that of harpists (v. 2). They will sing a song that only they will know (v. 3). Perhaps this means that because of their special, bold witness, no one else will be able to comprehend fully what they suffer.

In his vision John saw twelve thousand Jews from each tribe of Israel's twelve tribes (7:5–8). Why is the tribe of Joseph listed? And why is one of Joseph's sons, Manasseh, included and Ephraim left out? After the book of Genesis, there is no longer a tribe of Joseph. Also, why is the tribe of Dan omitted from this list?

The tribe of Ephraim may have been excluded because that tribe strongly influenced the northern tribes to go into idolatry (Judg. 17:1–13; 18:2, 30–31; 1 Kings 12:25–29). But in the recognition of the importance of Joseph in the family of the twelve sons of Abraham, John mentioned his tribe.

Concerning the tribe of Dan, Thomas writes:

> The only narrative in the OT in which Dan played a part is the one related to the worship of idols in Judg. 18:1–31. Idolaters will be excluded from the new Jerusalem (Rev. 22:15). Though Dan is included in the future distribution of the land (Ezekiel 48), it appears that this branch of the family will be excluded from the protective sealing prior to the trumpet judgments because of the blot upon Dan's history caused by idolatry. The other tribes were guilty of the same sin, but Dan was the leader in idolatrous practices.[5]

Are the 144,000 Jewish witnesses—with their twelve divisions of 12,000 each—to be taken literally or figuratively? Premillennialists argue that, as with all numerals in Revelation, 144,000 is a literal number—just as twelve is taken literally. Amillennialists, however, say the numbers are symbolic of the new Gentile church, though some Jews may also be included. Tuck argues that the 144,000 is "clearly a symbolical number. A goodly number, from all the tribes, had become members of the Christian Church."[6]

Amillenarians seek to deny the literalness of the 144,000 Jewish witnesses. For example, Alford writes, "I need hardly say that such an interpretation [the literal view] seems to me to be quite inconsistent with the usage of this book."[7] And Barnes adds, "If literal, it is necessary to suppose that this refers to the twelve tribes of the children of Israel. But on every supposition this is absurd. Ten of their tribes had been long before carried away, and the distinction of the tribes was lost, no more to be recovered, and the Hebrew people never have been since the time of John, in circumstances to which the description here could be applicable. These considerations make it clear that the description here is symbolical."[8]

The presupposition these writers make is that God is through with Israel. Though amillenarians say that some Jews will be saved, they say that God will never again deal with them as a distinct people.

The Woman and Satan

Who is the woman in Revelation 12 who will flee into the wilderness where she will be protected by the Lord for three and a half years? Roman Catholic theologians say she is Mary, claiming that this view has "solid arguments in its favor."[9] But nothing happened in the life of Mary that even remotely parallels the events of this chapter.

True, verse 5 says the woman gave birth to the "male child, who is to rule all the nations with a rod of iron; and her child was caught up to God and to His throne." But then the woman will flee to "a place prepared by God, so that there she might be nourished for one thousand two hundred and sixty days," that is, three and a half years (v. 6).

The Dragon, who is Satan, will persecute the woman (v. 13), attempting to sweep her away with a river of water from his mouth (v. 15). But she will be spared and hidden by the earth (v. 16). Enraged, the Dragon will make war with her offspring, who will "keep the commandments of God and hold to the testimony of Jesus" (v. 17).

These verses represent a historical sketch of the nation Israel, with "offspring" mentioned in the final verse (v. 17) referring to the Jews who will believe in the Lord during the Tribulation.

> The added expression "the remnant of her seed" (v. 17) describes those who have been already born again from the nation of Israel. Satan frustrated by divine intervention in his evil purpose to destroy the nation turns against these more accessible believers with redoubled fury. These are the ones identified by Christ as "my brethren" (Matt. 25:40) and who become the touchstone of faith to distinguish between the "sheep" and "goats" at the judgment before the throne as the kingdom is established (Matt. 25:31–46).[10]

By describing Israel as a woman, John garnered sympathy for his people just as one would be concerned for a woman in distress. Though the Jews turned against Christ and Christianity, in the Tribulation they will be looked on again with mercy as they face the intense, diabolical powers Satan will muster against them!

Why is the woman said to be "clothed with the sun, and the moon under her feet, [having] on her head a crown of twelve stars" (v. 1)? This colorful visual recalls Genesis 37:9–10, where eleven stars and Joseph are mentioned. The sun and the moon are seen as the epitome of God's creation in the universe, for they also "rule" over the earth and are pictured as the marvels of the Lord's providence. Along with the woman, they will appear as part of "a great sign" in heaven (12:1), and they will come up against "another sign" in the heavenlies, the red Dragon, having ten horns representing the revived Roman Empire (v. 3).

Measuring the Temple, and the Two Witnesses

John's measuring of the temple and the arrival of the two witnesses seem to take place as one event (11:1–3). John was told to measure the temple of God and the altar and to include "those who worship in it" (v. 1). The temple *(naos)* may have meant simply the sanctuary and not the entire structure with the extended outer courts. The apostle may have used a builder's measuring rod of about sixteen feet, or perhaps a staff-like tool of approximately five feet. This command to measure suggests that God will restore interest in the activity of the temple (though John did not record the measurements he made).

John was told to exclude the "court" in his calculations, because it was given over to the "nations," who will "tread under foot the holy city for forty-two months" (v. 2), or three and a half years. The court is probably the court of the Gentiles, where non-Jews would come, but they could not venture closer into the temple area.

In the chronology of the Tribulation, when will all this take place? The answer is found in 2 Thessalonians, where Paul wrote of the coming of the "man of lawlessness," or "the son of destruction," who "opposes and exalts himself above every so-called god or object of worship, so that he takes his seat in the temple of God, displaying himself as being God" (2:4).

This will happen midway through the Tribulation when the lawless one, the Antichrist, will make peace with the nation Israel and will allow them to begin constructing the new temple. Half way through the Tribulation, he will enter the temple and call himself God. Along with the nations of the world, he will tread Jerusalem under foot (Rev. 11:3) and will desecrate the temple by setting up an image of himself, "the abomination of desolation" (Matt. 24:15).

But in all this God will call forth two witnesses, who will receive "power to shut up the sky, in order that rain may not fall during the days of their prophesying" (Rev. 11:6). They will have authority over the waters of the earth to turn them to blood (pollution) and to smite the earth with plagues (v. 6). Besides, they will have power to kill those who would harm them (v. 5).

Who are these two witnesses of the Lord? Because of their great authority and prophetic power, some Bible teachers suggest that the two are Moses and Elijah. Moses is mentioned because of his power over plagues, and Elijah is mentioned because he did not die but was transported to heaven by a whirlwind (2 Kings 2:11) and because he will return to earth to herald the coming of the Messiah (Mal. 4:5). Though such arguments make sense, no one can be dogmatic as to the witnesses' identity.

When the testimony of the two will be completed, God will allow the Antichrist (the Beast) to prevail over them and they will be slain (Rev. 11:7). Their dead bodies will lie in the street of Jerusalem (v. 8).

Verse 9 makes an incredible statement that seems to imply the technology of global communications: "And those from the peoples and tribes and tongues and nations will look at their dead bodies for three days and a half, and will not permit their dead bodies to be laid in a tomb."

The whole world will then rejoice and will call for a holiday to celebrate the death of these two men (v. 10). Obviously, their testimonies struck spiritual and moral nerves that made the people of earth glad they were dead. But after three and a half days, the Lord will breathe life into their bodies, and they will come to life (v. 11). When they will ascend to heaven, an earthquake will strike Jerusalem, destroying a tenth of the city and killing seven thousand (vv. 12–13). But some will be terrified and will give "glory to the God of heaven" (v. 13). LaHaye observes, "This cataclysmic judgment of God upon the city of Jerusalem could be the event which triggers the revival that will sweep across Israel during the latter half of the Tribulation, for the message reads, 'and the remnant were terrified, and gave glory to the God of heaven.' This remnant . . . will turn in faith to embrace the message of the two witnesses so recently resurrected."[11]

The Heavenly and Earthly Temples

The books of Hebrews and Revelation both record certain facts about a heavenly temple and an earthly temple. The author of Hebrews wrote, "For Christ did not enter a holy place made with hands, a mere copy of the true one, but into heaven itself, now to appear in the presence of God for us" (Heb. 9:24). "We have such a high priest, who has taken His seat at the right hand of the throne of the Majesty in the heavens, a minister in the sanctuary, and in the true tabernacle, which the Lord pitched, not man" (8:1–2).

While Hebrews speaks of the throne of God four times (1:8; 4:16; 8:1; 12:2), His throne is mentioned more than forty times in Revelation. Christ spoke of His Father's throne (Rev. 3:21), and John wrote of the throne in heaven (4:2), a rainbow around the throne (4:3), God who sits on His throne (7:10), and the Lamb and God who share the same throne (22:3).

In pictorial language the book of Revelation is telling us that the Lord is sovereign, and that His throne is related to His tabernacle (or tent), where He spiritually dwells in heaven. Both the tabernacle and the temple are mentioned in Revelation. Before Solomon built the permanent temple, the great "tent" traveled about with the Israelites. So the tent *(skēnē)* and the temple *(naos)* both speak of Christ's dwelling with His people.

The Antichrist will blaspheme God, His name, His heavenly tent, and all who dwell in heaven as well (13:6). Because the tent and the temple are so closely related in heaven, John wrote, "I looked and the temple of the tabernacle of testimony in heaven was opened" (15:5), and "the temple was filled with smoke from the glory of God and from His power" (v. 8).

The temple and tabernacle are again mentioned as a place of comfort for those who will "come out of the great tribulation" (7:14): "For this reason, [the martyrs] are before the throne of God; and they serve Him day and night in His temple; and He who sits on the throne shall spread His tabernacle [tent] over them. . . . For the Lamb in the center of the throne shall be their shepherd, and shall guide them to springs of the water of life; and God shall wipe every tear from their eyes" (vv. 15, 17).

When John saw the New Jerusalem descending to the earth, he wrote, "And I heard a loud voice from the throne, saying, 'Behold, the tabernacle [tent] of God is among men, and He shall dwell [be tenting] among them, and they shall be His people, and God Himself shall be among them'" (21:3).

When the Jewish people will read Revelation in the Tribulation, they will not miss the connection between the throne, the tabernacle, and the temple. Because they understand the earthly temple, they will easily be able to visualize the heavenly presence of God.

As mentioned, Tribulation martyrs will serve the Lord in His temple (7:15). When the seventh trumpet will be blown and God prepares to show His wrath on earth, the heavenly temple will be opened, the ark of the covenant of heaven revealed, and the Lord's anger demonstrated with flashes of lightning, thunder, an earthquake, and a great hailstorm (11:19).

Going about their assignments, angels will come forth from the temple (14:15, 17; 15:6). And often God's commands will come directly from the temple (16:1, 17).

Though the tabernacle and temple seem to be close in John's thinking, in the eternal New Jerusalem there will be a throne but no temple. "And I saw no temple in it, for the Lord God, the Almighty, and the Lamb, are its temple" (21:22).

Mount Zion and Jerusalem

The word "Zion" is first used of the stronghold or fortress of the ancient city Jebus. Though the Jebusites considered their city impregnable, David was able to conquer it. He lived in the fortress and named the city "the city of David."

In time the word "Zion" took on a broader meaning. It came to mean the entire city of Jerusalem, not just the fortress in it. The word was even used at times of a group such as "the daughters of Zion" (Isa. 3:16–17), that is, female inhabitants in the city. Later the word came to mean the entire Jewish nation.

In prophetic passages "Zion" is often used of Jerusalem in the final days. For example, David exclaimed that the "salvation of Israel" "comes out of Zion" (Ps. 53:6), and concerning the Messiah the psalmist wrote, "I have installed My King upon Zion" (2:6). The prophets continue: "the LORD of hosts will reign on Mount Zion" (Isa. 24:23), the "Redeemer will come to Zion" (59:20), "let us go up to Zion, to the LORD our God" (Jer. 31:6), and "shout for joy on the height of Zion" (v. 12).

Joel wrote, "Then you will know that I am the LORD your God, dwelling in Zion My holy mountain" (Joel 3:17), and Micah and Zechariah predicted, "from Zion will go forth the law" (Mic. 4:2), and "I will return to Zion and will dwell in the midst of Jerusalem" (Zech. 8:3).

Yet surprisingly, Zion is mentioned only once in the entire book of Revelation: "And I looked, and behold, the Lamb was standing on Mount Zion, and with Him one hundred and forty-four thousand, having His name and the name of His Father written on their foreheads" (Rev. 14:1).

Here the apostle pictured the 144,000 redeemed Jewish witnesses standing on Zion, enjoying the presence of Jesus, the Lamb of God. Is this refer-ring to the gathering of these martyrs in the city of Jerusalem in the millennial kingdom, or is it used here as a reference to heaven? The verses that follow (vv. 2–5) seem to affirm that the martyrs will have just arrived in heavenly glory and will stand at that moment before Christ in adoration.

Interestingly, the book of Hebrews also speaks of a heavenly Jerusalem and Zion, where countless numbers of angels glorify the Lord. Hebrews also only mentions Zion one time. "But you have come to Mount Zion and to the city of the living God, the heavenly Jerusalem, and to myriads of angels" (Heb. 12:22). Though Revelation 14:1 and Hebrews 12:22 refer to the *heavenly* Zion and Jerusalem, this does not alter the fact that the Messiah will return to the earthly Zion, Jerusalem, and will reign there.

If Zion is so important in Bible prophecy, why did John refer to it only once? The answer may simply be that because the Old Testament speaks so often of the Jews returning to Zion and enjoying the Messiah there, it need not be repeated in the New Testament. Any Jew studying the book would under-stand that all the glorious promises to his nation will be fulfilled in that impor-tant place—Jerusalem.

Also, the city of Jerusalem is mentioned only four times in Revelation. The Jews and Christians of the early church knew well that the Messiah could return to Jerusalem. So there was no reason to mention the city repeatedly.

In the middle of the Tribulation, Jerusalem will become a tool in the hands of Satan and the Antichrist. When the two witnesses are slain, their dead bod-ies will be left in the street "of the great city which mystically is called Sodom and Egypt, where also their Lord was crucified" (Rev. 11:8). The other refer-ences speak of the New Jerusalem that will come down from heaven. This promise was to give hope to the church of Philadelphia by the Lord Himself: "I will write upon [the overcomer] the name of My God, and the name of the city of My God, the new Jerusalem, which comes down out of heaven from My God" (3:12).

With the new heavens and the new earth (21:1), John also saw the "holy city, new Jerusalem" coming down from glory (v. 2). The prophet was then led by the Spirit up to a high mountain, where he was shown the new eternal city (v. 10), radiating with brilliance and the glory of God (v. 11).

The Reign of Christ and the Millennium

When Christ returns to the earth to reign as Messiah and King, the heavens will open and He will come with "the armies which are in heaven," that is, angels (19:14). His regalia will consist of a robe dipped in blood, and His names are "Faithful and True" and "The Word of God" (vv. 11, 13).

He will come to judge ("His eyes are a flame of fire"), and He is granted great authority, signified by the wearing of "many diadems" (v. 12). Also written on His robe and thigh will be the title "King of Kings, and Lord of Lords" (v. 16).

As already stated the "armies" that will come with Christ are angels, for they will battle against the unbelieving nations (v. 15). When Christ returns, His angels will call forth His elect from the four winds. Of course, He will return also with His saints (1 Thess. 3:18).

The initial stages of His return will not be pleasant, for He will "tread the wine press of the fierce wrath of God, the Almighty" (Rev. 19:15), and a great slaughter of unbelievers will follow (vv. 17–21). This will occur in Armageddon, the battle that will conclude the final stages of the conflict. Isaiah graphically described this "day of vengeance" (Isa. 34:8): "For the LORD's indignation is against all the nations, and His wrath against all their armies; He has utterly destroyed them, He has given them over to slaughter. So their slain will be thrown out, and their corpses will give off their stench, and the mountains will be drenched with their blood" (vv. 2–3).

During the one-thousand-year earthly reign of the Messiah Satan will be confined to the abyss (Rev. 20:3). Without doubt this one-thousand-year period refers to the same earthly kingdom rule of the Messiah mentioned scores of times in the Old Testament.

Critics of a literal kingdom, however, sometimes ask, "Why does the New Testament not have more verses about this millennial kingdom?"

Beginning with the gospels, many verses follow in the New Testament that summarize the events of the Tribulation *and* the kingdom. For example, in Matthew 24:15 Jesus describes the abomination of desolation spoken of in Daniel 9:27; in Matthew 24:21 the horrors of the Great Tribulation are found as in Jeremiah 30:7 and Daniel 12:1. Further, in Matthew 24–25 Christ taught about the coming of the Lord (24:42), the reign of the Son of Man (v. 44), and the King (25:34).

When writing of the abomination of desolation, Jesus said it "was spoken of through Daniel the prophet" (Matt. 24:15). Christ did not need to add more. They either knew what Daniel had said or they could search it out for themselves. In other words, little more needed to be said than what was already written in the Old Testament.

The same is true about the King and kingdom promises the Lord speaks of in Matthew 25:31–46. The Son of Man sitting on His throne the Jews knew about from Isaiah 66:18–22 and Daniel 7. When He spoke of being the Shepherd who would divide the sheep from the goats, this was a clear fulfillment of Ezekiel 34:11–31.

The prophecies of the physical earthly and heavenly disturbances recorded in Revelation 6:12–17 all come from various detailed and lengthy Old Testament passages (Isa. 2:19; 34:1–4; Joel 2:11, 31; Nah. 1:2, 5–6). Even Jewish rabbinical scholars knew Revelation 21 was a summary of messianic kingdom passages coming from the writings of the ancient prophets. Patai writes,

> Entirely within the spirit of these Jewish apocalypses is the vision of the heavenly Jerusalem contained in Revelation . . . chapter 21. . . . Its author was a Judeo-Christian, well versed in the Scriptures [of the Old Testament], who, while he believed in the Messiahship of Jesus (whom he calls "the Lamb"), expected his return in the Future to Come, and described the heavenly Jerusalem in Jewish Apocalyptic . . . terms.[12]

When Jesus mentioned the kingdom of God, the Jews understood perfectly well what He meant. He did not have to repeat all the accumulated details about it to His Israeli audiences. The kingdom He spoke about was the same theocracy anticipated in the Old Testament. Bright notes,

> But for all his repeated mention of the Kingdom of God, Jesus never once paused to define it. Nor did any hearer ever interrupt him to ask, "Master, what do these words, 'Kingdom of God', which you use so often, mean?" On the contrary, Jesus used the term as if assured it would be understood, and indeed it was. The Kingdom of God lay within the vocabulary of every Jew. It was something they understood and longed for desperately.[13]

Pentecost summarizes this issue:

> The *literal* view [of prophecy], supported by the study of the New Testament, is that the kingdom announced and offered by the Lord Jesus was the same theocratic kingdom foretold through the Old Testament prophets.[14]

The righteous Jews clearly understood the words of Christ when He said: "Come, you who are blessed of My Father, inherit the kingdom prepared for you from the foundation of the world" (Matt. 25:34).

When the kingdom begins, thrones will be set up for judgment. Who are seated on the thrones? As John wrote, they will be those who "had been beheaded because of the testimony of Jesus and because of the word of God, and those who had not worshiped the beast or his image" (Rev. 20:4). Possibly this is a special judgment on Tribulation unbelievers who especially took action against the witnesses, the martyrs of the Lord. When they complete this judgment, they will reign "with Christ for a thousand years" (v. 4).

The "first resurrection" (v. 5) is the resurrection of the righteous of the Old

Testament period and of those believers who perished in the Tribulation. They will not die again, because "over these the second death has no power, but they will be priests of God and of Christ and will reign with Him for a thousand years" (v. 6). But the "rest of the dead," who are not given life until after the thousand years will end, are the unbelievers of all generations who will be judged at the Great White Throne (vv. 5; 11–15).

At the end of the Millennium Satan will be released from the abyss, and he will immediately marshal a great disgruntled population to come up against Jerusalem, "the beloved city" of the saints, in a futile attempt to dethrone Christ (vv. 7–9). This is a worldwide movement inspired by the forces of Gog and Magog (v. 8). These names are used in Ezekiel 38–39 to describe the coming invasion of Israel, after the Jews will have been regathered to the land of Palestine. Gog is a reference to the ruler of Magog, identified as the land north of the Black Sea.

Some scholars believe this invasion described in Revelation 20 is the same as that in Ezekiel, but though the names are the same, there are some important differences.

The Ezekiel passage makes no reference to the kingdom, the Messiah, or Satan's release. Instead, the passage indicates that the Jews will have recently been regathered to their land, and the peoples of Magog will come to plunder the land of Israel of its material goods (Ezek. 38:12–13). God will then bring down fire on Magog (39:6) so that the Lord's name might be made known in Israel (v. 7) and among the nations (38:16). When this Gog-and-Magog conflict is over, God's Spirit will be poured out on the house of Israel, and God will not hide His "face from them any longer" (39:29).

The event in Revelation 20 is entirely different. The Messiah will have reigned in peace for a thousand years. In Ezekiel Gog will bring a few other nations with him against Israel, but in Revelation he will bring rebel forces from "the four corners of the earth" (Rev. 20:8). In Revelation Israel will already know the Lord, and the Holy Spirit and His activities will certainly be known and recognized. Many place Ezekiel's Magog event near the beginning of the seven-year Tribulation. A few scholars place it at the midpoint of the Tribulation.

The event in Revelation is a case of history repeating itself, an act of vengeance on later generations of Gentiles living in the kingdom. Righteous Gentiles who enter the Millennium in their natural bodies will have children. Those offspring will produce future generations of people who must, as today, decide for or against receiving Christ as their Savior. Toward the end of the kingdom, many will rebel and refuse to make Him their spiritual Head. It is these whom Satan will easily encourage to join him in turning against the Messiah.

After the thousand-year kingdom, God will usher in the new heavens and the new earth (21:1).

The Millennial Temple

As mentioned, John was instructed to measure the temple area (11:1–2). He did not elaborate on the significance of this command or describe what would soon happen after it. This is where we must piece Scripture together with Scripture in order to understand it more fully. Ezekiel 40–48 describes the millennial temple in great detail. Since the apostle John abbreviates his description of the kingdom, starting with the coming of the Messiah (Rev. 19:11–20:9), he saw no need to elaborate on the millennial temple, for Christians and believing Jews of his day would understand from Ezekiel that the temple would be restored.

If Ezekiel's temple were an allegory, as some say, rather than a literal temple, it would be impossible to make any sense of Ezekiel 40–48. In fact, as much detail is given here as was given for the construction of the tabernacle and of the first temple.

Some argue against a literal view of the millennial temple by asking why a temple with sacrifices to be offered would be necessary since the Messiah has already died. However, if Ezekiel 40–48 is not to be taken literally, what would be its symbolic meaning? Nonliteralists must resort to mere subjective guesswork. The literal approach is the only sensible, objective way to understand Ezekiel 40–48.

What, then, is the purpose of the animal sacrifices in this temple in light of Christ's death? Fruchtenbaum reminds us that "the sacrificial system of the Mosaic Law did not remove sins either (Heb. 10:4), but only covered them (the meaning of 'atonement' in Hebrew). Its purpose was to serve as a physical and visual picture of what the Messiah would do (Isa. 53:10–12)."[15] In a similar way, the millennial temple and sacrifices in it would remind believers of Christ's sacrifice for them.

The New Jerusalem and Eternity

The Millennium will close world history as we know it. The eternal state following the Millennium will begin with a renovation of the universe and the introduction of the new heavens and the new earth (Rev. 21:1). Since the environment will be different, there is no longer a general need for water and "there is no longer any sea" (v. 1). The New Jerusalem will be holy (v. 2) and will come down from heaven adorned as a bride. God will dwell among His redeemed (v. 3). Called "the bride, the wife of the Lamb" (v. 9), the city will enjoy the glory of God in its full divine brilliance (v. 11). The new city of Jerusalem will be huge, measuring fifteen hundred miles in length, width, and height (v. 16).

Though water will no longer be necessary, a river will flow with "the water of life, clear as crystal, coming from the throne of God and of the Lamb" (22:1). No longer will there be a temple (21:22), but the throne of God and of the Lamb will be there in the New Jerusalem (22:3). No night will exist, and even the sun will not be needed. Instead, the "Lord God shall illumine [the saints]; and they shall reign forever and ever" (v. 5).

Jesus' bond servants will worship Him and will see His face, and His name shall be on their foreheads (22:3–4). Since He is God incarnate, seeing Him will be like seeing God Himself (John 14:9).

Peter wrote of the new heavens and the new earth this way: "But the day of the Lord will come like a thief, in which the heavens will pass away with a roar and the elements will be destroyed with intense heat, and the earth and its works will be burned up. Since all these things are to be destroyed in this way, what sort of people ought you to be in holy conduct and godliness, looking for and hastening the coming of the day of God, on account of which the heavens will be destroyed by burning, and the elements will melt with intense heat!" (2 Peter 3:10–12).

CHAPTER 16

THE RAPTURE OF THE CHURCH AND THE BOOK OF REVELATION

RUSSELL L. PENNEY

SOME MISTAKENLY BELIEVE THE doctrine of the Rapture of the church is some aberrant view of prophecy that has been invented recently. Though it is true that the Rapture of the church has become a prominent subject only in the last one hundred and eighty years or so, good reasons explain why.

The current revival of interest in prophecy studies began in England around 1820. Awareness of passages about the Rapture of the church caused scholars to rethink the prophetic outline of biblical end-time events. The prevalent and earlier views of amillennialism had clouded over the idea of the Rapture. But one reason interest was revived was the fact that 1 Thessalonians 4:13–18 and other passages were so unusual in their implications. This brought about a renewed interest in studying similar verses. Until that time these passages were simply lumped together with all references to the return of the Lord, without noting differences in their contexts.

Most prominent amillennial scholars ignored the idea that 1 Thessalonians 4 could be any different from other passages that speak of "the coming" *(parousia)* of Christ. In fact, to them the word *parousia* seemed to sum up the doctrine of only one return of Jesus.

In time it became clearer to some that, by contextual study, the coming of Christ to "rapture" away the church saints was an entirely different event than was His coming to judge sinners and to

187

rule and reign for a thousand years. Many great Bible teachers of the period saw that both events were to be taken as distinct, literal comings and could not simply be spiritualized away.

By studying various passages, it can be shown that there are two distinct resurrections connected to the Lord's return. There is the resurrection for those in Christ, who will be taken to glory before the Tribulation begins. There is also a raising of the Old Testament saints and the Tribulation-martyred believers to enjoy the blessings of the Lord's one-thousand-year literal kingdom reign.[1]

What Is the Rapture?

The word "Rapture" comes from the Greek word *harpazō*, which can be translated "to snatch away, pluck up, catch up" or "to be caught up" (1 Thess. 4:17). It is used of a thief who grabs one's possessions and runs. Other verses speak of the Rapture without using the word *harpazō*.

The church at Thessalonica learned "to wait for His Son from heaven, whom He raised from the dead, that is Jesus, who delivers us from the wrath to come" (1:10). "For God has not destined us for wrath, but for obtaining salvation through our Lord Jesus Christ" (5:9). And Paul wrote to the Philippian believers, "Our citizenship is in heaven, from which also we eagerly wait for a Savior, the Lord Jesus Christ; who will transform the body of our humble state into conformity with the body of His glory" (Phil. 3:20–21).

With just these few verses, one can see something is mentioned that is entirely different from Christ's returning to the earth to reign in Jerusalem. In these verses Paul wrote of a future catching away, or waiting to be delivered from the wrath to come, and the transforming of our body.

It has been estimated that over twenty-eight verses state similar facts about the Rapture. When these are compared with what most would agree are verses about Christ's second coming, the differences become more obvious.

What Are the Differences?

Thomas Ice and Timothy Demy briefly state the difference as follows: "The rapture is most clearly presented in 1 Thessalonians 4:13–18. It is characterized in the Bible as a 'translation coming' (1 Corinthians 15:51, 52; 1 Thessalonians 4:15–17) in which Christ comes for His church. The second advent is Christ returning with His saints, descending from heaven to establish His earthly kingdom (Zechariah 14:4, 5; Matthew 24:27–31)."[2]

Ice and Demy also chart thirteen differences between the Rapture and the Second Coming.

Contrasts Between the Rapture and the Second Coming

Rapture/Translation	*Second Coming*
1. Translation of all believers	No translation at all
2. Translated saints go to heaven	Translated saints return to earth
3. Earth not judged	Earth judged and righteousness established
4. Imminent, any moment, signless	Follows definite predicted signs, including tribulation
5. Not in the Old Testament	Predicted often in the Old Testament
6. Believers only	Affects all men
7. Before the day of wrath	Concluding the day of wrath
8. No reference to Satan	Satan bound
9. Christ comes for His own	Christ comes with His own
10. He comes in the air	He comes to the earth
11. He claims His bride	He comes with His bride
12. Only His own see Him	Every eye shall see Him
13. Tribulation begins	Millennial kingdom begins[3]

Figure 13

Some have argued that if the Rapture and the Second Coming are different, a scriptural reference should state this specifically. But the same kind of argument could be used against the Trinity. Why is there not one clear verse that says "Trinity"? The Rapture, like the doctrine of the Trinity, *is* demonstrated and proved by dozens of passages. It should also be pointed out again that until fairly recently few theologians were examining prophetic Scripture and teaching eschatology, much less attempting to differentiate what was being taught in different contexts. There was no effort made to understand fully all the details of future events, specifically the differences between the Rapture and the second coming of Christ.

The Rapture and Revelation

One of the arguments for some people against the Rapture is that this truth is not stated in the book of Revelation. True, John did not mention it. Paul certainly did. Why? Because Paul was the apostle "of the church." He was given great revelations on the nature of the church and the ending of the church age. John, on the other hand, was given detailed revelation about earth's final days.

After the Lord spoke through John to the seven churches, little else in Revelation could be called "church truth," except 5:8–10 and 20:4–6. John's vision of the twenty-four elders seems to be referring to church saints who in the future "will reign upon the earth" (v. 10). They will reign with the Lord in the Millennium as promised (2:26; 3:21; 20:4–6). The following facts are given in Revelation about the church.

1. Presently, the church is a kingdom of priests serving God (1:6).
2. The seven lampstands are the seven churches of Asia Minor (1:20).
3. The seven churches, along with their spiritual problems, are addressed in chapters 2–3.
4. The phrase "after these things" (4:1) refers to the fact that John was then going to write of things that are beyond the church age.
5. John is shown "what must take place after these things" (4:1).
6. The Rapture must happen at this point in Revelation because 5:8–10 describes a great company in heaven, redeemed and purchased for God "from every tribe and tongue and people and nation" (v. 9). These are church saints in heaven. And the Tribulation does not begin until chapter 6!
7. From chapter 6 on, no mention is made of the church. The only earthly witnesses are the 144,000 Jews (7:1–8) and a great company of saints in heaven who will be martyrs in the Tribulation (v. 14).
8. As promised in 2:26 and 3:21, church saints will reign with Christ in the Millennium (20:4–6).

Arguing from Silence

Some have criticized the pretribulational Rapture position by stating that Revelation is silent about the doctrine of the Rapture. "If the Rapture is true," they argue, "why is it not mentioned in the Apocalypse?" Pretribulationalists stress that there is an even larger question at issue: Where is the church in the book of Revelation? If the church is not mentioned in what are clearly Tribulational and "wrath" chapters, then it only makes sense that the Rapture would not be mentioned either. Strombeck gives helpful answers to this issue.

> In reading the record of the tribulation, beginning at the sixth chapter of Revelation and closing with the nineteenth, one cannot fail to be impressed with the fact that there is no mention made of the Church being on earth during that time. The record is not only silent about the presence of the Church on earth, it is also silent concerning any cause, or reason, why the Church should then be on earth. There is

complete silence respecting any purpose to be fulfilled thereby. There is also silence regarding any protection for the Church against the torment of those years. This silence, while not in itself a conclusive argument for the pre-tribulation rapture of the Church, adds great weight to the direct arguments. . . . When, however, the Bible supplies irrefutable reasons for this silence, then this silence does become important evidence in favor of the view that the Church will not be on earth during that time.[4]

Various Premillennial Views

As discussed earlier, premillennialism follows a normal, literal approach to interpretation. Looking at the Bible this way makes a premillennial, pre-tribulational Rapture view seem the most plausible. But among premillennialists different positions about the Rapture are espoused.

Premillennial Pretribulational Rapture

This view—that the church will be raptured before the Tribulation—seems to be the most consistent with all of prophetic revelation. Though not specifically stated in the book of Revelation, this seems to be the teaching of various New Testament passages. In this view when the Rapture occurs the souls of the dead in Christ will return from heaven with Him and will instantly receive new glorified bodies. In their new glorified state, they will go upward to meet the Lord. Immediately after that the living saints will be taken up to be with Him. Then at the end of the seven-year Tribulation these resurrected church saints of all generations will return with Christ to reign with Him on the earth in His millennial kingdom.

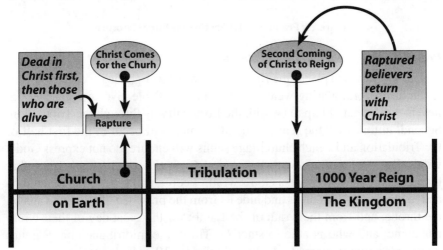

Figure 14: Premillennial Pretribulational Rapture

Premillennial Posttribulational Rapture

According to this view the church will go through the seven-year Tribulation period. At the end of the Tribulation when Christ returns, dead church-age saints will be raised and then the living saints will be transformed and raptured. It seems all church saints will return almost instantly back to the earth to be with Christ in the Millennium.

The problem with this view is that there is no evidence to suggest that the church will go through the Tribulation, the seventieth week of Daniel. That period is a judgment on the disbelieving world and a time of purging of the nation Israel. It is a period of wrath, and the church, those who are in Christ, are not destined for such judgment (1 Thess. 1:10; 5:9). Another problem is that it seems senseless for the church saints to be caught up in the Rapture and then instantly come right back down with Him to reign!

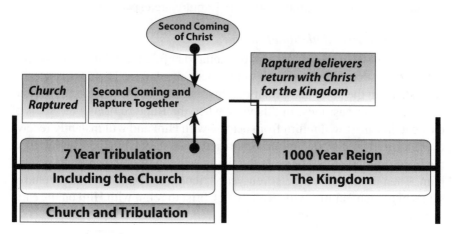

Figure 15: Premillennial Posttribulational Rapture

Premillennial Midtribulational Rapture

This view, which places the Rapture midway through the seven-year Tribulation has several glaring weaknesses. First, the Bible gives no hint that believers will be caught up to be with the Lord halfway through the Tribulation. Second, in this view the seal judgments, which will occur in the first half of the Tribulation and which church-age saints will endure, do not express God's wrath. But this conflicts with Revelation 6:16–17, which clearly state that these judgments will express God's wrath: People will say "to the mountains and to the rocks, 'Fall on us and hide us from the presence of Him who sits on the throne, and from the wrath of the Lamb; for the great day of their wrath has come; and who is able to stand?'" Third, the midtribulational Rapture theory also runs counter to 1 Thessalonians 1:10, which speaks of "Jesus, who delivers us from the wrath to come." Fourth, this view suggests that the

Lord's purposes for Israel and the church overlap. The church, they say, will take part in at least a portion of the Tribulation called "the time of Jacob's trouble," and the seventieth week of Daniel, but not in the more terrible judgments in Revelation 8 and 16.

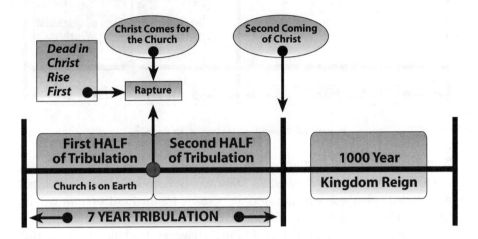

Figure 16: Premillennial Midtribulational Rapture

Premillennial Prewrath Rapture

This view is close to the midtribulational view, but there are some differences. Both views see the church going through a portion of the Tribulation.

> The prewrath view is different from the midtribulational view in that it does not have the Rapture exactly in the middle of the week. Midtribulationism places the Rapture with the sounding of the seventh trumpet (Rev. 11) while prewrath rapturism places it with the sounding of the first trumpet and at the same time as the Second Coming which is before the Day of the Lord begins.
>
> In brief it may be said that the view is built on the basic assumption that the seal judgments (Rev. 6) do not represent the wrath of God. The divine wrath begins with the trumpet judgments introduced by cataclysmic disturbances. Also, the view places the church within the Olivet Discourse as given by Jesus in Matthew 24 and 25.[5]

This view is different from the generally accepted premillennial position because it does not clearly distinguish between God's program with Israel and His working with the church. It differs too in that it places the church in part of Israel's seventieth week.[6]

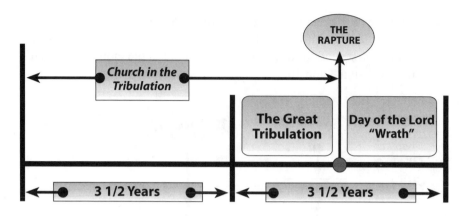

Figure 17: Premillennial Prewrath Rapture

Premillennial Partial Rapture

This view has also been called the "Spiritual Believer's Rapture" because it teaches that only those who are spiritually ready for the Lord's return will be raptured. One has to be ready for that event and be watching and waiting, in order to be taken with the raptured saints. However, Paul clearly wrote that "we who are alive" (1 Thess. 4:15) and "the dead in Christ" (v. 16) will be raptured. He made no distinctions among those who are to be raptured. Paul said that just before the Rapture and the Day of the Lord the unsuspecting world will say, "Peace and safety" (5:3). But that terrible time of Tribulation will come "just like a thief in the night." So the apostle warned believers "not

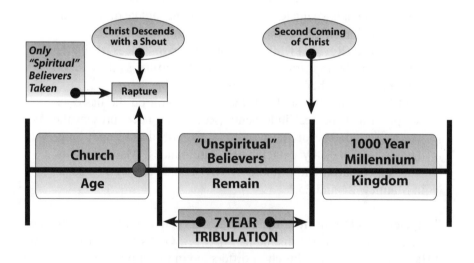

Figure 18: Premillennial Partial Rapture

[to] sleep as others do, but [to] be alert and sober" (v. 6). He was urging believers to continue to work and serve right up until the Rapture. But nowhere did he indicate that some would not be raptured if they were not alert. In fact, he said just the opposite: Those in Christ "are all sons of light and sons of day. We are not of night nor of darkness" (v. 5).

So the Rapture of God's children is not based on whether they are spiritually ready, but on the fact that they are part of the body of Christ. The Rapture is not on the basis of merit; it is based on Jesus' finished work at the cross. Thus "whether we are awake [prepared] or asleep [unprepared], we may live together with Him" (v. 10), because "God has not destined us for wrath, but for obtaining salvation through our Lord Jesus Christ" (v. 9).

The Imminency of the Pretribulational Rapture

In almost all the Rapture passages pronouns such as "we, you, us" indicate that the apostles and the early church believed the Rapture could take place at any time. In the following verses italics are added for emphasis:

> And if I go and prepare a place for *you,* I will come again, and receive *you* to Myself; that where I am, there *you* may be also. (John 14:3)

> So that *you* are . . . awaiting eagerly the revelation of *our* Lord Jesus Christ. (1 Corinthians 1:7)

> Behold, I tell *you* a mystery; *we* shall not *all* sleep, but *we* shall *all* be changed, in a moment, in the twinkling of an eye. (1 Corinthians 15:51–52a)

> When Christ, who is *our* life, is revealed, then *you* also will be revealed with Him in glory. (Colossians 3:4)

> . . . .to wait for His Son from heaven . . . that is Jesus, who delivers *us* from the wrath to come. (1 Thessalonians 1:10)

> For God has not destined *us* for wrath, . . . whether *we* are awake or asleep, *we* may live together with Him. (1 Thessalonians 5:9–10)

> . . . with regard to the coming of *our* Lord Jesus Christ, and *our* gathering together to Him. (2 Thessalonians 2:1)

> . . . that *you* keep the commandment without stain or reproach, until the appearing of *our* Lord Jesus Christ. (1 Timothy 6:14)

> Looking for the blessed hope and the appearing of the glory of *our* great God and Savior, Christ Jesus. (Titus 2:13)

> Be patient, therefore, *brethren,* until the coming of the Lord. . . . strengthen *your* hearts, for the coming of the Lord is at hand. Do not complain, *brethren,* against one another, that *you yourselves* may not be judged; behold, the Judge is standing right at the door. (James 5:7–9)

> Besides using the word *parousia* [the coming], James adds, this coming is at hand (James 5:8). From the Greek the expression, "is at hand" *(engizō)* could read, "The coming of the Lord has progressively been approaching, coming nearer, drawing nearer." The word has the idea "to be imminent" and can be translated "to be at the point of." The word *engizō* is related to the noun that has the idea of "in the vicinity of, close by." . . . Without doubt, the early church and the apostles hoped for Christ's soon return. The use of the terms "we, you, and us" are proof that the Rapture could have happened in Paul's own generation. As with some [marriage] engagements, a wedding date may not have been set, yet the bride and groom long for and anticipate their coming union. The disciples had this longing but were given no hint as to the time of the Rapture. Since it did not come upon them, we do not question their hope nor the Lord's revelation about the doctrine itself. It simply means that it is yet to come.[7]

Taking a normal, literal interpretative approach to prophecy, only the pretribulational Rapture position makes sense and fits with the premillennial, futurist view of the book of Revelation.

PART 3

A VERSE-BY-VERSE
BACKGROUND GUIDE TO THE
BOOK OF REVELATION

Churches of Revelation

Map courtesy of Three's Company, London

THE SALUTATION AND INTRODUCTORY VISION

Synopsis

(1:1–3) The apostle John reported the remarkable order in which the message of the book was transmitted to him and then to all the bond-servants of the Lord. The revelation of Jesus Christ is His ultimate revelation as King as witnessed in the final chapter of the book (22:13). God blesses those who study any portion of the Word of God, but a special blessing is attached to this prophecy for those who read, follow carefully, and practice what is taught within its pages.

(1:4–8) John, God the Father, the Holy Spirit, and Jesus Christ all give the salutation of grace and peace to the readers. Jesus is set forth in these verses as the Witness from the dead and the Ruler over the kings of the earth. And it is by His blood that His bond-servants are set free from sin. But the author, John the apostle, made verses 7–8 almost an anthem. Rushing into the future, he prophesied of Christ's glorious return, to be witnessed by the entire earth.

(1:9–20) John then was given a brilliant vision of the exalted Jesus, who stands in heaven as the One who has dominion over all. The Lord is not seen as a helpless and limited monarch, who is impotent to rule. He is presented as just the opposite. He is the Sovereign who will someday come as Judge. John was so overwhelmed with the Lord's appearance that he fell at his feet as if dead. Jesus then instructed him to write down all that he experienced.

1:1 The Revelation of Jesus Christ, which God gave Him to show to His bond-servants, the things which must shortly take place.

Revelation. Verses 1 and 2 are remarkable in that they record a kind of divine order for the inspiration of the book. The Revelation concerning Christ came from God the Father through the Son and finally to John, who bore witness to the Word of God. No other book of Scripture shows such an intricate order of how the writing was communicated. By this formula we learn how urgent and important the Apocalypse really is.

The word "revelation" *(apokalypsis)* literally means "a removal from *(apo)* the hidden." Lenski writes that "this Revelation deals almost entirely with the future. . . . The book before us presents the fullest revelation of the future which, therefore, also Jesus Christ himself made."[1]

The apostle Paul spoke of this revelation when he wrote to the Thessalonian church that God would "give relief to you who are afflicted and to us as well when the Lord Jesus shall be revealed from heaven with His mighty angels in flaming fire, dealing out retribution in those who do not know God and to those who do not obey the gospel of our Lord Jesus" (2 Thess. 1:7–8).

Which must shortly take place. The Greek phrase *en tachei* probably means that when these events begin, they will take place with "rapid fire" sequence or "speedily." This is its contextual usage here.

1:3 Blessed is he who reads and those who hear . . . and heed the things which are written in it; for the time is near.

Blessed. The Greek word *makarios* means "fortunate" or "happy" because of something positive that has occurred. Because of the promises in this book, a believer in Christ is especially fortunate. Believers are responsible to hear (that is, to absorb or take in) and heed (live out) the truths that are written in this book.

For the time is near. This can best be translated "the season *[kairos]* draws near *[engys]*." Each day brings us closer to the Lord's return.

1:4 Grace to you and peace, from Him who is and who was and who is to come; and from the seven Spirits who are before His throne.

Grace and peace. Though these words were common in letters of greeting, they should be taken seriously in scriptural letters. God wishes for His children graciousness and inner spiritual peace and contentment. The greeting is from

John, God the Father, the Holy Spirit, and from Jesus Christ Himself (v. 5). Again, this lengthy greeting reinforces the importance of this revelation.

Who is and who was and who is to come. See page 97.

The Seven Spirits. See page 114.

> **1:5** The first-born of the dead, and the ruler of the kings of the earth. To Him who loves us, and released us from our sins by His blood.

Firstborn. By being the first One to defeat death by coming out of the grave with a resurrected body, Jesus, the firstborn from the dead, paved the way for others to inherit eternal life.

The ruler of the kings of the earth. He presently rules by divine providence, but when the millennial kingdom will come, His rule will be a physical reality. At that time He will exercise clear and observable authority.

To Him who loves us, and released us from our sins by His blood. He continually loves us (present participle), having freed us from our sins by His blood. "He poured out Himself to death . . . yet He Himself bore the sin of many, and interceded for the transgressors" (Isa. 53:12).

> **1:6** He has made us to be a kingdom, priests to His God and Father; to Him be the glory and the dominion forever and ever. Amen.

Kingdom, priests. This does not mean that the church has become the millennial kingdom. Instead, the believers in the dispensation of the church act as kings and priests in serving God the Father.

To Him be the glory and the dominion. This refers to Jesus, the Son of Man. "His dominion is an everlasting dominion which will not pass away" (Dan. 7:14).

Forever and ever. John did not need to add "and ever," but he did so for emphasis. The Greek phrase reads, literally, "into the ages of the ages."

> **1:7** Behold, He is coming with the clouds, and every eye will see Him, even those who pierced Him; and all the tribes of the earth will mourn over Him.

He is coming with the clouds. Here John quoted from Daniel 7:13 and Zechariah 12:10, both messianic passages that testify of His coming. The entire world will witness His return, especially the Jews who were the chief agents in His death. The tribes of earth will mourn (*koptō,* "to beat one's breast") when they realize who He is and what they forfeited in not receiving Him as their Savior.

> **1:8** I am the Alpha and the Omega . . . who is and who was and who is to come, the Almighty.

I am the Alpha and Omega. Here the apostle paraphrased Isaiah 41:4, which reads: "I, the Lord, am the first, and with the last. I am He." The words "Alpha and Omega," the first and last letters of the Greek alphabet, parallel Isaiah's words "the first" and "the last."

Who is and who was and who is to come. These words could be rendered, "Who exists right now, who always was in the past, and who still will be existing tomorrow."

> **1:9** I, John, your brother and fellow-partaker in the tribulation and kingdom and perseverance which are in Jesus, was on the island called Patmos, because of the word of God and the testimony of Jesus.

I, John, your brother. By the words "the brother of all of you" (literal rendering) John identified with those who will read this prophecy. He wanted his readers to know that he was suffering along with them.

Fellow-partaker in the tribulation and kingdom and perseverance which are in Jesus. Johnson writes:

> John sees his plight as part of God's design and says he is a partner with Christians in three things: "suffering" ("ordeal," "tribulation," "distress," "agony"), "kingdom," and "patient endurance" (or "faithful endurance"). . . . Also [the believers] share with Christ in his "kingdom" (power and rule). In one sense they already reign (1:6), though through suffering. Yet, in another sense, they will reign with Christ in the eschatological manifestation of his kingdom (20:4, 6; 22:5).[2]

On the island called Patmos. This and other Aegean islands were used as prisoner settlements by the Romans. The island of Patmos is about forty miles west of the coast city of Miletus. In land area Patmos is only ten miles long and five miles wide at its widest point, with a shape like a crescent, which makes the island a safe harbor from storms. It was also used as a port haven on the journey from Ephesus to Rome. Church history records that John was sent to Patmos by Emperor Domitian (A.D. 81–96) and was forced to slave in the island's mines. Another tradition says John returned to Ephesus after Domitian died.

1:12 I saw seven golden lampstands.

Golden lampstands. These lampstands, or lampholders, represent the seven churches of Asia Minor (v. 20). The churches were to be lights to the pagan world. However, the flames of these congregations flickered and gave an unclear illumination. And yet the Lord saw fit to use them to serve Him on earth.

John saw Jesus standing among the lampstands (v. 13), holding the seven stars (v. 16), or messengers (angels), of the churches in His hand (v. 20). Each of the seven lamps was supported on a stand. In homes in the Roman world these lamps were actually bowls that held oil, which, when lit, illumined an entire room. It is difficult to escape the parallel of the seven lamps of the menorah that brought light to the tabernacle and then later to the temple. Writing of the menorah in the tabernacle, Haldemann notes: "As the light of the Candlestick was not the light of nature, but a light specially provided of God; as the light was fed and made possible only by the oil, and the oil is a symbol of the Holy Spirit, then the Church is not in the world to give the light of nature to men, but the light and truth that comes through the energy and revelation of the Spirit. In short the Church is to give the light of God's revealed truth to the world."[3]

1:13 One like a son of man, clothed in a robe reaching to the feet, and girded across His breast with a golden girdle.

One like a son of man. In Daniel's vision in Daniel 7:13–14 he saw the Son of Man in His glorious, eternal body, coming before God the Father, the Ancient of Days, to receive eternal dominion. The term "Son of Man" means "the Son who relates to mankind."

Here in Revelation 1:13, He is seen wearing His royal robe, and His chest is encircled with a royal (golden) girdle (leather or cloth cincher). This pictures Him as a conquering, kingly warrior, standing in heaven as guardian over His people.

1:14 His head and His hair were white like white wool, like snow; and His eyes were like a flame of fire.

Like white wool. Though this is speaking of Christ, the Son of Man, there is a surprising association with Daniel 7:9, where God the Father is described as having "the hair of His head like pure wool." These similar descriptions point to Jesus' deity.

His eyes were like a flame of fire. The Son of Man will judge with a burning righteousness that no one can escape. When He comes as the promised Messiah, He will reign "on the throne of David and over his kingdom, to establish it and to uphold it with justice and righteousness" (Isa. 9:7).

1:15 His feet were like burnished bronze . . . and His voice was like the sound of many waters.

His feet were like burnished bronze. This is bronze heated to the maximum "to glow in a furnace." In such heat bronze slag and impurities bubble to the surface so that the dross is easily removed. The Messiah stands like crafted and smelted bronze, pure, stable, and strong.

His voice like the sound of many waters. Just as rushing waters can be deafening, so the voice of Jesus is commanding and overpowering. He is certainly not "meek and mild."

1:16 He held seven stars; and out of His mouth came a sharp two-edged sword.

He held seven stars. These are the angels or messengers of the churches (v. 20). Like stars they illumine the churches to whom they minister.

Out of His mouth came a sharp two-edged sword. This picture of the Messiah was presented in Isaiah 49, a great messianic chapter. The Messiah called to the islands, Gentiles, that is, and said, "The LORD called Me from the womb; from the body of My mother He named Me" (v. 1). Then He warned the hearers, "He has made My mouth like a sharp sword" (v. 2). The sword portrays judgment and so does the rod (staff or club). "He will strike the earth with the rod [warrior's club] of His mouth, and with the breath of His lips He will slay the wicked" (11:4).

The Word of God is also called the "two-edged sword," by which God cuts deep into a person's soul and spirit and through which He "judges the thoughts and intentions of the heart" (Heb. 4:12).

Thus Christ is the coming Judge, and no evil will be able to hide from His searing scrutiny.

1:17 When I saw Him, I fell at His feet as a dead man. . . . "Do not be afraid; I am the first and the last."

I fell at His feet as a dead man. Though John had walked with Jesus, about sixty years had passed since he had seen Him face to face. But now he saw the Lord in all His resurrected glory. John, along with the apostles Peter and James, had years before witnessed Christ's kingdom brightness and glory. "He was transfigured before them; and His face shone like the sun, and His garments became as white as light" (Matt 17:2). Some have suggested that seeing the Savior in this manner again was too much for the elderly apostle, and so he fainted, falling at the Lord's feet.

I am the first and the last. These words are close in meaning to what is said of the eternal nature of God the Father, "I am the Alpha and the Omega" (v. 8). These words are said of God again in 21:6. Christ used both descriptions when presenting Himself at the end of Revelation as the eternal God, and also as the One who is coming quickly. "I am the Alpha and the Omega, the first and the last, the beginning and the end" (22:13).

1:18 I have the keys of death and of Hades.

I have the keys of death and of Hades. The word "Hades" is used ten times in the New Testament. It is often translated "hell," that is, the place of torment for the lost (Luke 16:23). Sometimes it is used graphically to describe the power of the grave and of death itself. "O death *[hadēs]*, where is your sting?" (1 Cor. 15:55). In quoting Psalm 16:10, Peter applied that verse to Jesus: "Thou wilt not abandon My soul to Hades [i.e., the grave], nor allow Thy Holy One to undergo decay" (Acts 2:27).

In Revelation, John was given a vision of how the power of death would end. He wrote, "And the sea gave up the dead which were in it, and death and Hades gave up the dead which were in them; . . . And death and Hades were thrown into the lake of fire" (20:13–14). Christ is the Judge who holds the keys to victory over the final enemy of humanity.

1:19 Write therefore the things which you have seen, and the things which are, and the things which shall take place after these things.

The things which you have seen. Most students of Scripture take these words to mean John's vision of the glory of the exalted Lord, reported in verses 13–18.

The things which are. This includes the struggles and victories of the seven churches the Lord addressed in chapters 2–3, and by extension "the things which are" could refer to all churches in the present church age.

The things which shall take place after these things. This phrase refers to end-time events, which John recorded in Revelation 4–22—the church in heaven (chaps. 4–5) after the Rapture, the Tribulation (chaps. 6–18), the Second Coming (chap. 19), the Millennium (chap. 20), and the eternal state (chaps. 21–22). Verse 19 of chapter 1 serves as the overall outline of the book of Revelation.

> **1:20** As for the mystery of the seven stars which you saw in My right hand . . . the seven stars are the angels of the seven churches.

As for the mystery of the seven stars. The Bible uses the word "mystery" to describe something not previously revealed, something that was a puzzle or that was not clearly understood. In this case, the seven stars (lights) are explained as representing seven angels or messengers of the churches.

The seven stars are the angels of the seven churches. Many think these were seven elders of the churches who came to the island of Patmos and, receiving John's finished revelation, took it back to the churches and read and taught the people the message. But others feel that these were godly, educated men who read Revelation to their churches and who also may have written down the letters from their churches that were then sent to other assemblies. The "angel" was "the messenger of the church, i.e., the delegate, who went to and fro between the church and the Apostle."[4]

THE PROBLEMS IN THE SEVEN CHURCHES OF ASIA

THINGS WHICH ARE . . .
MESSAGES TO EPHESUS, SMYRNA,
PERGAMUM, THYATIRA

Synopsis

(2:1–7) The Lord addressed the church in Ephesus where there were false apostles and those who had "left" the Lord, their "first love." This church had commendable deeds and did not tolerate evil men. They even tested and examined those who were presenting false doctrine, especially those of the sect of the Nicolaitans. But they no longer loved Christ as they did when they were first saved. The Lord said that if they did not repent, He would come and remove their lampstand, that is, their influence as witnesses for Christ.

(2:8–11) Christ reminded this church in Smyrna that He is deity, "the first and the last." The congregation was persecuted by tribulation and blasphemed by the local Jewish synagogue. But even more, He reminded them that some may die. But He told them that if some are faithful unto death, He would give them the crown of life. This is the only church that the Lord did not have to correct as to how they lived the Christian life.

(2:12–17) Satan, who had his "throne" in Pergamum, came against this assembly with great and determined opposition. But this church also had its problems. Some were guilty of idolatry, immorality, and even participation in the Nicolaitan cult. Christ warned them that, if they did not repent, He would come quickly to judge.

(2:18–29) To the assembly in Thyatira the Lord proclaimed Himself as the Son of God, who will judge with eyes like a flame of fire. He commended them for their love, faith, service, and perseverance, and for the increased zeal in their deeds. But they tolerated the prophetess Jezebel, who led many into acts of immorality. She and her followers will be judged, and her children will be slain with pestilence. The good news is that the entire body of believers will not be held responsible for those who are sinning.

Message to Ephesus: "Left Your First Love" (2:1–7)

2:1 To the angel of the church in Ephesus write:

Angel. See page 127.

Ephesus. Ephesus was a large, important city on the west coast of Asia Minor where the apostle Paul founded a church. A number of factors contributed to the prominence Ephesus enjoyed.

The first factor was economics. Situated at the mouth of the river Cayster, Ephesus was the most favorable seaport in the province of Asia and the most important trade center west of Tarsus. Today because of silting from the river the ruins of the city lie in a swamp five to seven miles inland.

Another factor was size. Although Pergamum was the capital of the province of Asia in Roman times, Ephesus was the largest city in the province, having a population of perhaps 300,000 people.

A third factor was culture. Ephesus had a large outdoor amphitheater that seated an estimated 24,000 people. A main thoroughfare, some 105 feet wide, ran from the theater to the harbor, at each end of which stood an impressive gate. The thoroughfare was flanked on each side by rows of columns fifty feet deep. Behind these columns were baths, gymnasiums, and impressive buildings.

The fourth, and perhaps most significant, reason for the prominence of Ephesus was religion. The temple of Artemis (or Diana, her Roman name) at Ephesus ranked as one of the seven wonders of the ancient world. As the twin sister of Apollo and the daughter of Zeus, Artemis was known variously as the moon goddess, the goddess of hunting, and the patroness of young girls. The temple at Ephesus housed the multi-breasted image of Artemis, which was reputed to have come directly from Zeus (Acts 19:35).

The temple of Artemis in Paul's day was supported by 127 columns, each of them 60 meters (197 feet) high. The Ephesians took great pride in this grand edifice. During the Roman period, they promoted the worship of Artemis by minting coins with the inscription, "Diana of Ephesus."

The history of Christianity at Ephesus began about A.D. 50, perhaps as a result of the efforts of Priscilla and Aquila (Acts 18:18). Paul came to Ephesus about A.D. 52, establishing a resident ministry for the better part of three years (Acts 20:31). During his Ephesian ministry, Paul wrote 1 Corinthians (1 Cor. 16:8).

The book of Acts reports that "all who dwelt in Asia heard the word of the Lord Jesus" (Acts 19:10), while Paul taught daily in the lecture hall of Tyrannus (v. 9). Influence from his ministry undoubtedly resulted in the founding of churches in the Lycus River valley at Laodicea, Hierapolis, and Colossae.

So effective was Paul's ministry at Ephesus that the silversmith's league, which fashioned souvenirs of the temple, feared that the preaching of the gospel would undermine the great temple of Artemis (v. 27). As a result, Demetrius, one of the silversmiths, stirred up a riot against Paul.

During his stay in Ephesus Paul encountered both great opportunities and great dangers. He baptized believers who apparently had come to believe in the Messiah through disciples of John the Baptist (vv. 1–5), and he countered the strong influence of magic in Ephesus (vv. 11–20).

After Paul left Ephesus, Timothy remained to combat false teaching (20:29; 1 Tim. 1:3; 2 Tim. 4:3). Many traditions testify that the apostle John lived in Ephesus toward the end of the first century. In his vision from the island of Patmos off the coast of Asia Minor, John described the church of Ephesus as flourishing, although it was troubled with false teachers and had lost its initial love for Christ (Rev. 2:1–7). In the sixth century A.D. the Roman emperor Justinian (A.D. 527–565) raised a magnificent church to John's memory in this city.

Ephesus continued to play a prominent role in the history of the early church. A long line of bishops in the eastern church lived there. In A.D. 431 the Council of Ephesus officially condemned the Nestorian heresy, which taught that Jesus Christ existed as two separate persons, one divine and one human.

2:2 I know your deeds and your toil and perseverance.

Deeds. The Greek word *ergon* has the idea of "expending energy." This church was serving the Lord with great diligence.

Toil. This word *(kopos)* suggests that the believers worked hard as they witnessed for Christ.

Perseverance. They had remained steadfast, remaining faithful under pressure.

2:3 [You] have endured for My name's sake, and have not grown weary.

My name's sake. They carried on because of their love for the Lord. His name and reputation were at stake.

Weary. With the opposition and persecution that came against them, these believers had not reached the point of weariness in their labor for the Lord.

2:4 You have left your first love.

You have left. The Greek expresses this a little more strongly than the English wording. They had forsaken *(aphēmi)*, that is, abandoned, their first love, who was Christ Himself. Apparently this church was active in the Lord's work, but their heart was not in it.

2:5 I am coming to you, and will remove your lampstand out of its place—unless you repent.

Lampstand. Without repentance, they would no longer be a beacon light of witness for the Lord Jesus. "The Christian who is unwilling to yield all his talents and capabilities to Jesus Christ has a love problem; that is, he does not sufficiently love Christ."[5]

2:6 Yet this you do have, that you hate the deeds of the Nicolaitans, which I also hate.

Nicolaitans. See page 139.

2:7 He who has an ear, let him hear what the Spirit says to the churches. To him who overcomes, I will grant to eat of the tree of life, which is in the Paradise of God.

He who has an ear, let him hear what the Spirit says to the churches. This clause closes each of the letters to the seven churches. It encourages the readers to "listen carefully" to what was written down and read. These words come from Christ and the Holy Spirit. But again, what was said by the Holy Spirit and then written down is applicable to all the churches, not simply to one.

Overcomes. See page 164.

Tree of life. See page 169.

Paradise. *Paradeios* occurs only three times in the New Testament. The

Lord promised the thief that he would be with Him in paradise (Luke 23:43); Paul wrote of himself as the "man" who was caught up into paradise (2 Cor. 12:4); and here in Revelation 2:7 the tree of life, John wrote, "is in the Paradise of God." "*Paradeios* is derived from a Persian word describing a pleasure garden and park with wild animals built for Persian monarchs. . . . What was originally a garden of delight has taken on the connotation of the new heavens and the new earth."[6]

Message to Smyrna: "I Know Your Tribulation" (2:8–11)

2:8 And to the angel of the church in Smyrna write: The first and the last, who was dead, and has come to life.

Smyrna. Smyrna's superb natural harbor in western Asia Minor made the city an important commercial center. In spite of keen competition from the neighboring cities of Ephesus and Pergamum, Smyrna called itself "the first city of Asia."

As early as 195 B.C., Smyrna foresaw the rising power of Rome and built a temple for pagan Roman worship. In 23 B.C., Smyrna was given the honor of building a temple to the Emperor Tiberias, because of its years of faithfulness to Rome. Thus the city became a center for the cult of emperor worship—a fanatical "religion" that later, under such emperors as Nero (A.D. 54–68) and Domitian (A.D. 81–96), brought on severe persecution for the early church. The apostle John encouraged the persecuted Christians of Smyrna to be "faithful unto death" and they would receive a "crown of life" (2:10).

Smyrna, known today as Izmir, is presently the chief city of Anatolia and one of the strongest cities in modern Turkey. Excavations in the central part of Izmir have uncovered a Roman marketplace from the second century A.D.

The first and the last. See 1:17. This phrase is repeated in 22:13, where it is clear Christ possesses deity, for He has the same eternal attributes as God the Father.

Who was dead, and has come to life. The resurrection (1:5) is a great demonstration that Jesus is the Son of God (Rom. 1:4; 1 Cor. 15:12–19), and He is the firstfruits of those who are asleep (v. 20) in that He leads the way to victory over death.

2:9 Those who say they are Jews and are not, but are a synagogue of Satan.

Synagogue of Satan. See page 143.

2:10 Be faithful until death, and I will give you the crown of life.

Crown of life. See page 167.

Message to Pergamum: "You Hold Fast My Name" (2:12–17)

2:12 And to the angel of the church in Pergamum write: The One who has the sharp two-edged sword says this:

Pergamum. Pergamum was the chief city of Mysia near the Cestris River in northwest Asia Minor. The city, situated opposite the island of Lesbos, was about fifteen miles from the Aegean Sea.

In its early history Pergamum became a city-state and then the powerful head of a region after Attalus I (241–197 B.C.) defeated the Gauls (Galatians). It stood as a symbol of Greek superiority over the barbarians. Great buildings were erected, and a library containing over 200,000 items was established. The Egyptians, concerned with this library that rivaled their own at Alexandria, refused to ship papyrus to Pergamum. As a result, a new form of writing material, "Pergamena charta," or parchment, was developed.

In the days of Roman dominance throughout Asia Minor, Pergamum became the capital of the Roman province of Asia. In a gesture of friendship, Mark Antony gave Pergamum's library to Cleopatra, and its volumes were moved to Alexandria.

Besides Pergamum being a government center with three imperial temples, it was also the site of the temple of Asklepius (the Greco-Roman god of medicine and healing). Here also was a temple to Athena and a temple to Zeus with an altar showing Zeus defeating snake-like giants. John wrote of Pergamum as a place "where Satan's throne is." This could be a reference to the cult of emperor worship, because Pergamum was a center where the Roman emperors were worshiped. "In 29 B.C. a temple had been built to the divine Augustus and the goddess Roma, which was served by a powerful priesthood. Especially abhorrent to the Christians was the local cult of Aesculapius, whose symbol was the serpent, which was called 'the god of Pergamum' but to the Christians was the symbol of Eden. . . . So much at least is certain that the Lord himself . . . regarded Pergamum as the one city among the seven where Satan even had his throne and thus ruled as king."[7]

Two-edged sword. See 1:16; 2:16.

2:13 I know where you dwell, where Satan's throne is; and you hold fast My name, and did not deny My faith, even in the days of Antipas.

Satan's throne. See 2:9.

You hold fast My name. See 2:3.

My faith. Believers in Smyrna refused to deny the gospel and the Christian faith, though opposition to the believers was so violent and hostile.

Antipas. See page 138.

2:14 You have there some who hold the teaching of Balaam.

Balaam. See pages 138–39.

2:15 You also have some who in the same way hold the teaching of the Nicolaitans.

Nicolaitans. See 2:6. See also page 139.

2:16 I will make war against them with the sword of My mouth.

Sword. See 1:16; 2:12.

2:17 To him who overcomes, to him I will give some of the hidden manna, and I will give him a white stone, and a new name written on the stone which no one knows but he who receives it.

Overcomes. See page 164.

Hidden manna. See page 165.

White stone. Much debate has revolved around the meaning of the white stone. Some connect it with the precious stones bearing the names of the twelve tribes on the breastplate of the high priest. Some see the white stone as a ticket of admission to the future heavenly feast. Another view relates it to elections in which white stones were used as ballots.

Concerning the new name, some have thought this was the name of Christ Himself. It could refer to the fact that a Christian is a new person with a new identity with Jesus Himself. As Johnson writes, "It seems best to link the stone to the thought of the manna and see it as an allusion to an invitation that entitled its bearer to attend one of the pagan banquets. The 'new name . . . known only to him who receives it' is either the name of Christ himself, now hidden from the world but to be revealed in the future as the most powerful of names (3:12; 14:1), or the believer's new name or changed character through redemption (Isa. 62:2; 65:15)."[8]

Message to Thyatira: "I Know Your Deeds" (2:18–29)

2:18 And to the angel of the church in Thyatira write: The Son of God, who has eyes like a flame of fire, and His feet are like burnished bronze, says this:

Thyatira. Thyatira was a city of the province of Lydia in western Asia Minor situated on the road from Pergamum to Sardis. The city was on the southern bank of the Lycus River, a branch of the Hermus River.

Although never a large city, Thyatira was a thriving manufacturing and commercial center during New Testament times. Archaeologists have uncovered evidence of many trade guilds and unions here. Membership in these trade guilds, necessary for financial and social success, often involved pagan customs and practices such as superstitious worship, feasts of union members who ate food sacrificed to pagan gods, and sexual immorality.

Verse 19 refers to a woman known as "Jezebel," who taught and beguiled the Christians at Thyatira to conform to the paganism and sexual immorality of their surroundings (1:11; 2:18–29). In the church in Thyatira Jezebel's followers seem to have been a minority, because the majority of Christians in this church are commended.

The apostle Paul's first convert in Europe was "a certain woman named Lydia, from the city of Thyatira, a seller of purple " (Acts 16:14). The modern name of Thyatira is Akhisar, which means "white castle."

Son of God. See page 107.

Eyes like a flame of fire. See 1:14.

Feet are like burnished bronze. See 1:15.

2:20 You tolerate the woman Jezebel, who calls herself a prophetess, and she teaches and leads My bond-servants astray, so that they commit acts of immorality and eat things sacrificed to idols.

Jezebel. See pages 139–40.

2:24 You . . . who have not known the deep things of Satan, as they call them—I place no other burden on you.

The deep things of Satan. Satan is a master at counterfeiting false spirituality. Some in the church at Thyatira had toyed with and sampled the false religions that Satan had under his power. But others in the congregation had not. The Lord would not hold them at fault. As God's wisdom and knowledge is spiritually deep (Rom. 11:33), so Satan has, in opposition, his false spirituality. And, as the Spirit searches all things for the believer's benefit, "even the depths of God" (1 Cor. 2:10), so the spirits who serve the deceiver can make people believe they are receiving true spiritual knowledge.

Walvoord observes, "Here reference is made to the satanic system often seen in great detail in false cults which compete with the true Christian faith. Just as there are the deep things of God (I Cor. 2:10) which are taught by the Spirit, so there are the deep things of Satan which result from his work."[9]

2:26 He who overcomes, and he who keeps My deeds until the end, to him I will give authority over the nations.

I will give him authority over the nations. Speaking to this church at Thyatira, the Lord quoted Psalm 2:8 in which God said to His Son, Jesus Christ, "Ask of Me [My Son], and I will surely give the nations as Thine inheritance." By quoting this remarkable psalm Jesus was telling His bondservants in Thyatira that they will coreign with Him in the millennial kingdom. He continued the promise in the next verse.

2:27 And he shall rule them with a rod of iron, as the vessels of the potter are broken to pieces, as I also have received authority from My Father.

In this verse Christ quotes several Old Testament promises that again point to His kingdom power and authority. But the thought is that the believers in Thyatira who are victorious will carry out His judgments with the authority the Father has given Him! Ruling the nations with a rod of iron recalls Psalm 2:9, and the potter's breaking the vessel to pieces recalls Isaiah 30:14. "The overcoming Christians are promised places of authority. They will share the rule of Christ over the nations of the world."[10]

2:28 And I will give him the morning star.

The morning star. As a morning star shining in the east gives assurance that the dawn is coming soon, so Peter used this expression to illustrate the assurance or guarantee that all will soon be brought to finality. "And so we have the prophetic word made more sure, to which you do well to pay attention as to a lamp shining in a dark place, until the day dawns and the morning star arises in your hearts" (2 Peter 1:19).

But in Revelation 2:28 the morning star is Jesus Christ Himself. Possibly the idea is that He will grant assurance to believers that all is well and that the end of pain and sin is near. Christ added in Revelation 22:16: "I am the root and the offspring of David, the bright morning star." "To the overcomers also is given the promise of 'the morning star.' While various explanations of this expression have been given, it seems to refer to Christ Himself in His role as the returning One who will rapture the church before the dark hours preceding the dawn of the millennial kingdom."[11]

THE PROBLEMS IN THE SEVEN CHURCHES OF ASIA (CONTINUED)

Synopsis

(3:1–6) Sardis was a spiritually dead church that needed to wake up. The ministry of the congregation was about to die, and the Lord said, "for I have not found your deeds completed in the sight of My God." The people were further reminded to recall what they had received and heard. They were to maintain this spiritual posture, and if they did not do so, Jesus would come like a thief "and you will not know at what hour I will come upon you." Apparently only a few in the assembly had not soiled their garments with sin. The Lord promised them, "They will walk with Me in white; for they are worthy." The one who overcomes the tug and pull of the culture will be clothed in white "and I will not erase his name from the book of life," and "I will confess his name before My Father, and before His angels."

(3:7–13) The Lord Jesus gave the church in Philadelphia an open door of ministry that could not be shut. This church had little power, but it kept His word and had not denied Jesus' name. The city of Philadelphia also had a synagogue of Satan (see 2:9) that must have resulted in terrible periods of spiritual and even physical persecution for new believers in Christ. But a day of reckoning would come in which the Jews of the city would come and bow down at the feet of the Christians. When this would happen is not explained.

Because of their perseverance, this church would be kept from the hour of testing that would eventually come on the entire earth. Finally, this congregation is instructed to "hold fast what you have, in order that no one take your crown." The overcomer would be made a pillar in the temple of God, and Jesus will also write on him "the name of My God, and the name of the city of My God, the new Jerusalem, which comes down out of heaven from My God, and My new name."

(3:14–22) To the church of Laodicea, Jesus presented Himself with the impressive titles, the Amen, the faithful and true Witness, the Beginning of the creation of God. He said this assembly was neither cold nor hot but was lukewarm spiritually. This congregation thought of itself as wealthy and in need of nothing. But the Lord said that spiritually they were wretched, miserable, poor, blind, and naked. He urged the people to buy from Him refined gold, white garments, and eyesalve so that they could again be clean and be able to perceive the truth about themselves. Christ reminded the readers that those whom He loves He reproves and disciplines; therefore, they were urged to be quick to repent. The Lord closed with a desire for fellowship expressed in His standing and knocking at the door. For the overcomers He will grant that they join Him on His throne, just as He was victorious and sat down on His Father's throne in heaven.

Message to Sardis: "Remember What You Have Received" (3:1–6)

3:1 And to the angel of the church in Sardis write: He who has the seven Spirits of God, and the seven stars, says this: "I know your deeds, that you have a name that you are alive, but you are dead."

Sardis. Sardis was the capital city of Lydia, a province of Asia in western Asia Minor. It was situated on the east bank of the Pactolus River about fifty miles east of Smyrna. It occupied a rocky spur of Mount Tmolus and a valley at the foot of this mountain. In ancient times Sardis was well fortified and easily defended. It became the capital of the ancient Lydian Empire, and then it passed successively to the Persians, the Greeks, and the Romans during their respective dominance of the ancient world.

The city was known for its trade in luxury clothing. During its days as a Roman city, Sardis became an important Christian center. However, the church at Sardis was evidently affected by the complacency of the city and its reliance on past glory: "You have a name that you are alive, but you are dead" (Rev. 3:1). The church there was like "whitewashed tombs which on the outside appear beautiful, but inside they are full of dead men's bones" (Matt. 23:27). Its thriving, healthy appearance masked an inner decay.

The most impressive building of ancient Sardis must have been its magnificent Temple of Artemis, built in the fourth century B.C. The temple was 327 feet long and 163 feet wide and had 78 Ionic columns, each 58 feet high. Some of these columns are still standing today.

The seven Spirits. See page 114.

The seven stars. These are the seven messengers (angels) of the seven churches. See 1:20.

You have a name that you are alive. By their profession of Christianity they expressed to the world their purpose to live for the Lord. They professed to have true spiritual life.

But you are dead. What they said and how they actually lived were two different things, for they were dead spiritually.

3:2 Wake up, and strengthen the things that remain.

Wake up. If they awakened spiritually, they could recover lost ground and get back on track. Apparently their works and deeds were carried out only halfheartedly.

3:3 Remember, therefore what you have received and heard; and keep it, and repent.

Remember, therefore what you have received and heard. They were to recall what they had been taught, to do what was right, and to repent of their sins. If not, Christ would come suddenly as a thief to judge them.

3:4 You have a few people in Sardis who have not soiled their garments; . . . they are worthy.

A few . . . have not soiled their garments. Because some had not dirtied themselves with sin, they were worthy. *Axios,* the word translated "worthy," means "equal in price, of comparable value." "They have shown themselves worthy to be regarded as followers of the Lamb; or, they have a character that is fitted for heaven."[12]

3:5 He who overcomes shall thus be clothed in white garments;

and I will not erase his name from the book of life, and I will confess his name before My Father, and before His angels.

Clothed in white garments. These comments about white garments and soiled garments are fitting in light of the fact that the city was known, as already stated, for its trade in luxury clothing. Verse 4 may be describing those in that congregation who were "professors" but not "possessors." Such people were not born again. However, those who received Christ as their Savior had overcome the pull of the culture and had experienced salvation victory.

I will not erase his name from the book of life. This expression "means that the names would be found there on the great day of final account, and would be found there for ever."[13]

I will confess his name before My Father, and before His angels. Jesus was saying that, in heaven, He would acknowledge that those believers were His followers!

Message to Philadelphia: "I Have Put Before You an Open Door" (3:7–13)

3:7 And to the angel of the church in Philadelphia write: He who is holy, who is true, who has the key of David, who opens and no one can shut, and who shuts and no one opens, says this:

Philadelphia. Like Sardis, Philadelphia ("brotherly love") was a city of the province of Lydia. It was situated on the Cogamus River, a tributary of the Hermus (modern Gediz) River, and was about twenty-eight miles southeast of Sardis. It was founded by Attalus II (Philadelphus), who reigned as king of Pergamum from 159 to 138 B.C. Philadelphia was a center of the wine industry. Its chief deity was Dionysus, in Greek mythology the god of wine (the Roman Bacchus).

In the book of Revelation John described the church in Philadelphia as the faithful church and the church that stood at the gateway of a great opportunity (3:7–13). The "open door" means primarily access to God, but it also refers to opportunity for spreading the gospel of Jesus Christ. Still a city of considerable size, Philadelphia is known today as Alasehir, or Allah-shehr ("the city of God").

[He] who has the key of David. Here Christ was quoting Isaiah 22:22, which speaks of God's faithful servant and prime minister Eliakim (v. 20), who replaced unfaithful Shebna, the minister or steward during Hezekiah's reign sometime before 701 B.C. Though he was not king, Eliakim was given kingly responsibility, as if he were receiving the mantle of the house of David. Christ now has that authority as the ultimate Son of David's line.

[He] opens and no one can shut, and who shuts and no one opens. Jesus' authority and power are absolute!

> **3:8** I have put before you an open door which no one can shut, because you have a little power, and have kept My word, and have not denied My name.

I have put before you an open door. The congregation had ample opportunity to witness and share the gospel, and yet their ability to carry this out must have been limited.

You have a little power. The opposition against them must have been tremendous. They had a great struggle, apparently against the Jewish community that so opposed Christianity (v. 9).

[You] have kept My word, and have not denied My name. Despite the forces against them, these believers were faithful in what they could accomplish. They had not stained the name of Christ in their ministry efforts.

> **3:9** Behold, I will cause those of the synagogue of Satan, who say that they are Jews, and are not, but lie—behold, I will make them to come and bow down at your feet, and to know that I have loved you.

Synagogue of Satan. See page 143 and 2:9, 13. The Jews in this synagogue must have had a violent hatred of the church. Under the influence of Satan, they were not responding as should the descendants of Abraham.

I will make them to come and bow down at your feet. Unbelieving Jews will fall prostrate before the believers, but there is no indication as to when this would happen. Possibly later these Jews were touched by the Holy Spirit and received the gospel, and so they fell in gratitude before their Christian brothers. Or, it could mean that someday in the far future they will fall before them in an act of repentance.

> **3:10** I will keep you from the hour of testing, that hour which is about to come upon the whole world, to test those who dwell upon the earth.

I will keep you from the hour of testing. The preposition "from" can mean "out of" in the sense of not entering something. Some have said this verse is a promise that only this one local church will experience the Rapture. However, because the issues addressed are applicable to all the seven churches (v. 13), this Rapture promise is likely valid for all church-age believers.

Which is about to come. The Greek verb *mellō,* "to be about," has the idea of "inevitable, with certainty." "It serves to express in general a settled futurity."[14]

To test those who dwell upon the earth. This is referring to the Tribulation testing that is meant to produce repentance on the part of unbelievers, but in which the world will harden itself and continue on in its sin (9:20–21).

3:11 Hold fast what you have, in order that no one take your crown.

Crown. Many believe this is the crown of life, but others say this is the crown of righteousness that Paul wrote about in 2 Timothy 4:8, and which will be given to all those who have loved (longed for) Christ's appearing and who also have fought the good fight, finished the course, and kept the faith (v. 7).

3:12 He who overcomes, I will make him a pillar in the temple of My God, and he will not go out from it any more; and I will write upon him the name of My God, and the name of the city of My God, the new Jerusalem, which comes down out of heaven from My God, and My new name.

I will make him a pillar in the temple of My God . . . and I will write upon him the name of My God. Overcomers will be marked by the Lord by direct identification with God, His name, and the New Jerusalem. Also they will become pillars. This is probably a hyperbole, used to affirm that the faithful will have a permanent place in God's presence. "The honour thus conferred on him 'who should overcome' would be as great as if the name of that God whom he served, and whose favour and friendship he enjoyed, were inscribed on him in some conspicuous manner. The meaning is that he would be known and recognized as belonging to God."[15]

Message to Laodicea: "You Are Lukewarm" (3:14–22)

3:14 And to the angel of the church in Laodicea write: The Amen, the faithful and true Witness, the Beginning of the creation of God, says this:

Laodicea. Laodicea was a city in the fertile Lycus Valley of the province of Phrygia. It was about forty miles east of Ephesus and about ten miles west of Colossae. Laodicea was built on the banks of the river Lycus, a tributary of the Maeander River.

Jesus' words to Laodicea contain allusions to the economic prosperity and social prominence of the city. Founded by the Seleucids and named for Laodice, the wife of Antiochus II (261–247 B.C.), Laodicea became extremely wealthy during the Roman period. For example, in 62 B.C. Flaccus seized the annual contribution of the Jews of Laodicea for Jerusalem, amounting to twenty pounds of gold. Moreover, when the city was destroyed by an earthquake in A.D. 60 (along with Colossae and Hierapolis), it alone refused aid from Rome for rebuilding (compare the self-sufficient attitude of the church of Laodicea in 3:17). Laodicea was known for its black wool industry; it manufactured garments from the raven-black wool produced by the sheep of the surrounding area.

Apparently the apostle Paul did not seem to have visited Laodicea at the time he wrote Colossians 2:1. Epaphras, Tychicus, Onesimus, and Mark seem to have been the early messengers of the gospel there (Col. 1:7; 4:7–15). A letter addressed to the Laodiceans by Paul (4:16) has apparently been lost. Some consider it to be a copy of the Ephesian letter. A church council was supposedly held at Laodicea (A.D. 344–363), but all that has come down to us are statements from other councils. The site of Laodicea is now a deserted heap of ruins that the Turks call Eskithsar, or "old castle."

The Amen. The apostle Paul calls Jesus "our Amen to the glory of God" (2 Cor. 1:20b). "In Judaism the use of Amen is widespread and firmly established. An extraordinary value is attached to its utterance. . . . Apart from divine service it was to be used in response to any prayer or praise uttered by another. The concluding Amen signified concurrence."[16]

Jesus then is the confirmation of what is right and absolute.

The faithful and true Witness. Jesus is the witness for God and His truth, and He can verify what the Father has approved.

The Beginning of the creation of God. Though this at first is difficult to understand, the most compatible meaning with the rest of Scripture is that Christ presides over creation as its Prince or Head. Many passages seem to carry this thought. For example, "All power is given unto Me in heaven and in earth" (Matt. 28:18 KJV). And all things are "put under His feet" (Heb. 2:8). The Father also gave Him authority over all mankind (John 17:2). In this, the Lord Jesus is the Starting Point (*archē*, "Beginning") of all of God's creation.

3:17 Because you say, "I am rich . . . and have need of nothing,"
and you do not know that you are wretched and miserable and poor
and blind and naked.

"I am rich . . . and have need of nothing." This church measured itself by
the physical and the external; they overlooked the internal and the spiritual.

3:19 Those whom I love, I reprove and discipline; be zealous therefore, and repent.

Whom I love, I reprove and discipline. The Lord never leaves us where
we are. He is constantly moving believers toward maturity. "For those whom
the Lord loves He disciplines" (Heb. 12:6).

3:21 He who overcomes, I will grant to him to sit down with Me
on My throne, as I also overcame and sat down with My Father on
His throne.

On my throne. A throne in New Testament times often included the plat-
form and steps, as well as the chair. The son of Peter the Great used to sit on
the steps of the throne when his father held court. This way, the ministers
knew who was in line as sovereign, because the next son was "on the throne"
by his father. This verse promises the overcomers that they will sit down by
Christ, who is on His throne. Jesus now is sitting with His Father on the heavenly throne. "The LORD says to my Lord: 'Sit at My right hand, until I make
Thine enemies a footstool for Thy feet'" (Ps. 110:1). This verse is quoted
more often in the New Testament than any other Old Testament verse.

Some say the Father's heavenly throne is the same as the Davidic reign.
This passage, however, separates these two. The heavenly throne is the Father's,
and "My throne" is the Messiah's earthly Davidic reign. These are clearly two
different thrones.

JOHN CALLED INTO HEAVEN: "COME UP HERE"

Synopsis

(4:1–3) John is one of the few prophets of Scripture who was transported in spirit into heaven itself to receive a prophecy. He would be shown things that must take place "after these things," that is, he was given a unique vision of what will take place after the church age. John was standing in heaven before the Lord in all His majestic splendor!

(4:4–5) John saw twenty-four elders sitting on twenty-four thrones. With peals of thunder and lightning, the apostle witnessed the glory of the seven-fold Spirit of God.

(4:6–11) Around the throne was a crystal sea and the four living angelic creatures who have spectacular characteristics and attributes. They stand before the Lord day and night saying the anthem of glory, "Holy, Holy, Holy, is the Lord God, the Almighty."

4:1 The first voice which I had heard, like the sound of a trumpet.

Trumpet. The voice the apostle John heard was like that of a trumpet. This is one of only two instruments that are used in heaven in worshiping God (the other is the harp/lyre). When God gave the Ten Commandments to the nation Israel, His presence was preceded by trumpets. The trumpet was used by God to summon the Israelites to the tent of meeting (Num. 10:2). Depending on the count of the trumpets used (one or two) it would summon either the elders of the tribes to the tent or the entire congregation before they moved on in their journey through the wilderness.

The trumpet the apostle John heard can be traced back to Revelation 1:10 where the revelation began. There he wrote that the voice of Jesus Christ sounded like a trumpet.

Some have equated the scene in 4:1 with that of the Rapture of the church as recorded in 1 Thessalonians 4:16. This is unlikely, however, since John's body remained on Patmos; and the Rapture of the church has nothing to do with receiving revelation.

4:2 Immediately I was in the Spirit.

In the Spirit. John's conscious state changed immediately to that of an expectant state in which he could receive the instruction and revelation God had for him. Some have suggested that John's experience in chapter 4 simply continues the vision he received from 1:10 through 3:22. This, however, does not seem to account for the word "immediately" in 4:2, which suggests a change of some kind.

Before this experience John was "in the Spirit," but apparently a greater work was needed for him to comprehend what the Lord would show him now. Overall, it can be said that John's ecstatic state spiritually brought him to the throne room of God, although physically he was in Patmos. John's experience is similar to that of Paul described in 2 Corinthians 12:1–2. In John's ecstatic state he had the ability to hear and see.

4:3 He who was sitting was like a jasper stone and a sardius in appearance; and there was a rainbow around the throne, like an emerald in appearance.

Jasper stone, sardius. These stones point to various aspects of heaven's throne room. Many have said this scene describes God's awesome creative and providential power over creation.

The jasper (green chalcedony) stone has been hotly debated over the centuries, since jasper stones today are opaque. It could be argued that the form of this stone in antiquity had characteristics that, as John wrote, are clear, almost like that of a diamond. The jasper was the last stone on the breastplate of the Levitical high priest's garment (Exod. 28:20; 39:13), and was the sixth stone in the headdress of the king of Tyre (Ezek. 28:13). The jasper is also one of the stones that will be in the foundation of the New Jerusalem (Rev. 21:19–20).

The sardius stone is less debated, since it is more commonly known as the carnelian (or ruby). It has a deep red appearance and is the first stone listed on the Levitical breastplate. Together the jasper and the sardius stones may represent God as the Alpha and Omega. Or they may represent God's overall goodness and His just judgment, His deity and His humanity, and/or His holiness and justice.[17]

Perhaps these two stones picture the Lord reacting in His holiness to the sinfulness of humankind, with "purity" of the jasper depicting His holiness and the "blood red" nature of the carnelian depicting His wrath.

Rainbow. John also saw a rainbow around God's throne. In the Old Testament the rainbow was a sign from God that He would not destroy the world by water again (Gen. 8:13).

Some writers say the rainbow in Revelation 4:3 is semicircular, like rainbows we see in the clouds today. Others say it was circular like a halo. If so, this would again point to the fact that God is the Alpha and the Omega, the First and the Last, since a circle has no beginning and no end.

Why was the rainbow emerald green in appearance? Lenski suggests it is because "green is . . . the color of hope and the rainbow is the symbol of peace."[18] And, he adds, this color shows that God's rule shines like a rainbow of grace.[19]

> **4:4** I saw twenty-four elders sitting, clothed in white garments, and golden crowns on their heads.

White garments. The Levites were given white garments to wear as they performed their service at the tabernacle of God. Jesus at His transfiguration was wearing a robe that was whiter than any garment made by human hands. Also the saints who will come out of the Tribulation will wear white robes (7:13). What then do the white garments of the twenty-four elders represent? The idea conveyed is that the wearers of these garments are considered morally pure and set apart from others. Because of their purity they are allowed to enter heaven's throne room in the very presence of God.

Golden crowns. These crowns *(stephanos)* are the types of crowns given by the Greeks to the victors of a contest such as a footrace or a wrestling match. They symbolize that the group of elders either overcame something or that they were rewarded for something they had done.

> **4:5** Seven lamps . . . are the seven Spirits of God. See page 114.

> **4:6** Before the throne there was, as it were, a sea of glass like crystal.

Sea of glass like crystal. Perhaps this clear sea, by its transparent nature and limitless boundaries, speaks of God's purity and majesty. He is in control and nothing is a mystery to Him; everything is crystal clear because He decrees it. The "sea of glass, similar to crystal, pictures the splendor and majesty of God on His throne that sets Him apart from His creation, a separation stemming from His purity and absolute holiness which he shares with no one else."[20]

> **4:7** And the first creature was like a lion, and the second creature like a calf, and the third creature had a face like that of a man, and the fourth creature was like a flying eagle.

See page 153.

> **4:8** And the four living creatures, each one of them having six wings, are full of eyes around and within.

See page 153.

THE BOOK TAKEN BY CHRIST: "A BOOK WRITTEN INSIDE AND ON THE BACK"

Synopsis

(5:1–4) John's vision shifted to God on the throne holding a book written inside and on the back, and sealed by seven seals. A powerful angel asked the question, "Who is worthy to open the book and to break its seals?" John was so moved by this drama that he began to cry, because no one appeared worthy to open the book.

(5:5–7) But one of the twenty-four elders answered that only the Lion, the Root of David, who has overcome, was capable of opening the book and the seals. The elder instructed John to stop weeping. Next he saw Christ the Lamb who had been slain, "having seven horns and seven eyes," which symbolize the sevenfold Spirits of God. "The seven Spirits" are sent into all the earth, and the Lamb took the book from God Himself. The Lamb was the only one worthy!

(5:8–12) Suddenly there was a host of heavenly beings praising and falling down before the Lamb—the four living creatures, the elders, other angels, altogether myriads of myriads and thousands of thousands. A new song was sung with this heavenly host crying a new anthem: The Lamb is worthy to open the seals, because He was slain and purchased for God by His blood men from every tribe and tongue. He is worthy to receive power, riches, and wisdom, and more!

(5:13–14) God and the Lamb received more praise from every created thing in heaven, on earth, under the earth, and even on the sea.

5:2 Who is worthy to open the book and to break its seals?

Seals. Most legal documents in the New Testament times were sealed with several imprints in order to disclose different parts of the document to different individuals. The seal was usually an inscription on a signet ring or cylinder belonging to the one granting the contract and was to be opened only by the person to whom it was sent. The inscription was often imprinted on wax.

Normally a rolled-up scroll would be sealed with only one seal on the outer edge. The scroll John saw, however, had been rolled up part way and a seal was placed on the edge; then more of the scroll was rolled up and sealed; then another portion, and so forth, till the entire scroll was rolled up and a final seal of wax was placed on the outer edge. So as the scroll was opened, seven wax seals in sequence had to be broken.

The fact that God gave the authority to the Lamb to open the seven seals should not be understated. Jesus told His disciples that He had been given authority over all things under heaven by God His Father (Matt. 28:18). That is, He has the title deed to exercise justice.

The number seven indicates the completeness of God's wrath in the coming judgment.

5:5 The Lion that is from the tribe of Judah, the Root of David, has overcome so as to open the book and its seven seals.

Lion. See page 107.

Tribe of Judah. See page 107.

Root of David. See page 107.

5:6 And I saw . . . a Lamb standing, as if slain, having seven horns and seven eyes, which are the seven Spirits of God, sent out into all the earth.

Lamb. At His first coming the Lamb of God was a sacrifice for the sins of the world (John 1:29). Now He is seen as a Lamb with power (seven horns) and much wisdom (seven eyes). See page 107.

Seven Spirits of God. See page 114.

5:8 Twenty-four elders fell down before the Lamb, having each one a harp, and golden bowls full of incense, which are the prayers of the saints.

Harp. This is one of only two instruments that are used in the worship of God in the book of Revelation.

> The musical instrument of the elders *kitharan* ("a harp") is the traditional one associated with the psalmody in the OT. It, like the lyre, is associated with joy and gladness (cf. 1 Chron. 25:1, 6; 2 Chron. 29:25; Pss. 71:22; 92:3; 149:3). It also is regularly connected with prophecy (cf. 1 Sam. 10:5; 1 Chron. 25:3; Ps. 49:4). More than any other musical instrument, the harp is employed in Scripture in direct praise and worship of God. Later in the Apocalypse it is used to describe celestial music in 4:2 and 15:2.[21]

According to Genesis 31:27, Laban accused Jacob of not letting Laban send him off with joy and singing with a timbrel and a lyre. See also Revelation 14:2.

Golden bowls full of incense. Each golden bowl held by one of the twenty-four may have been a small slim bottle with a narrow neck. Or they may have been more like the bowl-like dishes that were used to offer up incense, much like the ones given by the tribes as tributes to God in the dedication of the tabernacle (Num. 7). These bowls were filled with incense that represented prayers offered at the time of sacrifice.

In the Bible incense is often associated with prayer. It added a sweet aroma to the earthly sacrifices offered in the temple. The Levites were responsible to offer incense to God. Aaron's sons, Nadab and Abihu, offered "strange" fire to God and were consumed by God's wrath (Lev. 10:1–2).

5:9 [You] didst purchase for God with Thy blood men from every tribe and tongue and people and nation.

From every tribe and tongue and people and nation. John saw this great crowd of Gentiles in heaven just before the beginning of the Tribulation. They are church saints who will be raptured before God's wrath is poured out on the world.

5:10 Thou hast made them to be a kingdom and priests to our God; and they will reign upon the earth.

Kingdom and priests. See 1:6; 3:21; 20:4.

5:14 And the four living creatures kept saying, "Amen."

Four living creatures. See page 153.

Amen. The word "Amen" means completely trustworthy and sure. It could be rendered "So be it." The fact that the four living creatures kept repeating "Amen" adds emphasis to the song of the heavenly hosts in which all will join in worshiping the Lamb and God the Father (5:13). The fact that the same worship is offered to both the Lamb (Jesus Christ) and to God the Father is another evidence that Christ possesses full deity, for only God is to be worshiped (see 19:10; 22:8–9).

THE SIX SEALS OPENED

Synopsis

(6:1–2) The first seal was broken, and on a white horse a warrior rode with bow and crown to conquer men on the earth.

(6:3–4) When the second seal was broken, a red horse came forth with another warrior wielding a great sword. He was given power to remove peace from the earth, and people began to kill each other.

(6:5–6) The third seal was broken, and a black horse appeared with a rider carrying a pair of scales in his hand. The food supply of earth seemed to be diminished with the most common grains for human consumption limited and nearly exhausted.

(6:7–8) The fourth seal was broken with one named Death riding on a pale-colored horse. Hades followed with authority to kill a fourth of the earth's population by means of the sword, famine, pestilence, and animals.

(6:9–11) The fifth seal was broken, and from the heavenly altar a cry came forth from martyrs who were slain because of the word of God and their testimony. They asked how much longer it would be before their blood would be avenged on those on earth who killed them. Given white robes, they were told to rest and wait a little longer, because more of their fellow servants must die.

(6:12–17) When the sixth seal was broken, a terrible earthquake occurred with the sun and moon darkened and the moon looking blood-red in color.

Compounding the terror, the stars (probably an asteroid shower) blanketed the earth, and the sky (or atmosphere) was somehow split apart. People on every level of society cried out to the mountains to fall on them and hide them from the wrath of God and of the Lamb. They recognized that the great day of God's wrath against them had come and that they were unable to endure it.

6:2 I looked, and behold, a white horse, and he who sat on it had a bow; and a crown was given to him; and he went out conquering, and to conquer.

A white horse. The rider on a white horse is the first of the "Four Horsemen of the Apocalypse" who will be released when the first seals of the scroll are broken by the Lamb. They are called into action by one of the four living beings that will be around the throne of God. The four horsemen parallel those in the book of Zechariah 1:7–11, although the horsemen in Zechariah are sent only to patrol the earth rather than to inflict God's wrath. As animals of war, horses signified the ability to attack swiftly and with frightening results against the enemy's foot soldiers. The first horse will go forth with its rider to seek, destroy, and conquer. Its rider will hold a bow and will wear a victor's crown. When an army general paraded through the streets of Rome after some conquest, he rode a white horse to signify victory. Some have said the first rider in Revelation 6 will be Christ at His second coming, because the white horse is a symbol of victory. This view, however, seems unlikely, because Christ the Lamb had just broken the seal. And it would seem strange to have Christ depicted in this way at the beginning of the Tribulation, when He will come on a white horse after the Tribulation is over, not at its beginning.

The rider then will be "the prince who is to come" (Dan. 9:26), the false messiah or the Antichrist, as revealed in Revelation 13:1–10. Here in chapter 6, the Antichrist will appear as a world conqueror.

6:4 And another, a red horse, went out; and to him who sat on it, it was granted to take peace from the earth, and that men should slay one another; and a great sword was given to him.

Red horse. When the second seal of the scroll is broken, a red horse will go out. The fiery red color denotes war and conquest. The rider of this horse will be equipped with a sword and will have the ability to remove peace from the earth. This corresponds to Jesus' introduction of the seven-year Tribulation (Matt. 24:6–8; Mark 13:7–8; Luke 21:9–10). As Jesus said, this is "the beginning of birth pains," which probably points to the first half of the Tribulation.

The prophet Isaiah also wrote about God's using a sword to bring judgment on Israel (Isa. 51:19; 65:12).

> **6:5–6** Behold, a black horse; and he who sat on it had a pair of scales in his hand. And I heard as it were a voice in the center of the four living creatures saying "A quart of wheat for a denarius, and three quarts of barley for a denarius; and do not harm the oil and the wine."

Black horse. The opening of the third seal revealed a black horse with a rider holding a set of scales in his hand. This black horse, as the color implies, depicts a great famine (see Lam. 4:8–9) that God has said will come on the earth in the Tribulation.

Scales. The scales denote a measurement commonly used in Bible times. After the war depicted by the red horse (Rev. 6:4) the price of food in the famine will be so great that an entire day's wages (a denarius) will be required to purchase enough wheat (a quart) for means for one day or enough barley (three quarts) for three meals. At these prices a family would have no money left for either oil or wine.

These inflationary prices will be inevitable in the face of war and conquest. The average worker will be unable to afford the simple necessity of food for himself and his family.[22]

A denarius. A denarius, a silver coin, was the amount paid for a day's work by a common laborer (Matt. 20:2). It was worth about 15 cents by today's standards. Used throughout the Roman Empire, the denarius is the most mentioned denomination of coin in the Bible and is sometimes called a penny or a cent.

> **6:8** And I looked, and behold, an ashen horse; and he who sat on it had the name "Death"; and Hades was following with him.

Ashen horse. The color of this horse and its rider will be a pale green (Greek, *chloros*). The same word is used several times in the New Testament to describe grass (Mark 6:39; Rev. 8:7; 9:4), but here it most likely refers to the pale color of decay and death, much like that of a corpse.

The name "Death." Unlike the riders on the first three horses, this one will be given a name. "Death" will be an appropriate name because this rider will have the power to kill people by means of sword, famine, pestilence, and animals. Hades will be not far behind this rider. Hades is personified as a person who is ready to engulf death's victims. Death and Hades will work together to insure that people will die and will then be buried.

This horse and its rider will be responsible for the death of twenty-five percent of the world's population. Some have suggested that this percentage will result from the atrocities of the horsemen, but the natural antecedent of "them" suggests that the responsible parties are death and Hades.[23] In all of its horror death will come on mankind as it has never done before at any time in history.

> **6:9–10** And when He broke the fifth seal, I saw underneath the altar the souls of those who had been slain. . . . and they cried out . . . "How long, O Lord, holy and true, wilt Thou refrain from judging and avenging our blood on those who dwell on the earth?"

How long, O Lord . . . This prayer of these saints contrasts with the prayer of Stephen in Acts 7:60. Living near the beginning of the church age of grace, it is understandable that his prayer would have been for God's grace and mercy on his murderers. The prayer of the saints from beneath the altar, however, is quite different. This is because at that hour the judgment of the wicked of the earth will have begun. This indicates that this is sometime in the Tribulation period. The judgment asked for by the saints is not in retribution for their deaths, but for God's wrath to come on those who have completely rejected their Creator and martyred His followers.

> **6:12** When He broke the sixth seal . . . there was a great earth-quake; and the sun became black as sackcloth.

Black as sackcloth. Sackcloth was made from the hair and hides of goats or camels and was worn as a tunic or loincloth as a sign of mourning and anguish. When sackcloth was worn, the mourner often fasted and put ashes on himself (Isa. 58:5; Dan. 9:3).

Several Old Testament prophets also wrote that the sun will be darkened in the coming "Day of the Lord" (Isa. 13:10; 24:23; Ezek. 32:7–8; Joel 2:10, 31; Amos 5:20; 8:9; Zeph. 1:15).

> **6:13** And the stars of the sky fell to the earth, as a fig tree casts its unripe figs when shaken by a great wind.

Stars. The word "stars" translates the Greek word *asteres* which can refer to what we think of as stars, but it can also refer to asteroids or meteors.[24] From John's point of view, it appeared that the very heavens will rain down on the earth. This spectacle of an asteroid or meteor shower will be so enormous that from a human perspective it will seem as if all the stars are falling to the earth. This will certainly strike great fear in the hearts of everyone. As the Lord Himself said, there will be "great signs from heaven" (Luke 21:11) that will strike terror in the hearts of men. The scope of this astral event will be so violent that it is likened to a fig tree losing its unripe figs in a severe windstorm.

6:14 And the sky was split apart like a scroll when it is rolled up.

And the sky was split apart like a scroll. This in the fourth great sign that will occur in the heavens at the breaking of the sixth seal. The other three are the sun, the moon, and the stars. The sky is compared to a scroll or book *(biblion),* much like the one that the Lamb will unroll as these events occur. The heavens will look as if they are split in half, and each half will appear to be rolled up like a scroll. Isaiah, too, wrote that in the day of God's wrath "the sky will be rolled up like a scroll" (Isa. 34:4). People will think that the universe is falling apart.

6:16 Fall on us and hide us from the presence of Him who sits on the throne, and from the wrath of the Lamb.

The wrath of the Lamb. In the Tribulation unbelievers will want to escape these evidences of the wrath of both God the Father ("Him who sits on the throne") and Jesus Christ, the Lamb of God. Some Bible teachers say that the wrath in the early part of the Tribulation will come from nature, man, and/or Satan, but not from God. They suggest that His wrath will not begin until around 14:9–10, 19. However, 6:16–17 clearly indicate that the early years of the Tribulation will reveal God's wrath. Therefore since believers will not be subject to God's wrath (1 Thess. 1:10; 5:9), the Rapture of the church will occur before the Tribulation will begin. This is a strong argument for the pretribulational Rapture.

6:17 For the great day of their wrath has come; and who is able to stand?

God has acted so dramatically and His power has been displayed on such an astronomical scale in the shaking of earth and heaven that men recognize for the first time their weakness and nothingness. Ranged against God men must inevitably fall, they cannot possibly stand! The rhetorical question is strategically placed and the next chapter will describe those who through divine grace will be able to stand through the dark days of the tribulation period.[25]

PARENTHESIS: SAVED PEOPLE COMING OUT OF THE TRIBULATION

Synopsis

(7:1–3) The chronology of Revelation is interrupted here in order to seal the Lord's bond-servants on their foreheads. The earth, sea, and trees will not be harmed further until the 144,000 Jewish witnesses are set aside for service.

(7:4–8) The 144,000 witnesses will be from every tribe of Israel. Twelve thousand from each of the twelve tribes will be sealed, that is, given special protection until the Lord calls them home.

(7:9–17) The slaughter of righteous people on the earth will continue. Thousands of saints from all nations and peoples will stand before God's heavenly throne and before the Lamb clothed in white. They will cry out, "Salvation to our God who sits on the throne, and to the Lamb." The question will be asked, "From where have they come?" The answer is that they will have come out of the great Tribulation and will have washed their robes in the blood of the Lamb. They will serve the Lord day and night in His temple. Also they will never again face hunger or thirst. The Lamb will be their shepherd and will guide them to the water of life. And God shall wipe away the tears from their eyes.

7:1 I saw four angels standing at the four corners of the earth, holding back the four winds of the earth.

Four corners of the earth. Some have used this verse to try to prove that the earth is flat. However, this simply means that angels will stand at the north, south, east, and west portions of the globe.

The winds that the angels will restrain are personified as if they are eager to be set free to inflict devastation on the earth. But angels will restrain them in order to prevent a premature outbreak of God's fury that will devastate the earth. Once the sealing of the 144,000 is complete, the fifth angel will release the winds, and Jewish witnesses will be safe from the coming immediate carnage.

7:2 The four angels to whom it was granted to harm the earth and the sea.

To harm the earth and the sea. The Greek verb *adikeō* ("to harm") is a strong word meaning "to harm viciously or vigorously." The verse also stresses God's sovereignty against injustice. He will give authority to His angels to bring harm on the earth and the sea.

7:3 Do not harm the earth or the sea or the trees, until we have sealed the bond-servants of our God on their foreheads.

Foreheads. It was not uncommon for members of certain workers' guilds to place a mark on their foreheads to identify with the group. This would mean that whoever placed the mark on the worker would stand by him, even though the one making the mark would not condone all the worker's actions. Also the bearer of the seal would be identified with the one who sealed him. Since one's forehead is a conspicuous portion of one's body, this mark on the foreheads of the 144,000 Jews will be readily visible. People will know they belong to God. Though it is not known what the seal or mark will be like, others will know they are God's bond-servants.

7:4 One hundred and forty-four thousand sealed from every tribe of the sons of Israel.

One hundred and forty-four thousand. See page 175.

7:9 A great multitude . . . standing before the throne and before the Lamb . . . and palm branches were in their hands.

Palm branches. The palm tree *(phoenix dacyliera)* was a blessing in biblical times because of its fruit (dates) and its shade from the sun. Palm trees are tall and have rough and unbranched trunks, and at the tip they have a tuft of huge feathery leaves. Because of its many palm trees Jericho was known as the city of palms (Judg. 1:16). In Bible times people waved palm leaves as a sign of conquest, peace, and salvation. Orientals thought of the palm tree, which could live up to two hundred years, as the perfect tree because of its longevity, shade, and fruit.

During Jesus' triumphal entry into Jerusalem (our Palm Sunday), the Jews waved palm branches to signify that their salvation and Messiah had come. Similarly the 144,000 Jews will praise God for their salvation and their Messiah.

> **7:10** They cry out with a loud voice, saying, "Salvation to our God who sits on the throne, and to the Lamb."

Salvation. Both God the Father and God the Son are called our Savior (1 Tim. 1:1; Titus 1:4). This further supports the doctrine of the deity of Christ. See page 111.

> **7:14** These are the ones who come out of the great Tribulation.

These are the ones. . . . See page 175.

THE FOUR TRUMPETS SOUNDED

Synopsis

(8:1) The seventh seal will be opened in heaven.

(8:2–6) Seven angels will blow trumpets that will bring on more wrath from God on the earth. The prayers of martyred saints that are on the golden altar in heaven will come up before God as a sweet smelling incense. Fire from the altar will be tossed on the wicked earth below, followed by peals of thunder, lightning, and an earthquake. The Lord will thereby respond to the death of His righteous saints who have perished for their witness.

(8:7) When the first trumpet is sounded, there will follow hail and fire, mixed with blood (pollution), thrown on the earth. A third of the trees will be consumed, and all the green grass will be burned up.

(8:8–9) When the second angel sounds the second trumpet, the sea will become polluted as blood. One third of sea life will die, and one third of the ships in the ocean will be destroyed.

(8:10–11) At the sound of the third angel trumpet, a great asteroid will fall to earth from heaven, affecting a third of the rivers on earth and also the springs of water. The great asteroid will be called Wormwood. Many people will die from the waters, because they will become polluted.

(8:12–13) When the fourth angel blows the fourth trumpet, a third of the light

from the sun, moon, and stars will be smitten so that the light from space will be dimmed. But a flying eagle will give a warning to earth, shouting, "Woe, woe, woe, to those who dwell on the earth." The warning is that the remaining trumpet blasts will bring on the earth greater wrath and terror than has gone before.

8:1 There was silence in heaven for about half an hour.

Silence. As the seventh seal is broken, while praise is going on in the throne room of God, complete silence will occur. John's human finiteness is apparent as he tried to explain time as he understood it from his human senses. Being transcendent, God is above time, but He created it for our benefit. This half-hour of silence will anticipate the coming trumpet and bowl judgments that the seventh scroll will reveal when opened.

8:2 And seven trumpets were given to them.

Trumpets. The initial use of the trumpet in the history of Israel was at Mount Sinai. It was first used to call the entire nation to the mountain of God to receive the Ten Commandments (Exod. 20:18). Later trumpets were blown to call the entire nation (two trumpet blasts) or the leaders (one trumpet blast) to the tabernacle in anticipation of journeying onward to a new location (Num. 10:1–18). Other trumpets have been used throughout Israel's history to call the nation to war (10:9), for special feasts (10:10), in ceremonial processions (1 Chron. 15:24), and in announcing that the Day of the Lord is coming (Joel 2:1).

The purpose of the trumpets in Revelation 8, however, is different in three ways. First, they will be given to the angels for the purpose of announcing great calamity. Second, these trumpets will relate to the breaking of the seventh seal. Third, these trumpet blasts will not expect anyone to respond. Instead they introduce what God will send on the earth.

8:3 And another angel came and stood at the altar, holding a golden censer; and much incense was given to him.

The Altar. Some Bible students say there are two altars in heaven and that this angel will take coals from the first and deliver them to a second angel, who will use a golden censer much like the ones Solomon placed in the temple (1 Kings 7:15; 2 Kings 25:15; 2 Chron. 4:22; Jer. 52:18–19).

However, just as there was only one golden altar of incense in the tabernacle, and since the tabernacle was constructed after a heavenly pattern (Exod. 25:40; Heb. 8:5), it is preferable to say that John saw only one altar. This is consistent with the visions recorded in Isaiah 6:6 and Ezekiel 10:2. The fact that the saints' prayers will be on the altar like incense suggests that the saints are near the throne of God and that there is only one altar. Incense played a major role in worship in the Old Testament. This incense offering would be a reminder of the sweet smell of intercessory prayer.

8:5 And the angel took the censer; and he filled it with the fire of the altar and threw it to the earth.

The fire of the altar. The fire will be followed by thunder, lightning, and an earthquake. The terror on the earth will continue and will seem unending. These fighting phenomena will come as divine retribution against those who will martyr saints in the Tribulation. This act of retribution will be God's response to the martyrs' cries and prayers.

8:7 And the first [trumpet] sounded . . . and a third of the earth was burnt up, and a third of the trees were burnt up, and all the green grass was burnt up.

A third of the earth . . . trees . . . green grass . . . was burned up. One can hardly conceive how frightening this will be to people, for such a widespread conflagration will obviously upset the earth's ecology. Some take these statements as figurative, but there is no reason to deny their literalness.

8:8 Something like a great mountain burning with fire was thrown into the sea; and a third of the sea became blood.

Some have suggested that the apostle saw a huge atomic cloud that will boil into the sky and then fall into the sea. Whatever the "mountain" is, it will pollute the ocean, destroying sea life and sinking ships. When the number "a third" is mentioned, as also in verse 7, there is no reason to say this is not a precise figure.

8:10–11. A great star fell from heaven, burning like a torch . . . the name of the star is called Wormwood.

Wormwood. This is a large celestial body that will fall from the heavens after the third trumpet blast and will cause a third of the earth's water to become bitter. The wormwood is a nonpoisonous but bitter plant and is common in the Middle East in several varieties. Wormwood is mentioned seven times in the Old Testament to depict bitterness and sorrow.

8:12 A third of the sun and a third of the moon and a third of the stars were smitten, so that a third of them might be darkened.

Darkened. There are two suggestions as to how to understand this verse. One is that these heavenly bodies will be simultaneously cursed so that they give off a third less light than normal. Another view, which may be preferable, is that the atmospheric pollution, caused by the first three trumpet judgments will reduce the amount of light from the sun, moon, and stars.

8:13 I heard an eagle flying in midheaven, saying with a loud voice, "Woe, woe, woe, to those who dwell on the earth."

Eagle. Some wonder how an eagle (or the Greek word may be translated "vulture") could speak, but elsewhere in Scripture animals—a serpent and a donkey—had been given the ability to speak (Gen. 3:1–5; Num. 22:28–30). The words of this strong bird anticipate the next three judgments—the fifth, sixth, and seventh trumpets.

If the bird is a vulture, it may be flying in the sky in anticipation of the carnage and decaying flesh to come in the sixth trumpet judgment (see 9:15).

Woe. The Greek word *ouai* is what one might scream when under intense pain or suffering. There will be three times when people will moan and cry out in intense agony (9:12; 11:14; 12:12).

THE FIFTH AND SIXTH TRUMPETS SOUNDED

Synopsis

(9:1–12) With the blowing of the fifth trumpet, horrible demonic, locust-like creatures with strange appearances will come from a terrible bottomless pit and will swarm on the earth, having the power of scorpions to harm unsaved people on the earth. Those who have the seal of God on their foreheads will be protected from these creatures. They will torment people for five months but will not be able to kill people. They follow a leader named Abaddon (in Hebrew) or Apollyon (in Greek). The releasing of these demonic beings is the first of the three predicted terrible woes to fall on earth.

(9:13–21) When the sixth angel will sound the next trumpet, a voice will speak from the heavenly golden altar, "Release the four angels who are bound at the great river Euphrates." These angels will be let loose to carry out judgment on a third of mankind. Apparently they will be used of God to turn loose two hundred million warriors who will form a terribly destructive army. These horsemen and their steeds will bring destruction by fire, smoke, and brimstone, which will come out of their mouths. People who will not be killed by this army will continue in their sins, refusing to repent.

9:1 I saw a star from heaven which had fallen to the earth; and the key of the bottomless pit was given to him.

A star. More than likely this refers to an angelic being since he is given a specific task. Since the angel had fallen (perfect tense), possibly some time in the past, many scholars believe this will be a fallen angel who followed Satan in his rebellion and was cast out of God's presence. Others believe this will be an elect angel. In either view the angel will carry out an order from the Lord Himself.

Key to the bottomless pit. The key represents authority to unlock the pit, implying that these creatures who are confined in the pit will not be able to come out until they will be released. The "bottomless pit" in Greek is literally the "shaft of the abyss."

> **9:2** And smoke went up out of the pit, like the smoke of a great furnace.

Smoke of a great furnace. This furnace "is waterless, birdless, chaotic, horrible, fiery, and is situated beyond the confines of earth and heaven. . . . It is the temporary place of punishment for the fallen angels, the stars and hosts of heaven. . . . It is beyond the bounds of earth and heaven, xviii. 11, xxi. 7. It is [connected] with the world of space above by a great shaft."[26]

> **9:3** Out of the smoke came forth locusts upon the earth; and power was given them, as the scorpions of the earth have power.

Locusts. See pages 159–60.

Scorpions. See pages 159–60.

> **9:4** And they were told that they should not hurt the grass of the earth, nor any green thing, nor any tree, but only the men who do not have the seal of God on their foreheads.

The seal of God on their foreheads. The seal of God was placed on the foreheads of the 144,000 Jews during the sixth seal judgment (7:4–8). This seal marked the Jews, much as did the blood on the doorposts during the first Passover. The demonic beings will be given liberty to harm only non-sealed humans and will be restrained from harming trees or plants. This seal will keep believers from being tormented during the five-month oppression of these locust-like demons.

> **9:7** And the appearance of the locusts was like horses prepared for battle; and on their heads, as it were, crowns like gold, and their faces were like the faces of men.

The locusts. See pages 159–60.

9:11 They have as a king over them, the angel of the abyss; his name in Hebrew is Abaddon, and in the Greek he has the name Apollyon.

Apollyon. See page 160.

9:12 The first woe is past.

Woe. See 8:13; and 11:14.

9:13 I heard a voice from the four horns of the golden altar which is before God.

Golden altar. See 8:3 and page 242.

9:14 Release the four angels who are bound at the great river Euphrates.

Four angels. See page 160.

Euphrates. See page 160.

9:16 And the number of the armies of the horsemen was two hundred million.

Two hundred million. Walvoord remarks, "If considered a literal enumeration of the army, it would represent the largest armed force ever known to man. Considering the millions of people in the Orient, the literal interpretation is not impossible, especially in view of the population explosion."[27] Swete, however, believes the number is not literal. "These vast numbers forbid us to seek a literal fulfillment, and the description which follows supports this conclusion."[28]

But as Thomas points out,

> The fact that the horses rather than the riders are the destructive agents and that they and their riders wear brightly colored breastplates matching the destructive forces proceeding from their mouths suggests that the combination of horse and rider is of superhuman origin. The determining aspect in favor of these being demons is the description of the horses that differ so greatly from

any ordinary horse that these horses must be of another order. . . . these armies are demonic, not human, so the largeness of the number is no obstacle.[29]

9:17 The riders had breastplates the color of fire and of hyacinth and of brimstone; and the heads of the horses are like the heads of lions; and out of their mouths proceed fire and smoke and brimstone.

Horses. The lion-like appearance of the horses' heads indicates that these horses, which will be instruments of warfare, will be ferocious like lions. In Revelation the lion is a sign of terror (10:3) and destructiveness (13:2).

Hyacinth and brimstone. The Greek word translated "hyacinth" refers to a deep blue gem, so that this color would suggest a sulfurous-type smoke. Throughout the Bible, brimstone, with its yellowish color, has been used by God as a vehicle of judgment on those who have despised His righteousness.

Fire and smoke and brimstone. Fire, of course, is red in color. Together these three colored elements (red, deep blue, and yellow) depict great destruction by heat. These beasts of warfare will emit from their mouths these elements of fire and smoke and brimstone on people.

9:18 A third of mankind was killed by these three plagues, by the fire and the smoke and the brimstone, which proceeded out of their mouths.

A third of mankind was killed. "Further light is cast on the character of the warfare in verse 18, where it is repeated that the third part of men are killed by the invading force; special mention is made of the means, namely, 'by the fire, and the smoke, and by the brimstone, which issued out of their mouths.'"[30]

9:20 The rest of mankind, who were not killed by these plagues, did not repent of the works of their hands.

Plagues. The Greek term translated "plague" was used in a nonfigurative sense for a blow or a stroke. Thus figuratively it came to mean "a plague, or a misfortune."[31] These plagues, then, were more of a lashing or a series of blows that were inflicted, rather than sickness or disease. Some have suggested that these plagues refer to the entire set of trumpet judgments. However, it seems as if John was referring exclusively to the lion-headed horses and their riders.

These plagues, stripes, or lashings, then, would have been the result of the sixth trumpet alone. Even with the loss of one third of the remainder of the human race the survivors will still not repent and change their wicked ways. This hardness will make the remaining seven bowl judgments all the more deserved and righteous.

PARENTHESIS: TRIBULATION HORROR INTENSIFIES

Synopsis

(10:1–7) Another powerful angel is involved in this vision. He had in his hand an open small book (scroll). Placing his feet on the land and the sea, he instructed John not to write in detail about the seven loud peals of thunder he has just heard. But the prophet was told that he was about to see the mystery of God finished, a reference to the completion of the terrible Tribulation period. John was then told to consume the little book.

(10:8–11) The small scroll tasted good to John, but it was bitter to his stomach. The angels then instructed him to continue to prophesy concerning many peoples, nations, tongues, and kings.

10:1 And I saw another strong angel coming down out of heaven, clothed with a cloud; and the rainbow was upon his head, and his face was like the sun, and his feet like pillars of fire.

Strong angel. The identity of this angel is not specifically given in this passage, but he is compared to (*allon*, "the one similar to" or "one of the same type") the strong angel in 5:2. Some have suggested that this is Christ, but this seems unlikely in light of 10:5–6. Although Christ is referred to in the Old Testament as "the Angel of Yahweh," nowhere in the New Testament is He referred to as simply "an angel."

Clothed with a cloud. This angel's appearance is enhanced by the fact that he is adorned in the majesty of a cloud.

The rainbow. Here the word "rainbow" is a translation of the Greek *iris*. This rainbow, much like the one that was in the throne room (4:3), encircles the angel's head like a warrior's headdress. While the rainbow in the throne room of God was emerald in color, this rainbow is much like the one that adorned the sky in the days of Noah and indicates mercy in the midst of God's wrath.

His face was like the sun. The angel's face is compared to that of sunshine, which is also the way Jesus' face is described in 1:16. Perhaps the angel's face shone because he had been in God's presence, just as Moses' face shone after he spoke with God.

Pillars of fire. The angel's legs are likened to fire, which is suggestive of judgment.

10:2 And he placed his right foot on the sea and his left on the land.

His right foot on the sea and his left on the land. This suggests that the judgments to come will encompass both land and sea, that is, the entire world.

10:4 Seal up the things which the seven peals of thunder have spoken, and do not write them.

Seal up the things. This seal recalls the command given to Daniel to seal up his vision until the end (Dan. 12:4). However, this command for John to "not write" about the peals of thunder differs from the command given to Daniel in that these utterances were not to be written at all, whereas Daniel's prophecies were written and were to be sealed until the end.

10:9 Take it, and eat it; and it will make your stomach bitter, but in your mouth it will be sweet as honey.

Take it, and eat it. John was commanded to approach the angel that had the scroll, and the angel told him that it would make his "stomach bitter." While John thoroughly devoured the scroll, the angel anticipated its overall effect on him.

Sweet as honey. The sweet taste John experienced was like honey. This recalls the way God's Word is described in Psalm 119:103, "How sweet are

Thy words to my taste! Yes, sweeter than honey to my mouth." Perhaps the honey-like taste in the apostle's mouth represented his being joyful that God had informed him of things to come. However, this was short-lived, for this taste quickly became bitter in his stomach because of the coming apostasy, the persecutions of believers, and God's righteous judgments on mankind.

"The bitterness and the sweetness, then, do not pertain to different parts of the little scroll, but to the sensations of the prophet at different stages regarding the totality of it."[32]

THE TEMPLE, THE TWO WITNESSES, AND THE SEVENTH TRUMPET

Synopsis

(11:1–2) John was instructed to measure the temple of God, the altar, and the crowd of worshipers who had gathered. He was told not to measure the outer court, the court of the Gentiles, because it would be under the control of the nations, who will subjugate it for forty-two months or three and a half years.

(11:3–14) Suddenly two special prophets and witnesses were introduced. They will minister and prophesy for the same three and a half years. In their witness for the Lord, they will become like lampstands of truth and dependable olive trees on the earth. Unsaved people will attempt to kill them, but they will possess power and authority to slay those who will come against them. They will also perform miracles such as stopping the rain, causing water to become polluted, and bringing all kinds of plagues on the land.

When their ministry will be completed, the Lord will allow the Beast to slay them. Their bodies, lying in the streets of Jerusalem, will be seen by the entire world. The whole world will see their dead bodies and rejoice. But God will call them to heaven, saying, "Come up here." When they are taken to heaven, a powerful earthquake will strike the city, killing seven thousand people. Many will be so frightened that they will give glory to God.

(11:15–19) When a seventh angel sounds the seventh trumpet, loud voices will suddenly be heard from heaven. The voice will announce that the kingdom will soon come and that the reign of Christ will soon begin! In heaven the twenty-four angels will fall on their faces, worshiping God and giving Him thanks. This will make the pagan nations more enraged, because the inhabitants of earth will realize that more wrath will be coming on them for their sin and rebellion. After this announcement the temple of God in heaven will be opened, followed by flashes of lightning, peals of thunder, an earthquake, and a terrible hailstorm.

11:1 And there was given me a measuring rod like a staff; and someone said, "Rise and measure the temple of God, and the altar."

Measuring rod. The Greek word *kalamos,* translated "measuring rod," is literally "reed." Combined with the following phrase "like a staff" *(omoios rabdō),* we have the literal rendering, "reed like a staff." "This served for a surveyor's rule or measuring rod and it might have been the cane which grows along the Jordan valley and was known as the 'giant reed' of Mediterranean lands. It grows in swampy areas and sometimes it may reach the height of twelve or even fifteen or twenty feet."[33]

The altar. The Greek for altar, *thusiastērion,* simply means the place where offering or sacrifices are made.[34] In the Jewish temple there were two altars. One was the brazen altar, located in the outer court of the temple, and the other was the altar of incense in the Holy Place. Walvoord points out that the altar previously mentioned in 8:3, 5 seems to be the altar of incense,[35] and that altar is probably the one in view here. We also need to keep in mind that John was asked to measure the "temple *[naos]* of God," which refers to the temple proper (the Holy of Holies and the Holy Place) and not the court. Lenski writes, "The word is not *ieron,* 'the Temple' (our versions), for this includes all courts; but *naon,* 'the Sanctuary,' the one building that contained the Holy and the Holy of Holies where God is present."[36] So this suggests that this altar was the altar of incense in the Holy Place.

11:4 These are the two olive trees and the two lampstands that stand before the Lord of the earth.

Two olive trees. The two witnesses mentioned in verse 3 are said here to be two olive trees. The symbolism goes back to Zechariah 4:3, which refers to "two olive trees" as well as a lampstand.

In that context "the two olive trees represent 'the two anointed ones,' Zerubbabel and Joshua, king and priest."[37] "Just as these two witnesses were raised up to be lampstands or witnesses for God and were empowered by olive oil representing the power of the Holy Spirit, so the two witnesses of Revelation 11 will likewise execute their prophetic office. Their ministry does not rise in human ability but in the power of God."[38]

11:6 They have power . . . to smite the earth with every plague, as often as they desire.

Plague. See 9:20. The term here refers to what results from the supernatural abilities of the two witnesses to bring about drought, transform water into blood, and other supernatural catastrophes. Their power will be similar to that of Moses in his confrontation with Pharaoh.

11:8 And their dead bodies will lie in the street of the great city which mystically is called Sodom and Egypt, where also their Lord was crucified.

Sodom. Sodom is the Old Testament city located at the southern tip of the Dead Sea. It was said of the city during Abraham's day, "The outcry of Sodom and Gomorrah is indeed great, and their sin is exceedingly grave" (Gen. 18:20). Genesis 19:4–5 reveals that homosexuality was prevalent in the city. The city was so evil that God chose to annihilate it and its inhabitants from the face of the earth (19:13). Only Lot and his daughters were righteous enough to be saved from the devastation. In Revelation 11:8 Jerusalem because of its sin was metaphorically likened to Sodom. This is not the first time in Scripture that "Sodom" is used to exemplify spiritual and moral degradation (Isa. 1:10; Ezek. 16:46, 49).

Egypt. Egypt enslaved God's chosen people for over four hundred years, and it was also a center of idolatry at the time. When the Exodus occurred, Egypt was seen as a battleground of the gods versus God. Each plague showed a sound defeat of the Egyptian gods. Later the prophet Ezekiel said that harlotries originated in Egypt (Ezek. 23:3–4, 8, 19).

Mystically. This word in Greek is literally "spiritually" *(pneumatikōs)*. In a spiritual sense Sodom and Egypt both depict the spiritual degradation of the people of Jerusalem.

The introduction of this word "spiritually" settles the literalness of the narrative. Only the names "Sodom and Egypt" are to be spiritualized, or taken in a sense different from the letter. Men mistake God's mind, and pervert God's word, when they refuse to accept and interpret the Bible as it reads. When he means it to be taken otherwise, he gives us indication to that effect. Jerusalem is not Sodom; and yet, "spiritually" considered, Jerusalem in apostasy is a Sodom, and is repeatedly so called by the prophets. (Isa. 1:9, 10; 3:8, 9; Deut. 32:30–33; Jer. 23:14.) So also is it "spiritually" likened to an Egypt, because of its idolatries. (Ezek. 23:3, 4, 8, 19.) But to identify the place beyond mistake, it is further described as the city "where also their Lord was crucified," which was none other than the literal Jerusalem.[39]

11:14 The second woe is past; behold, the third woe is coming quickly.

Woe. See 8:13. The Greek term *ouai* is "an interjection denoting pain or displeasure."[40] Here the word is used as a substantive (a noun) and carries the sense of a calamity that occurs.[41] Walvoord writes, "As an aftermath to the resurrection of the two witnesses, the Scriptures record that a great earthquake occurs in which a tenth part of the city of Jerusalem falls and seven thousand men are killed. . . . With this event, the second woe is brought to its completion and is evidently regarded as the final phase of the sixth trumpet. The third woe contained in the seventh trumpet is announced as coming quickly. The end of the age is rapidly approaching."[42]

11:15 The kingdom of the world has become the kingdom of our Lord, and of His Christ; and He will reign forever and ever.

The kingdom of the world. This will be the kingdom of the Antichrist, which is mentioned in Daniel 7:23: "The fourth beast will be a fourth kingdom on the earth, which will be different from all the other kingdoms, and it will devour the whole earth and tread it down and crush it."

The kingdom of our Lord, and of His Christ. But the messianic kingdom will supersede the kingdom of the Antichrist. To the Son of Man will be "given dominion, glory and a kingdom, that all the peoples, nations, and men of every language might serve Him. . . . And His kingdom is one which will not be destroyed" (Dan. 7:14).

11:17 Thou hast taken Thy great power and hast begun to reign.

This verse and verse 15 may seem at first glance to be saying that right at that moment Christ will begin to reign. However, this should be understood instead as a heavenly preview of what will happen soon after the Tribulation.

11:18 The nations were enraged, and Thy wrath came, and the time came for the dead to be judged, and the time to give their reward to Thy bond-servants the prophets and to the saints and to those who fear Thy name.

The nations were enraged. The world will know the end is drawing near. Being under the severe wrath of God, people will sense that a climactic moment is coming soon, and so they will be further enraged against God.

Thy wrath came. This may refer to the beginning of the Tribulation. The world will realize that it is in a period of trial that will end in judgment on those who rebel against God.

The time came for the dead to be judged. The word "came" is not in the Greek, so the phrase reads, "the time for the dead to be judged." In other words, as stated in 20:11–15, the dead will be raised to be judged, and that will occur after the millennial kingdom.

The time to give their reward. The Lord's bond-servants, that is, the prophets and the saints, will be rewarded. This is probably referring to those believers who will have suffered during the Tribulation and will have been faithful to the Lord. Verse 18 is a kind of preview of events yet to come.

SATAN, THE WOMAN WHO IS ISRAEL, AND THE MESSIAH

Synopsis

(12:1–2) John saw the woman Israel wrapped in the glory that God originally gave to the twelve tribes. And she was about to give birth to a child.

(12:3–4) But when the nation was about to bring forth the promised Messiah, Satan, the red Dragon, pursued her to devour the child.

(12:5–6) But the prophesied Son came forth, who will rule the nations with a rod of iron. And the woman, the nation Israel, will flee into the wilderness and be hidden by God for three and a half years.

(12:7–12) The scene moves into the heavenlies where the archangel Michael and his angelic host will battle with the Dragon and his fallen angelic forces. The demons and Satan will be cast from the heavens down to earth, where they will deceive the nations. The Dragon, Satan, the accuser of believers, will be defeated when Christ will come and establish the kingdom of God on earth. Knowing that his time will be short, the Devil will come against the earth with great wrath.

(12:13–17) The Dragon will persecute the woman Israel, but in the Tribulation many of the Jewish people will be protected from him. And yet Satan will be enraged in his attempt to destroy the Jewish nation and her offspring, especially those who at that time will be trusting in Jesus.

12:1. And a great sign appeared in heaven: a woman clothed with the sun, and the moon under her feet, and on her head a crown of twelve stars;

Great sign. This is the first of two "signs" mentioned in this chapter (see also v. 3). Although there are many interpretations as to whom this sign is referring, the most consistent with the context is that the "woman" represents Israel. Walvoord states:

> The description of the woman as clothed with the sun and the moon is an allusion to Genesis 37:9–11, where these heavenly bodies represent Jacob and Rachel, thereby identifying the woman with the fulfillment of the Abrahamic Covenant. In the same context, the stars represent the patriarchs, the sons of Jacob. The symbolism may extend beyond this to represent in some sense the glory of Israel and her ultimate triumph over her enemies.
>
> This identification of the woman as Israel seems to be supported by the evidence from this chapter. Israel is obviously the source from which have come many of the blessings of God including the Bible, Christ, and the apostles. The twelve stars seem to refer to the twelve tribes. The persecution of the woman coincides with the persecution of Israel.[43]

12:3 And another sign appeared in heaven: and behold, a great red dragon having seven heads and ten horns, and on his heads were seven diadems.

Another sign. Satan attempted to upstage Israel by being a counter sign, "another sign." The seven heads on the Dragon represent seven kings, who will increase their aggression and their control over the nations of the earth (17:10–11). The ten horns represent the nations over which these kings rule. They will soon consolidate their power and receive a kingdom with the Beast for a short period (v. 12).

12:4 And his tail swept away a third of the stars of heaven, and threw them to the earth.

A third of the stars of heaven. Some commentators say this verse describes something that will occur in the Tribulation, but it may be preferable to say that this is recalling what happened in Satan's original fall, the same thing Jesus referred to when He said, "I was watching Satan fall from heaven like lightning" (Luke 10:18). Ezekiel, too, spoke of this fall: "I have cast you [the anointed cherub] as profane from the mountain of God" (Ezek. 28:16). See page 153.

12:6 [The woman will] be nourished for one thousand two hundred and sixty days.

Be nourished. This verse looks again to the second half of the Tribulation, so that obviously a great period of time will lapse between verses 5 and 6, when God will protect Israel from Satan's attempts to destroy her. This is not unusual in Bible prophecy. Walvoord notes, "Insomuch as Israel is in comparative tranquillity and safety in the first three and one-half years of Daniel's seventieth week (Dan. 9:27), the reference must be to the preservation of a portion of the nation Israel through the great tribulation to await the second coming of Christ."[44]

12:7 And there was war in heaven, Michael and his angels waging war with the dragon. And the dragon and his angels waged war.

War in heaven. Verses 7–9 may be a kind of flashback to the fall of Satan in eternity past. Or more likely, Satan will be cast down from heaven to the earth in the middle of the Tribulation. He has always deceived the nations (v. 9) and weakened them (Isa. 14:12). But his most energetic efforts to deceive the world will come about in the second half of the Tribulation. See page 157.

12:10 The accuser of our brethren has been thrown down.

Accuser of our brethren. See page 156.

12:11 And they overcame him because of the blood of the Lamb and because of the word of their testimony, and they did not love their life even to death.

The blood of the Lamb. Believers in the Tribulation who will be accused by Satan will overcome him. His accusations will be fake because they will have trusted in the fact that the Lamb, Christ, shed His blood for them, and because they will be faithful to the Lord. Seiss writes:

A Lamb has bled, whose meritorious blood, weighed in all the strictness of eternal right, by which the carping malignity of hell itself is silenced, covers the whole amplitude of their deficiencies, and cleanses away all account of their sins. "Who shall lay anything to the charge of God's elect? It is God that justifieth. Who is he that condemneth? It is Christ that died." . . . This is the everlasting fortress of the saints; and this stands foremost of all the means by which the accuser and his hosts are driven back.[45]

12:12 Woe to the earth and the sea; because the devil has come down to you, having great wrath, knowing that he has only a short time.

Only a short time. At the time of this "casting down" of Satan, he will have only three and a half years left in the Tribulation period. This is determined by noting the next two verses, which state that Satan will intensify his attack on the Jews, and yet God will sovereignly protect them for "a time and times and half a time" (v. 14; cf. Dan. 7:25; 12:7). Since Satan knows the Scriptures, he will realize that his time is short before he will be bound (Rev. 20:1–2). Satan's "coming down" (12:12) does not refer to his original fall from the presence of God, for he has been roaming the earth since at least the time Adam was created and accusing believers before God in heaven. The "coming down" more than likely refers to the fact that in the Tribulation he will intensify his efforts on the earth to destroy Israel.

12:14 And the two wings of the great eagle were given to the woman.

The great eagle. God will supernaturally enable Israel to escape quickly into the wilderness where God will protect her from Satan's attacks. As Walvoord writes, "The woman is described as being given two wings of a great eagle in order to enable her to fly into the wilderness into her place. . . . The same flight is indicated in Matthew 24:16 where Christ exhorts those in Judea to flee to the mountains. . . . Verse 14 implies that there is some supernatural care of Israel during this period."[46]

12:15 And the serpent poured water like a river out of his mouth after the woman, so that he might cause her to be swept away with the flood.

The serpent poured water like a river. In the Old Testament, Satan, the Dragon, is portrayed as a sea monster (Ezek. 29:3; 32:2–3; Ps. 74:13). Some have surmised that in the Tribulation Satan will employ water in some way in an attempt to drown or destroy the woman Israel. Others suggest the water is a figurative way of referring to human armies that Satan will use against Israel.

12:16 The earth helped the woman, and the earth opened its mouth and drank up the river which the dragon poured out of his mouth.

The earth helped the woman. "Whether the exact meaning of these two verses can be determined with certainty, the implication is that Satan strives with all his power to persecute and exterminate the people of Israel. By divine intervention, both natural and supernatural means are used to circumvent this program and to carry a remnant of Israel to safety through their time of great tribulation."[47]

> **12:17** The dragon was enraged with the woman, and went off to make war with the rest of her offspring.

The dragon was enraged with the woman. When Satan realizes that God is moving to intervene and deliver the Jewish people from his grip, he will be furious. Satan still will think he will be capable of defeating the Lord's plans to deliver Israel. The Devil believes he can win!

[He] went off to make war with the rest of her offspring. This seems to imply that Satan will move across the earth to find believing Jews so that he can kill them. His first attack may begin with those Israelites who will flee to the desert for safety. But now all Jews everywhere will be his target.

THE KINGDOM OF THE BEAST AND THE FALSE PROPHET

Synopsis

(13:1–10) This entire chapter addresses the revelation of the Beast (or Antichrist), who is first mentioned in 11:7, and the "other beast" who later is called the False Prophet (16:13). This first Beast is part of the seven-head and ten-horn confederation controlled by Satan, the red Dragon. The Beast is described as a powerful being with multiple strengths characteristic of a leopard, bear, and lion. Satan will give him great power and a throne having great authority. The Beast will appear to be assassinated but will live. This supposed miracle gives him added authority to lead people to worship him. For three and a half years he will have miraculous-like authority, while uttering arrogant words and blasphemies. He will make war against God's saints, and everyone on earth will worship him except those whose names are written in the Book of Life.

(13:11–18) This second Beast has been called the religious beast. He will cause the entire world to worship the "first beast, whose fatal wound was healed." He will perform what will appear to be great signs, even having fire come down out of heaven. By these signs he will deceive people and incite them to make an image to the first Beast who will be wounded but who will "come to life." This religious leader will even be able to make the image speak. Those who do not pay homage to the first Beast will be slain. Followers of the first Beast must place a mark on their right hand or on

their forehead to show their allegiance to him. The "number" of the Beast will be 666. Only believers who are living at that time may fully understand the significance of this number.

13:2 And the beast which I saw was like a leopard, and his feet were like those of a bear, and his mouth like the mouth of a lion. And the dragon gave him his power and his throne and great authority.

And the beast . . . was like a leopard . . . a bear . . . a lion. No doubt the animal symbolism in this verse is drawn from Daniel 7:4–8. In that passage the lion referred to Babylon, the bear to Medo-Persia, and the leopard to Greece, the empire of Alexander the Great. All these were world empires of greater or lesser power. In Daniel the lion represents royal power, the bear power and ferociousness, and the leopard great speed. All the characteristics of these world empires will be wrapped up into one, in the future world ruler—the Beast. In the Great Tribulation the revived Roman Empire will have the majesty of the lion, the power of the bear, the quickness of the leopard.

Dragon. The Dragon is Satan himself (see 12:9 and 20:2). In 12:3 he is called the "great red dragon." He will empower the Beast, the Antichrist.

13:3 And I saw one of his heads as if it had been slain, and his fatal wound was healed.

Fatal wound was healed. One of the Beast's heads, not necessarily the Beast himself, will receive a fatal wound. Since the Beast will be the ruler of a ten-empire confederacy, this one head would simply be one of his empires. As Walvoord notes, "It is significant that one of the heads is wounded to death but that the beast itself is not said to be dead. It is questionable whether Satan has the power to restore to life one who has died, even though his power is great. Far more probable is the explanation that this is the revived Roman Empire in view."[48]

13:4 And they worshipped the dragon, because he gave his authority to the beast.

They worshiped the Dragon. This is what Satan has desired all along. Before the creation of the world he had said, "I will ascend above the heights of the clouds; I will make myself like the Most High" (Isa. 14:14). In the Tribulation satanic worship will occur. God gave His authority to His Son, and so Satan will give his authority to the Beast.

13:5 And there was given to him a mouth speaking arrogant words and blasphemies; and authority to act for forty-two months was given to him.

A mouth speaking arrogant words and blasphemies. The Beast will have free reign to blaspheme God and all that is sacred. Paul called the Antichrist the "man of lawlessness . . . the son of destruction, who opposes and exalts himself above every so-called god or object of worship" (2 Thess. 2:3–4). He will sit in the temple displaying himself as God and he will act "in accord with the activity of Satan, with all power and signs and false wonders" (v. 9). The reason people will so easily follow the Beast is that the world will be deceived by gross wickedness: "they did not receive the love of the truth so as to be saved" (v. 10).

13:7 And it was given to him to make war with the saints and to overcome them.

Make war with the saints. The Beast will attempt to slay all believers in the Tribulation. Many of them will become martyrs because of his great hatred of them and the Lord.

13:10 If anyone is destined for captivity, to captivity he goes; if anyone kills with the sword, with the sword he must be killed. Here is the perseverance and the faith of the saints.

To captivity he goes. This verse seems difficult at first, but Allen explains it this way, "This is a restatement of the law of sowing and reaping that is taught clearly throughout Scripture. There are various statements of it and allusions to it in many Scriptures and most obviously in Jer 15:2; 43:11; Zech. 11:9. . . . The beast, in implacable hatred of Israel and the saints, will introduce unjust detention (captivity) and unrighteous execution using legal processes (the sword) for the 'crime' of refusing worship to the state."[49]

Here is the perseverance and the faith of the saints. Allen adds, "In the confidence that God is working out His purposes and that their persecutors are moving to just retribution from God the saints display a supernatural 'endurance' and 'faith,' as saints have done down the ages. . . . Suffering right to the point of death by martyrdom, these saints cling with unshakable confidence to the fact that Christ is coming and that the wrongs of earth will be finally righted."[50]

13:11 And I saw another beast coming up out of the earth; and he had two horns like a lamb, and he spoke as a dragon.

Another beast. This second beast will be a partner with the political Beast. He is apparently a religious leader who will have a certain docility (like a lamb), but yet he will be violent and will have dragon-like authority. This second beast is also called the False Prophet (20:10).

13:14 And he deceives those who dwell on the earth because of the signs which it was given him to perform in the presence of the beast, telling those who dwell on the earth to make an image to the beast who had the wound of the sword and has come to life.

Image. The Greek *eikōn* is used nine times in Revelation (13:14, 15 [twice]; 14:9, 11; 15:2; 16:2; 19:20; 20:4), and each time it refers to the image of the first Beast. Thomas writes:

Following the anarthrous eikona *(eikona),* the rest of the references are pointing back to this first mention. Whether this is an image of an emperor on a coin as that of Caesar in Christ's time (Matt. 22:20) or a statue to which people must bow down, much [like] that of Nebuchadnezzar in Daniel 3, is not clear. Since the pattern of this demand for worship comes from Daniel (Dan. 3:4–6), the latter appears more probable. In John's day, the cities of Asia, Pergamum in particular, had temples erected for the worship of emperors. Why should this great ruler of the future not have at least a full-blown statue toward which people could direct their worship?[51]

13:15 And there was given to him to give breath to the image of the beast, that the image of the beast might even speak.

The word translated "life" (Gr., *pneuma*) [v.15] as in the Authorized Version, is obviously an incorrect translation, as *pneuma,* commonly translated "spirit" or "breath," is quite different from *zōē,* which means "life." Expositors usually hold that the extraordinary powers given by Satan to the false prophet do not extend to giving life to that which does not possess life, because this is a prerogative of God alone. The intent of the passage seems to be that the image has the appearance of life manifested in breathing, but actually it may be no more than a robot. . . . Whether completely natural in its explanation, or whether some supernatural power is used to create the impression of life, the image apparently is quite convincing to the mass of humanity and helps to turn them to a worship of the first beast as their god.[52]

13:18 Here is wisdom. Let him who has understanding calculate the number of the beast, for the number is that of a man; and his number is six hundred and sixty-six.

Six hundred and sixty-six. Many attempts have been made to identify the Antichrist based on the meaning of this number. However, this verse seems to suggest that the number will be understood only by those who in the Tribulation will be spiritually wise (through their knowledge of Scripture) and thus able to discern that this is a false Christ. Thomas writes, "The inescapable conclusion is that the expression means this is a mysterious hint about a man whose name gives them number 666. It is the name of the beast as well as that of one of the beast's heads. He is a king or emperor who at times in the narrative is emblematic of the empire he rules."[53]

PARENTHESIS: PREVIEW OF THE END OF THE TRIBULATION

Synopsis

(14:1–5) These verses seem to leap ahead to the glorious day when the 144,000 Jewish martyrs will stand before Christ on Mount Zion. On their foreheads they will be marked by the name of Christ and of His Father. These righteous witnesses will sing a new song before the throne of the Lord and other heavenly beings. Only they will know the meaning of the song and have a right to sing it. These witnesses will have kept themselves morally clean while on earth, and they will be counted as firstfruits to God and the Lamb.

(14:6–7) At this stage in the Tribulation a final universal appeal to salvation will be given by an angel who will fly in midheaven preaching the gospel to those on earth. This most dramatic event will demonstrate the grace of God in calling people to turn to the Lord.

(14:8–12) Another angel will announce an important event in the progress of the Tribulation. Babylon the great, who will make the nations take part in her immorality, will be forced to drink of the wine of God's wrath, and she will be brought down. A third angel will add the fact that all who will have consorted with the Beast and who will have received his mark will also drink the wine of the wrath of God, and they will be tormented with fire and brimstone forever.

(14:13) In the middle of John's reminders of coming judgment, the prophet John wrote of the blessedness of those "who die in the Lord from now on!" They are promised rest from their labors, and their deeds will be rewarded.

(14:14–20) John continued to write about the imminent wrath of God that will come as sure as the reaper's sickle cuts down the grain. A call for the sharp sickle will come from the strong angel who is over the altar, saying, "The earth's grapes are ripe for harvest." The sickle of God's wrath over the earth will be swung, and its harvesting will be completed at the final conflict, the battle of Armageddon, where outside of Jerusalem the blood will come up to the horses' bridles, "for a distance of two hundred miles."

14:1 The Lamb was standing on Mount Zion, and with Him one hundred and forty-four thousand, having His name and the name of His Father written on their foreheads.

Mount Zion. This was the ancient residence of the kings of Israel in Jerusalem. The 144,000 Jewish witnesses (7:1–8) will have a special rendezvous with Christ on Mount Zion after their testimony on earth is finished. Probably they will be martyred, as suggested by the clause "they were purchased from the earth" (14:3), and the words "as many as do not worship the image of the beast [were] to be killed" (13:15). See page 175. "The vanguard who had borne the brunt of the struggle would enjoy a special bliss of their own. . . . Instead of the beast, the Lamb; instead of the beast's followers and their mark, the Lamb's followers with the divine name; instead of the pagan earth, Mount Zion. . . ."[54]

His name and the name of His Father written on their foreheads. The 144,000 will belong to Christ and to the heavenly Father in a very special way. Their presentation of the gospel in the Tribulation will have great authority and apparently will be heard worldwide. Newell calls their martyrdom "a beautiful badge of blessedness."[55]

14:2 And I heard a voice from heaven, like the sound of many waters and like the sound of loud thunder, and the voice which I heard was like the sound of harpists playing on their harps.

Harps. The harp *(kithara)* is mentioned in 5:8 and in 15:2 ("harps of God"). Thomas writes that harps are "the traditional instruments of Psalmody (e.g., Pss. 33:2; 92:3)."[56] The quality of the voice from heaven was like melodious harp music.

According to Josephus, the harp was played with the fingers and had 12 strings, in contrast to ten strings of the lyre, which was played with a plectrum.

These two instruments were the most important ones in the temple orchestra, and without which no public religious ceremony could be held. The harp seems to have been a vertical angular harp, larger in size, louder, and lower in pitch than the lyre. The harp is mentioned frequently in the Book of Psalms: 33:2; 57:8; 71:22; 81:2; 92:3; 108:2; 144:9; 150:3.[57]

14:4 These are the ones who have not been defiled with women, for they are chaste.

Chaste. Expositors are split over whether the word "chaste" (Greek, *parthenos,* literally "virgin") means spiritual virginity (i.e., nonidolatrous) or physical virginity. Thomas favors the latter view. "The most probable explanation of *parthenoi* is that it refers to celibates, i.e., it excludes married men. The peculiar demands of the time require celibacy. This is the basic meaning of the word, and it also agrees with the meaning of defilement reached earlier in v. 4. . . . This in no way degrades marriage, but is in special recognition of the critical times through which this group must pass."[58]

14:6 And I saw another angel flying in midheaven, having an eternal gospel to preach.

Eternal gospel. The only way people in the Tribulation will be saved is by the gospel that is here labeled "eternal." What Christ did at the cross carries over into all ages of history.

14:7 Fear God, and give Him glory, because the hour of His judgment has come.

Judgment has come. Unbelievers living in that terrible period will experience the terror of the wrath of God. So an angel will plead with them to fear God and receive the salvation offered before it is too late.

14:8 Fallen, fallen is Babylon the great.

Babylon the great. This is a preview of what is discussed in Revelation 17–18. By this time, deep into the Tribulation, the influence of Babylon will have become pervasive and seductive. See page 147.

14:14 And I looked, and behold, a white cloud, and sitting on the cloud was one like a son of man, having a golden crown on His head, and a sharp sickle in His hand.

Sickle. Sickles were used in biblical days for cutting grain, but on occasion they were used for pruning grapevines (14:18). Cleveland writes that, "The earliest type seems to have been constructed of wood. It resembled our modern scythes, though smaller, and its cutting edge was made of flint. Later sickles were constructed of metal."[59] Here John used the sickle as a symbol of God's judgment on the unbelieving earth.

14:18 Put in your sharp sickle, and gather the clusters from the vine of the earth, because her grapes are ripe.

Grapes are ripe. The fact that the grapes will be "in the prime" or "at the peak"[60] indicates that the earth will be due for God's judgment in the Tribulation because of its inhabitants' unrighteousness.

14:20 And the wine press was trodden outside the city, and blood came out from the wine press, up to the horses' bridles, for a distance of two hundred miles.

Horses' bridles. There is no reason to take the "horses' bridles" as figurative here, as some writers do. Newell writes:

> Ah, such a fearful sight! Rivers of human blood "unto the bridles of the horses"! Yet it will be. If Josephus could say that when Jerusalem was taken by Titus, the Roman soldiers "obstructed the very lanes with dead bodies; and made the whole city run down with blood, to such a degree indeed that the fires of many of the houses were quenched with these men's blood" (Wars: 6, 8)—what folly to doubt this word of God that *a river* of Blood will run when the Son of God tramples the nations of *all the earth* in the Almighty's anger![61]

THE GREAT CHORUS
OF VICTORY BEFORE
THE LORD

Synopsis

(15:1–8) This short chapter introduces the final stage of wrath on the world, described as the seven golden bowls full of the wrath of God. With these judgments, the wrath of God will be finished. The prophecy begins with John observing a large number of saved people standing before God holding harps. They will sing the song of Moses, which speaks of the great and marvelous works of the Lord God, the Almighty. The song tells of the Lord's glorious name and holiness and how His righteous acts will cause the nations to come and worship before Him. The temple in heaven will be opened and will be filled with smoke "from the glory of God and from His power." No one can enter the temple until these seven bowl judgments are completed.

15:2 And I saw, as it were, a sea of glass mixed with fire.

Sea of glass. See 4:6. The Greek word for "glass" could be translated "glassy, [or] crystal."[62] The same phrase is used in 4:6, where Rienecker states, "It was a pavement of glass resembling an expanse of water which was clear as rock crystal."[63] Thomas writes this about the sea of glass: "A sea of glass, probably the one already encountered in 4:6 even though no article appears, is the first thing to meet John's eye. The four living beings are here (15:7) just as they were in the earlier picture of heaven. As stated earlier, this sea of glass is an emblem of 'the splendor and majesty of God on His throne that sets Him apart from all His creation, a separation stemming from His purity and absolute holiness, which He shares with no one else.'"[64]

15:3 And they sang the song of Moses the bond-servant of God and the song of the Lamb.

Song of Moses. This hymn of praise, to be sung by the martyred saints in heaven, is called the "song of Moses" as well as the "song of the Lamb." This has often been identified with the song recorded in Exodus 15, although others have suggested that Moses' song recorded in Deuteronomy 32 may be the one referred to here. As Walvoord writes, "Both passages, however, ascribe praise to God and are similar in many ways to the hymn here recorded."[65]

15:6 And the seven angels who had the seven plagues came out of the temple, clothed in linen, clean and bright.

Clothed in white linen. The garments of God's elect angels reflects their righteousness. Thomas writes:

> *Linon* is a product from which linen is made (i.e., flax), and *byssinon* is the material itself (i.e., linen). Both καθαρὸν (*katharon*, "clean") and λαμπρὸν (*lampron*, "bright") appear again to describe the garments of the bride of Christ (19:8) who composes His army that is so clothed when they return with Him (19:14). The purity of their clothing befits the purpose of their mission which is purification. "Bright" or "glistening" is a way to describe angelic clothing (cf. Acts 10:30).[66]

15:8 And the temple was filled with smoke from the glory of God and from His power; and no one was able to enter the temple until the seven plagues of the seven angels were finished.

Temple filled with smoke. In the Old Testament smoke has often been a symbol of God's glory and presence (Exod. 19:18; 40:34–38; 1 Kings 8:10–11; 2 Chron. 5:11–14; 7:1–3; Ezek. 11:23; 44:4). This "Shekinah" glory filled the tabernacle when it was completed, and later filled Solomon's temple when it replaced the tabernacle as the worship center of Israel. Ezekiel saw this manifestation of God's glory depart from the temple just before the Babylonian captivity (10:1–22; 11:22–23).

THE SEVEN BOWLS OF WRATH

Synopsis

(16:1–2) The first bowl of wrath will affect the entire world and will bring malignant sores on people who will have the mark of the Beast and worship his image.

(16:3) When the second angel pours out his bowl, the ocean will become blood-like, or polluted, so that "every living thing in the sea" will die.

(16:4–7) When the third bowl is poured out, it will pollute the rivers and springs of water. This action will be justified because the enemy "poured out the blood of saints and prophets, and Thou hast given them blood to drink. They deserve it." The judgments of the Lord are "true and righteous."

(16:8–9) The fourth bowl will be poured out on the sun, and people on earth will be scorched with fire. Instead of repenting and giving glory to God, they will blaspheme Him.

(16:10–11) The fifth bowl will be poured out on the Beast by the angel. His kingdom will become darkened, and people will gnaw their tongues because of the intense pain. Again, they will blaspheme God and will not repent.

(16:12) The sixth angel will pour out the sixth bowl on the Euphrates River, and it will dry up so that kings and their armies from the east may cross.

(16:13–16) Then John saw unclean spirits coming from the mouths of the Dragon, the Beast, and the False Prophet. These spirits will influence the kings of the earth to come together for war against God in the Battle of Armageddon.

(16:17–21) The seventh and final bowl of wrath will be poured into the air, and a voice from heaven will announce, "It is done." After flashes of lightning, peals of thunder, and an earthquake, "the great city" will be torn into three parts. Other cities will fall, and Babylon the great will be remembered before God. Huge hailstones will fall on people, but they will continue to blaspheme God and refuse to repent of their sins.

16:2 And the first angel went and poured out his bowl into the earth . . . upon the men who had the mark of the beast and who worshiped his image.

Who worshiped his image. It is amazing how blind humanity will become, how superstitious and spiritually ignorant. For they will turn to an image rather than to God.

16:3 And every living thing in the sea died.

Every living thing. Revelation is full of such phrases that clearly tell us that the Tribulation is worldwide in scope and not simply some localized happening. This is a horrible scene, picturing the death of all biological life in the oceans.

16:5 Righteous art Thou . . . because Thou didst judge these things.

Righteous art Thou. God is declared righteous and just in bringing all judgment on the unsaved world.

16:8 It was given [to the sun] to scorch men with fire.

Scorch men. It has been suggested that one of the means God will use to bring this about is the removal of the ozone layer that encircles the earth. Ozone retards the sun's radiation, and if it is depleted, such scorching would take place.

16:12 The great river, the Euphrates; and its water was dried up, that the way might be prepared for the kings from the east.

The Euphrates. Running for almost two thousand miles from Turkey through present-day Syria and Iraq to the Persian Gulf, the Euphrates River serves as a kind of cultural barrier to armies to the east. In places it is almost two-thirds of a mile wide. In the Tribulation God will dry it up so that kings from the east will be able to cross it on their way to Israel.

> **16:15** Blessed is the one who stays awake and keeps his garments, lest he walk about naked and men see his shame.

Blessed is the one who stays awake. Several times John stopped in the reporting of his visions to warn the reader to consider all that will happen and to remain alert. His words will have direct, personal application for those who will face these horrible events in the Tribulation. The apostle was urging those readers to consider the salvation that is available only in Christ.

> **16:16** And they gathered them together to the place which in Hebrew is called Har-Magedon.

They gathered them together. Demonic spirits will perform miraculous signs (vv. 14–15) to influence Israel. Their purpose will be to exterminate once and for all the Jewish people, who belong to the Lord.

Har-Magedon. The "hill of Megiddo" lies at the northwestern tip of the Esdraelon or Jezreel Valley in northern Israel about fifteen miles southwest of the Sea of Galilee. The valley is a flat plain that makes the land of Israel vulnerable to invasion forces. The hill is a mound or tel on which more than twenty ancient cities have been built on top of each other. This was a defensive fortress even during the time of Solomon and before. Megiddo, which means "place of crowds," was originally a Canaanite fortified area. On this plain and down toward Jerusalem, the final great world battle, with millions of troops involved, will be fought when Christ returns to the earth.

> **16:18** There were flashes of lightning and sounds and peals of thunder; and there was a great earthquake, such as there had not been since man came to be upon the earth.

A great earthquake. This earthquake will be one of the most horrendous events to strike the earth since the Flood in Genesis 6–9. Islands will vanish, mountains will be leveled (Rev. 16:20), huge hailstones will fall (v. 21), and the planet itself will reel under the terrible wrath of God.

> **16:19** And the great city was split into three parts, and the cities

of the nations fell. And Babylon the great was remembered before God.

The great city was split into three parts. Some scholars believe this city is Jerusalem, and others suggest that it is Babylon. Scott believes it is the city of Rome.[67] However, since "Babylon the great" is mentioned in this verse, it makes more sense to say that "the great city" here is Babylon.

The cities of the nations fell. Scott writes:

> The seats and centres of Gentile commerce—the political world apart from and outside the Roman earth—are involved in the general ruin, which overtakes all human combinations. From the building of Babel (Gen. 11.1–9) till the day and hour of the seventh [bowl] human progress in civilization, in religion, in social and political government, in the arts, in science, in literature, has been the aim. Here we witness judgment on all that men have built up in these and other spheres of life. . . . What a blow to the pride and ambition of man![68]

Babylon the great. Central to this seventh bowl judgment is the fall of Babylon. This event was mentioned in 14:8 and even prefigured in the harvesting mentioned in 14:14–20. Though it seems sometimes as if God forgets, He remembers the persecution and oppression of His own. But Babylon's final days are yet to come in John's prophecy. Punishment is reserved for Babylon, and her downfall will come (17:16; 18:8), with the final collapse narrated in 19:18–21.

THE DOOM
OF BABYLON

Synopsis

(17:1–6) Babylon and her religion is described here. She is called the great harlot who makes the kings and inhabitants of earth drink of her immorality. In a vision John saw her sitting on the scarlet beast who has control of the seven heads and ten horns. She will be decked out in expensive apparel, but the golden cup in her hand will be full of the unclean things of her immorality. She is called "Babylon the great, the mother of harlots and of the abominations of the earth." She will be drunk with the blood of the saints and witnesses of Jesus.

(17:7–13) John paused in his narration to describe the seven heads and ten horns who are part of the kingdom of the Beast. Their one purpose will be to give their power to the Beast.

(17:14–18) In their combined efforts they will wage war against Christ the Lamb. But He will overthrow them "because He is Lord of lords and King of kings." Returning to the subject of Babylon the harlot, John explained that she will have great influence over "peoples and multitudes and nations and tongues." The ten horns and the Beast will turn on her "and will burn her up with fire."

17:1 Come here, I shall show you the judgment of the great harlot who sits on many waters.

The great harlot. See page 147.

Many waters. See verse 15.

17:3 I saw a woman sitting on a scarlet beast, full of blasphemous names, having seven heads and ten horns.

Scarlet beast. Here, even the Antichrist, the Beast, is pictured wearing the purple garb of royalty.

Seven heads and ten horns. Temporarily, the Beast and the revived Roman Empire will support Babylon. They will use her for their purposes. See pages 145–49.

17:4 And the woman was clothed in purple and scarlet.

Purple and scarlet. Though a harlot, she will act as if she is royalty to be honored rather than scorned.

17:5 A name was written, a mystery, "BABYLON THE GREAT, THE MOTHER OF HARLOTS AND OF THE ABOMINATIONS OF THE EARTH."

A mystery. The word *mystery* was actually a part of her name (see NIV). This suggests that there is now given new revelation about Babylon, and this probably has to do with the great evil nature of the system itself. In addition, Babylon is probably the place from which all false religious beliefs had their beginning. From Babylon stemmed a religious rebellion that has blinded people everywhere so that they are in opposition to the true God. Thus Babylon is a place, but it is much more. Man's widespread rebellion against God began at the town of Babel (Gen. 10:9–10), where later the city of Babylon was built. Its false teachings have continually plagued Israel, the church, and the world.

17:6 I saw the woman drunk with the blood of the saints, and with the blood of the witnesses of Jesus.

Drunk with the blood of the saints. John pointed out that many of the believers who will be martyred in the Tribulation will be slain by this system. To be drunk means that she will be satiated with the blood of the saints and will take great pleasure in their deaths. It must be remembered that the leaders of the revived Roman Empire will be working with her in this slaughter, and they will be pleased with the results of her killing.

17:8 The beast that you saw was and is not, and is about to come up out of the abyss and to go to destruction.

Was and is not, and is about to come up. Thomas best explains this puzzle: "Each head of the beast is a partial incarnation of satanic power that rules for a given period, so the beast can exist on earth without interruption in the form of seven consecutive kingdoms, but he can also be nonexistent at a given moment in the form of one of an empire's kings. The nonexistent beast in verse 8 must therefore be a temporarily absent king over the empire that will exist in the future."[69]

17:9–10 The seven heads are seven mountains on which the woman sits, and they are seven kings; five have fallen, one is, the other has not yet come.

Seven mountains. While writers have suggested many interpretations of these seven mountains, it seems best to understand the seven heads and mountains as seven empires that follow each other, and that the seven kings (v. 10) will be the heads and personifications of those empires. These would be seven Gentile kingdoms that have dominated the world throughout human history. They could be Egypt (or Babylonia, Gen. 10:8–11), Assyria, Babylon, Persia, Greece, Rome, and this coming future kingdom of the Beast.[70] If this view is correct, then the angel was saying to John that the harlot religion of Babylon has dominated these kingdoms.

17:14 These will wage war against the Lamb, and the Lamb will overcome them, because He is Lord of lords and King of kings, and those who are with Him are the called and chosen and faithful.

Wage war against the Lamb. These kings will seek together to prevent the reign of Christ on earth. They will make His defeat their one purpose, but because He is the Almighty Lord and King, their efforts will all come to nothing (see 19:15–19).

The called and chosen and faithful. When Christ returns to the earth, church-age saints will return with Him. They are those who have been chosen by Him in eternity past. In addition, Tribulation saints will accompany Him when He defeats His enemies. Though facing terrible persecution in the Tribulation, they will still be faithful, even as many face martyrdom and death. Yet, many of those who will believe in Christ in the Tribulation will survive that terrible time and will enter the kingdom without facing death.

17:16 And the ten horns . . . and the beast . . . will make her desolate and naked, and will eat her flesh and will burn her up with fire.

Will make her desolate and naked. The dominant Babylonian system will not last forever. After using her for their purposes, the confederation of nations and the Beast will bring her to her end. It is easy for false loyalty to turn to hatred and envy. The apostle John was not informed as to the source of that hatred, but it could be envy and opposition to her control of the nations. The violence by which they will destroy her is excessive, to say the least.

17:17 For God has put it in their hearts to execute His purpose by having a common purpose, and by giving their kingdom to the beast, until the words of God should be fulfilled.

For God has put it in their hearts to execute His purpose. God is sovereign even in His providential and mysterious manipulation of evil. He is not the author of sin, but He can use it to serve His purposes. In Romans 9:17 the apostle Paul minced no words about this when he quoted Exodus 9:16: "For the Scripture says to Pharaoh, 'For this very purpose I raised you up, to demonstrate My power in you, and that My name might be proclaimed throughout the whole earth.'"

Giving their kingdom to the beast. Each king and leader will turn over his realm to the Beast for the betterment of the empire. Together the "beast and the kings of the earth and their armies" (19:19) will come against Christ when He returns to earth.

17:18 And the woman whom you saw is the great city, which reigns over the kings of the earth.

The great city, which reigns over the kings of the earth. The identification of Babylon has been an issue of contention for generations among biblical scholars. The Reformers and other older writers held that Babylon represents the Roman Catholic system. More recent evangelical scholars contend that, to be consistent hermeneutically, we must interpret Babylon as a revival of the ancient system that was geographically located in the Middle East, because she is called a city (17:18; 18:10, 16, 19, 21). The next chapter seems to give weight to this argument.

However, one could argue that John was focusing on the religious and immoral nature of Babylon to such an extent that he was referring to more than the mere rebuilding of the ancient city. Though chapter 18 seems to highlight her commercial wealth, John continued to stress her immoral influence on the nations and how she was involved in slaying the prophets and saints (18:24). This would seem to rule out the view that Babylon is a code name for Rome. Perhaps the identity of Babylon "the great city" will not be known until these things come to pass.

THE TERRIBLE FALL
OF BABYLON

Synopsis

(18:1–8) More pronouncements were given against Babylon by a second angel who came from heaven with great authority. He shouted "Fallen, fallen is Babylon the great!" He described how she will be dominated by demons and unclean spirits and will make the nations drink of the wine of her immorality. God's people will be urged not to take part in her sins. Plagues will come on her since her sins will have piled up as high as heaven. Babylon will be paid back with plagues, pestilence, mourning, and famine, and will be burned up by the Lord God.

(18:9–19) The kings of the earth, standing at a distance, will cry, "Woe, woe, the great city, Babylon, the strong city!" The merchants of earth, who have purchased her cargo, will also lament her torment and will say, "for in one hour such great wealth has been laid waste!" When shipmasters, passengers, and sailors see the smoke of her burning, they will say, "What city is like the great city?"

(18:20–24) Heaven, the saints, apostles, and prophets will rejoice over her because "God has pronounced judgment for you against her." Babylon will be thrown down, her musicians and craftsmen will be no longer, and the light from her will no longer shine, because "in her was found the blood of prophets and of saints and of all who have been slain on the earth."

18:2 A dwelling place of demons and a prison of every unclean spirit, and a prison of every unclean and hateful bird.

Demons and a prison of every unclean spirit. "Demons" and unclean spirits both refer to the fallen angels who now roam the earth, bringing torment and leading people into all kinds of sin. The adjective "unclean" implies that they foster and promote the most vile kinds of sin and impurity. See pages 158–59.

A prison of every unclean and hateful bird. These words may allude to Isaiah 13:21 in which Isaiah wrote that houses of the Babylonians "will be full of owls, ostriches also will live there." Isaiah added that Babylon's "fateful time also will soon come and her days will not be prolonged" (v. 22).

> **18:3** For all the nations have drunk of the wine of the passion of her immorality . . . and the merchants of the earth have become rich by the wealth of her sensuality.

The passion of her immorality. This theme about Babylon's immorality, which she spread to all the nations, is stated repeatedly in chapters 17 and 18. The Greek word for "immorality" *(porneia)* can be translated "fornication" or "lasciviousness" and refers to various forms of sexual sin.

The wealth of her sensuality. The word translated "sensuality" refers to fleshly luxury and self-indulgence. Babylon traded in both sin and "all things that were luxurious and splendid" (v. 14), including numerous kinds of expensive goods (vv. 12–16), and even the trade of "slaves and human lives" (v. 13).

> **18:7** To the degree that she glorified herself and lived sensuously, to the same degree give her torment and mourning; for she says in her heart, "I sit as a queen and I am not a widow, and will never see mourning."

She glorified herself. Because of her self-centered pride and her murdering of God's prophets and saints, she will be paid back double (v. 6) and will be consumed by fire (v. 8).

> **18:9** The kings of the earth, who committed acts of immorality and lived sensuously with her will . . . see the smoke of her burning.

The smoke of her burning. The city of Babylon will be burned (cf. 17:16), and it will apparently happen quickly. The rulers of the world will be "standing at a distance" when this judgment comes within a period of one hour (v. 10). Three times in this chapter John heard that judgment on Babylon will fall in "one hour" (vv. 10, 17, 19). And three times those who will see her fall (kings, merchants, and sailors) are said to be observing from a "distance" (vv. 10, 15, 17). Because Rome is only about fifteen miles from the sea, some interpreters say this viewing from a distance suggests that the city is Rome, not Babylon. They say it would be impossible for sea merchants in the Mediterranean Sea to see a conflagration of a city like Babylon several hundred miles away. However, since Babylon is on the Euphrates River, sea merchants will no doubt be near the city, having navigated up the Euphrates from the Persian Gulf.

18:19 All who had ships at sea became rich by her wealth.

Became rich by her wealth. In the Tribulation Babylon will be exporting both immorality and materialism. Her cargoes being sent out by ship will include many kinds of riches.

18:20 Rejoice over her, O heaven, and you saints . . . because God has pronounced judgment for you against her.

Judgment for you against her. There is a place for righteous indignation and vengeance. God's justice dictates that evil be punished. When Babylon is destroyed, the martyred in heaven will rejoice because justice will finally be carried out against her.

18:21 Thus will Babylon, the great city, be thrown down with violence, and will not be found any longer.

The destruction of Great Babylon is an illustrious exhibition of the truth and righteousness of the divine administrations. Often it would seem as if God had forgotten his word, or quite abandoned the earth, so great is the prosperity of the wicked, the triumph of injustice, the wrongs and afflictions which those who most honour him suffer. But it is not so. He is true. His ways are just. . . . The harlot has her day; but then comes her night with never a star of hope to rise upon her any more.[71]

18:23 All the nations were deceived by your sorcery.

Sorcery. The nations will think it will be safe to engage in commercial trade with Babylon. However, they will be deceived. Sorcery (Greek, *pharmakeia*) probably refers to pagan religious ceremonies, probably enhanced by drug-induced trances and mind-altering substances.

18:24 And in her was found the blood of prophets and of saints and of all who have been slain on the earth.

All who have been slain on the earth. In some way Babylon will have been responsible for all the Tribulation martyrs, even from the beginning of the seven-year period. Babylon may well be on the scene at the beginning of the Tribulation, though it is not mentioned until 14:8.

THE DEMISE OF
BABYLON AND THE
COMING OF CHRIST

Synopsis

*(19:1–6) From a great heavenly host the Lord will receive thunderous praise
for His great salvation, power, and glory. He will have judged with truth
and righteousness the great harlot who had corrupted the entire world,
and He will have avenged the blood of His bond-servants who died because of her. The twenty-four elders and the four living creatures will fall
down before His throne and say, "Amen, Hallelujah!" Another great multitude of His servants will shout praises to "the Lord our God, the Almighty, [who] reigns."*

*(19:7–10) Then the preparation for the marriage of the Lamb will take place.
The bride will be given fine linen, bright and clean, which are the righteous
acts of the saints. When the angel pronounced a blessing on those who are
invited to the marriage supper, John fell before his feet to worship him. The
angel responded by reminding John that he, too, is but a servant of God
just like John and the other brothers. "Worship God," the angel said.*

*(19:11–16) Suddenly heaven will open with Christ coming forth, riding on a
white horse. Called "Faithful and True," He will judge with righteousness.
His eyes will be like fire, He will wear many crowns, and His robe will have
been dipped in blood. And His name is the Word of God. With armies following Him from heaven, He will come to earth to smite the nations with*

*judgment and to rule them with a rod of iron. Other names of His are King
of Kings and Lord of Lords.*

*(19:17–18) Birds will be called together for the great supper of God, where
the lost will be slain at the Battle of Armageddon.*

*(19:19–20) The Beast, the False Prophet, and those who will have received
the beast's mark will all be cast into the lake of fire.*

(19:21) The rest of the unsaved will be slain by Christ Himself when He returns.

19:1–2 Hallelujah! Salvation and glory and power belong to our
God; because His judgments are true and righteous; for He has
judged the great harlot.

Hallelujah! This is a Hebrew composite word meaning "Praise the ever-
existing One!" The word is a triumphant shout used at the end of many of the
Psalms. The apostolic church picked this up for its use from the Hellenistic
synagogues, and it became familiar even to the most unlearned of the early
Christians. In this verse the thought of the coming doom of Babylon will
bring forth such praise. This is in fulfillment of Jeremiah 51:48–49: "'Then
heaven and earth and all that is in them will shout for joy over Babylon, for
the destroyers will come to her from the north,' declares the LORD. Indeed
Babylon is to fall for the slain of Israel, as also for Babylon the slain of all the
earth have fallen."

19:2 He has judged the great harlot who was corrupting the earth.

He has judged the great harlot. The religious influence and power of this
revived Babylon will be pervasive in the Tribulation. This is why two chapters
(17–18) describe her religious seduction on the entire world.

19:6 Hallelujah! For the Lord our God, the Almighty, reigns.

Hallelujah! This is the fourth time "Hallelujah" occurs in this chapter (vv.
1, 3–4, 6). The joy and praise of the saints at the Lord's return will be
magnificent.

19:7 The marriage of the Lamb has come and His bride has made
herself ready.

The marriage of the Lamb. This seems to relate to Matthew 25:1–13, which pictures the coming of the groom, the Messiah, to establish the kingdom of heaven on the earth. The ten virgins, five prepared for His coming and five unprepared, seem to represent Israel. Not all of the Jews will be ready for His arrival. Who then is the bride? Matthew did not specify who the bride will be, and neither is her identity given here in Revelation 19.

His bride has made herself ready. Probably the "marriage supper of the Lamb" (19:9) is the "wedding feast" that will begin the one-thousand-year kingdom.

> **19:9** Write, "Blessed are those who are invited to the marriage supper of the Lamb."

Blessed are those who are invited. Jesus said something similar in Luke 14:15: "Blessed is everyone who shall eat bread in the kingdom of God!" Comparing the wedding in Revelation 19 to weddings in the first century can help us identify the bride, as Walvoord explains:

> A wedding normally included these stages: (1) the legal consummation of the marriage by the parents of the bride and of the groom, with the payment of the dowry; (2) the bridegroom coming to claim his bride (as illustrated in Matt. 25:1–13 in the familiar Parable of the 10 Virgins); (3) the wedding supper (as illustrated in John 2:1–11) which was a several-day feast following the previous phase of the wedding.
>
> In Revelation 19:9 "the wedding supper" is phase 3. And the announcement coincides with the second coming of Christ. It would seem, therefore, that the wedding supper has not yet been observed. In fulfilling the symbol, Christ is completing phase 1 in the Church Age as individuals are saved. Phase 2 will be accomplished at the Rapture of the church, when Christ takes His bride to heaven, the Father's house (John 14:1–3). Accordingly it would seem that the beginning of the Millennium itself will fulfill the symbolism of the wedding supper *(gamos)*. It is also significant that the use of the word "bride" in 19:7 *(gynē,* lit., "wife")* implies that phase 2 of the wedding will have been completed and that all that remains is the feast itself.[72]

> **19:11** And I saw heaven opened; and behold, a white horse, and He who sat upon it is called Faithful and True; and in righteousness He judges and wages war.

A white horse. In the first seal judgment the Antichrist appears on a white horse like a conquering Roman general. But he comes to remove peace from the earth and bring war (6:2). The true Messiah also appears on a white horse, but He is accompanied by armies from heaven clothed in fine linen, white and clean (v. 14). He is the Prince of Peace (Isa. 9:6), who will bring judgment to the earth (v. 7) and rule with a scepter of iron (Ps. 2:9).

> **19:12** He has a name written upon Him which no one knows except Himself.

A name . . . no one knows. This is probably a reference to the fact that He has not been seen in this light before, that is, as Potentate, King, and absolute Monarch, who will dispense righteous judgment with total authority. As Allen comments, "The fact that only Christ knows this name shows that there are resources of infinite power in deity available only to Christ as He acts for God in this judgment on earth; men, even redeemed men, may not share in this aspect of divine power."[73]

> **19:13** He is clothed with a robe dipped in blood; and His name is called The Word of God.

Robe dipped in blood. Some think this refers to Christ's blood, which He shed for humanity at the cross. But it is more likely a fulfillment of Isaiah 63:1–6, a messianic passage, that pictures the King coming with wrath and vengeance with His garments sprinkled with the blood of His enemies (v. 3). He comes to "speak in righteousness, mighty to save" (v. 1) during His year of redemption (v. 4). Further, He will say, "I trod down the peoples in My anger . . . and I poured out their lifeblood on the earth" (v. 6). Walvoord writes, "His vesture is declared to be 'dipped in blood,' as if anticipating the bloodshed to come (cf. Isa. 63:2–3; Rev. 14:20). Christ as the slain Lamb in Revelation speaks of redemption by blood; here blood represents divine judgment upon wicked men."[74]

The Word of God. See John 1:1 and 1 John 1:1. See also page 109.

> **19:15** From His mouth comes a sharp sword, so that with it He may smite the nations; and He will rule them with a rod of iron; and He treads the wine press of the fierce wrath of God, the Almighty.

From His mouth comes a sharp sword. See 1:16 and 2:12. This seems to be a fulfillment of Isaiah 49:1–7, another messianic passage. God "has made

My mouth like a sharp sword" (v. 2). And God the Father will reply, "I will also make You a light of the nations so that My salvation may reach to the end of the earth" (v. 6).

He will rule them with a rod of iron. See Psalm 2:9.

He treads the wine press of the fierce wrath of God. This is a messianic fulfillment of Isaiah 63:2–3, "Why is Your apparel red, and your garments like the one who treads in the wine press? 'I have trodden the wine trough alone . . . I also trod [the people] in My anger, and trampled them in My wrath.'"

19:16 He has a name written, "King of Kings, and Lord of Lords."

King of Kings. Because of His resurrection, He is declared to be Israel's King or Messiah (the Christ) (Acts 2:29–33, 36). So when He returns He will rule over Israel and over all the kings of the earth (Rev. 1:5).

Lord of Lords. And because He has been seated at the right hand of His Father's throne (Ps. 110:1; Acts 2:34–36), He is declared to be the Lord![75]

19:17 Come, assemble for the great supper of God.

Great supper of God. A terrible carnage will take place when Christ returns to the earth. In the Battle of Armageddon (16:16) the Beast and the kings of the earth will vent their anger toward Jerusalem. However, their armies will be stopped and completely destroyed at the plain of Megiddo.
Christ, seated on a white horse (vv. 11, 19, 21), will defeat these forces, along with the Beast, the False Prophet, and those who had received the mark of the Beast. The Beast and the False Prophet will be cast into "the lake of fire which burns with brimstone."

19:21 The rest were killed with the sword which came from the mouth of Him who sat upon the horse, and all the birds were filled with their flesh.

The rest were killed with the sword . . . and all the birds were filled with their flesh. "The carnage of men and beasts at Christ's return is so great that God calls forth all the vultures in the air to come and dine at this revolting supper. What a needless tragedy! All of these who are slain could have had eternal bliss and happiness. But now they have become a feast of fools!"[76]

THE KINGDOM REIGN
OF CHRIST AND
SATAN BOUND

Synopsis

(20:1–3) Just before the millennial kingdom begins, Satan will be confined and bound for a thousand years in the abyss. A seal will be placed over this prison-like place until the thousand years are completed. Then Satan will be released for a brief time.

(20:4–6) Thrones will be set up for judgment. Also the martyrs who had died for the sake of Jesus during the Tribulation will be resurrected and will reign with Him. The rest of the dead, those without Christ, will not be resurrected until the thousand years are finished. Those raised for the kingdom will be especially blessed and will reign with Christ as priests before God.

(20:7–9) Following the Millennium, Satan will be released, and he will deceive the nations again. Gog and Magog come together to make war. This will be an enormous force; "the number of them is like the sand of the seashore." They will come up to a broad plain and surround the camp of the saints, the beloved city. But fire will come down from heaven and devour them.

(20:10–15) The Devil will be cast into the lake of fire and brimstone, where the Beast and the False Prophet are confined. The Lord will then set up the

Great White Throne, where the unbelieving dead of all generations will be gathered and judged. They will be tried for their deeds before the Lord from the things that were written in a special set of books. Even the sea, death, and Hades will give up their dead so that everyone can be judged according to their works. What death and Hades give up will be cast into the lake of fire, which is the second death. Every person whose name will not be in the Book of Life will be cast into the lake of fire.

20:2 [The angel] laid hold of the dragon, the serpent of old, who is the devil and Satan, and bound him for a thousand years.

The dragon, the serpent of old, who is the devil and Satan. See pages 155–56, and 12:3, 9, 17; and 13:2.

Bound him for a thousand years. Those who do not believe in a literal, future, earthly kingdom attempt to give the Greek word *chilia* ("thousand") an allegorical or spiritualized meaning, that is, to make it mean simply a long period of time. And they apply this term to the church. On this Barnes writes, "There are but three ways in which the phrase 'a thousand years' can be understood here: either *(a)* literally; or *(b)* in the prophetic use of the term, where a day would stand for a year thus making a period of three hundred and sixty thousand years; or *(c)* figuratively, supposing that it refers to a long but indefinite period of time. It may be impossible to determine which of these periods is intended."[77]

But Walvoord correctly states: "The expositor is not free to spiritualize the interpretation of the vision but must accept the interpretation in its ordinary and literal meaning. If this is done, there is no other alternative than the premillennial interpretation which holds that at the second coming of Christ, Satan will be bound for a thousand years. This will constitute one of the major features of Christ's righteous rule upon the earth."[78]

20:3 So that [Satan] should not deceive the nations any longer.

Not deceive the nations any longer. This seems to be the main reason he is imprisoned for this long period of time—to give humanity a breather from his evil work. When the kingdom begins, all who enter it will be saved. Though the kingdom is a period of near perfect peace, people who will be born then will be born as sinners. As the generations pass, more and more in the kingdom will not be loyal to the Messiah. But still, Satan will not have direct influence on people until the very end of the thousand-year period, when he will be released for a short time.

20:4 And I saw thrones, and they sat upon them, and judgment was given to them.

Judgment was given to them. Those who will be beheaded for Christ's sake in the Tribulation will be resurrected and will become judges at "war-crime" trials at the beginning of the kingdom period. They will also reign with Christ as a reward for their faithfulness to Him during the Tribulation.

Something else will occur at the beginning of the kingdom. Jesus spoke of it in His Olivet Discourse message. "But when the Son of Man comes in His glory, and all the angels with Him, then He will sit on His glorious throne. And all the nations will be gathered before Him; and He will separate them from one another, as the shepherd separates the sheep from the goats" (Matt. 25:31–32).

This judgment focuses on how Gentiles treated or mistreated the Lord's brothers (v. 40) during the Tribulation. To mistreat the Jewish people during this time is tantamount to disbelieving in Him. Lindsey writes,

> Jesus predicted in Matthew 25 that when He came the second time as Judge of the universe He would separate the sheep from the goats. The sheep would be those people who had evidenced their faith in Him by the way they treated a group He called "these brothers of mine."
>
> Jesus called these benevolent helpers "the righteous" and "sheep," and invites them into the kingdom of God as mortal beings.
>
> The "goats" are those kings, captains, mighty men and slaves who opposed the returning Christ and persecuted His evangelists during the Tribulation. They are now judged and sentenced to eternal fire and then slain with the sword of the Lord.[79]

20:6 Blessed and holy is the one who has a part in the first resurrection; over these the second death has no power, but they will be priests of God and of Christ and will reign with Him for a thousand years.

The first resurrection. This first resurrection will include not only the righteous who suffered in the Tribulation but also the Old Testament righteous dead, the many who sleep in the dust and who awaken to everlasting life (Dan. 12:2). Since the church-age saints, who will be resurrected and raptured, will "always be with the Lord" (1 Thess. 4:17), the first resurrection will certainly include church saints as well.

The second death has no power. The second death will be the final death, that is, eternal and spiritual separation from God and heaven (v. 14; 2:11). The righteous, saved by the blood of Christ, will be spared this dreadful fate.

They will be priests of God and of Christ and will reign with Him for a thousand years. All the redeemed will be serving as priests during this millennial period and will also be reigning as administrators and officials, doing the Lord's bidding. Though they will be representing the Lord, they will not necessarily take part in the ceremonial affairs in the millennial temple. That will be the task of the Levitical priests, the sons of Zadok, who "shall come near to Me to minister to Me; and they shall stand before Me to offer Me the fat and the blood." And "They shall enter My sanctuary; they shall come near to My table to minister to Me and keep My charge" (Ezek. 44:15–16).

> **20:8** [Satan] will come out to deceive the nations which are in the four corners of the earth, Gog and Magog.

To deceive the nations. By the end of the thousand years, many people who will be perhaps twenty generations away from those righteous mortals who entered the kingdom in their natural bodies will rebel against Christ. They will be required to make a decision for or against Him as their Savior, similar to what one must do now in the present age. But their natural hearts will go cold and complacent and will turn against Christ. The nations that surround the land of Magog will rise up and follow Satan against Jerusalem.

The four corners of the earth. See 7:1.

Gog and Magog. See page 134.

> **20:9** [They] surrounded the camp of the saints and the beloved city.

The beloved city. Almost all commentators agree that this is Jerusalem. This will be a kind of repeat of Armageddon! But God will waste no time in destroying the forces involved in this rebellion.

> **20:10** The devil who deceived them was thrown into the lake of fire and brimstone, where the beast and the false prophet are also; and they will be tormented day and night forever and ever.

The lake of fire and brimstone. When Christ returns to reign, He will say to the unrighteous on His left, "Depart from Me, accursed ones, into the eternal fire which has been prepared for the devil and his angels" (Matt. 25:41). And here at the end of the millennial reign, Satan, the Beast, and the False Prophet will follow the lost into eternal fire.

20:11 And I saw a great white throne.

Great white throne. More than likely the Judge will be Jesus, because He stated that the Father "has given all judgment to the Son, in order that all may honor the Son, even as they honor the Father. . . . For just as the Father has life in Himself, even so He gave to the Son also to have life in Himself; and He gave Him authority to execute judgment, because He is the Son of Man [the Messiah]" (John 5:22–23, 26–27).

20:12 And books were opened; and another book was opened, which is the book of life.

Book of Life. See pages 167–68. See also 17:4 and 21:27.

20:14 And death and Hades were thrown into the lake of fire.

Death and Hades. See pages 235–36. Lenski argues, "Of the ten instances of the use of hades four appear in Revelation, and each of the four joins 'the death' and 'the hades.' We see why. Because "the death" separates the body of the wicked from the soul and, while the body of the wicked lies in the grave (or the sea, v. 13) until judgment day, the wicked soul is kept in the hades until that day. It is thus that 'the death' and 'the hades' are companions in Rev. 1:18; 6:8; 20:13, 14."[80]

20:15 And if anyone's name was not found written in the book of life, he was thrown into the lake of fire.

Anyone's name was not found written. All who do not know Jesus as their Savior will be given a fair trial at this heavenly court hearing. They will be tried on the only basis available to them, and that is the merit of their own deeds (vv. 12–13). But this will be of no avail, because human righteousness is likened to nothing more than filthy rags (Isa. 64:6), and no one can be saved "on the basis of deeds which we have done" (Titus 3:5).

Only those covered by the blood of Christ will be recorded in the Book of Life. All others will be cast into the lake of fire.

THE REVEALING OF THE NEW HEAVENS, THE NEW EARTH, AND THE NEW JERUSALEM

Synopsis

(21:1–8) Suddenly, John saw in a vision the new heavens and the new earth. The first will pass away, immediately followed by the revealing of a new Jerusalem that will come down from heaven. The cry is that now the tabernacle of God will be dwelling among men; in fact, God Himself will abide among them. There will be no more crying, mourning, pain, or death. The Lord on His eternal throne will make "all things new." To the reader of Revelation there is an additional promise that He "will give to the one who thirsts from the spring of the water of life without cost." And "he who overcomes shall inherit these things, and I will be his God and he will be My son."

(21:9–27) Carried away by the Spirit, John was shown the bride, the wife of the Lamb, Jerusalem, coming down out of heaven from God. Her brilliance is described, and the dimensions of the city are given. In the eternal city there will be no temple, because the Lord and the Lamb will be its temple. There will be no sun, moon, or light as now known on the earth, because the Lamb will provide the needed light. The saints will have access to the city, because its gates will never be closed. Nothing sinful will pollute its streets. Only those whose names are written in the Lamb's Book of Life will ever come into the city.

21:1 And I saw a new heaven and a new earth; for the first heaven and the first earth passed away, and there is no longer any sea.

A new heaven and a new earth. In some providential way the form remains but the substance will be eternally changed, and this system as we know it will be redeemed from the curse of sin. Isaiah was the first to whom God revealed this great cosmic renovation. The prophet wrote, "For behold, I create new heavens and a new earth; and the former things shall not be remembered or come to mind" (65:17). Peter repeated this and says that this new creation will be blessed "in which righteousness dwells" (2 Peter 3:13).

Peter further wrote that this "day of the Lord will come like a thief, in which the heavens will pass away with a roar and the elements will be destroyed with intense heat, and the earth and its works will be burned up" (v. 10). He reminded his readers that because "these things are to be destroyed in this way" (v. 11), we are to be "looking for and hastening the coming of the day of God, on account of which the heavens will be destroyed by burning, and the elements will melt with intense heat!" (v. 12).

There is no longer any sea. Water is essential for life, as we know it. But conditions in the eternal state will be different. A "river of the water of life," will flow from the throne of God and of the Lamb (22:1), and it will apparently water the tree of life in the city of Jerusalem. But apart from this, water is not needed for the new resurrected bodies of those in the eternal state.

21:2 I saw the holy city, new Jerusalem, coming down out of heaven from God, made ready as a bride adorned for her husband.

I saw the holy city, new Jerusalem. Though Isaiah also mentioned the creation of a new Jerusalem (Isa. 65:18), his reference may be to the millennial capital and not the eternal city. Apparently the millennial city will simply be replaced by the everlasting one which will come down from God out of the heavens.

Made ready as a bride adorned for her husband. The city is actually called "the bride, the wife of the Lamb" (v. 9), dressed in the regalia of a glorious bride (vv. 10–11).

21:3 Behold, the tabernacle of God is among men, and He shall dwell among them, and they shall be His people, and God Himself shall be among them.

The tabernacle of God is among men. God Himself will be present in the

New Jerusalem, and this will be in the person of Jesus, who is Immanuel, "God with us" (Matt. 1:23).

> **21:4** He shall wipe away every tear from their eyes; and there shall no longer be any death; there shall no longer be any mourning, or crying, or pain; the first things have passed away.

He shall wipe away every tear. This too refers to the second Person of the Trinity, who will be "among them" (v. 3) in bodily presence.

There shall no longer be any death. All the things listed here are the products of death on "the old earth and under the old heaven which pressed out so many, many tears. Summing it all up: 'The first things went away' (our idiom: have gone away), all the first things of the first heaven and the first earth."[81]

> **21:5** Behold, I am making all things new.

All things new. Tucker expresses this fact well: "It will be a Divinely and eternally fixed condition. There will be no variableness, no changing. Throughout the past change and decay in all around we see but here never again disorder, change or chaos. The trail of the serpent shall never mark or mar this fair creation. We are standing as it were at a mountain's peak, looking a landscape over. What we shall see will beggar human language to express."[82]

> **21:6** It is done. I am the Alpha and the Omega, the beginning and the end.

It is done. When God says something will occur, it is just as well as done. Since God is not bound by time as we humans are, He looks at things as if they are completed. We as mortals sluggishly move through time, limited in vision and understanding. But to God everything is completed.

I am the Alpha and the Omega, the beginning and the end. At the beginning of Revelation (1:8) God is referred to as the Alpha and Omega. Here at the end of the book Jesus applied to Himself the same title and description that was used of His Father. These words describing God's attribute of eternality were long ago recorded by Isaiah the prophet: "I am He, I am the first, I am also the last" (48:12b; cf. 41:4). Jesus is God.

> **21:7** He who overcomes shall inherit these things, and I will be his God and he will be My son.

He who overcomes. As with Christ's words for the seven churches (Revelation 2–3), this is probably a reference to overcoming the pull of the culture and receiving the Lord Jesus as one's personal Savior.

Shall inherit these things. "'Inherit' is correct even as Christ adds, 'he shall be to me a son.' A son inherits. We are now in our minority; on that day we shall be of age and shall inherit. The heir must wait until the inheritance laid up for him may be duly his. . . . Wondrous shall be this inheriting. . . . This shall be the inheritance even as Jesus says in the parable: 'Son, thou art ever with me and all that I have is thine.' Luke 15:31. Yes, Christ here calls himself 'God.' Let the modernists note this."[83]

21:9 Come here, I shall show you the bride, the wife of the Lamb.

The bride, the wife of the Lamb. See 19:7; 21:2.

21:11 Her brilliance [the New Jerusalem] was like a very costly stone, as a stone of crystal-clear jasper.

Crystal-clear jasper. God described Himself as a jasper stone (4:3). Whatever the color, this stone is gleaming and transparent, or crystal-clear.

21:12 It had a great and high wall, with twelve gates, and at the gates twelve angels; and names were written on them, which are those of the twelve tribes of the sons of Israel.

Twelve gates . . . of the twelve tribes. The tribes of Israel are here memorialized for eternity. Despite the failures of the nation, the Jewish people were used of God throughout history as His historic, earthly people. As eternity begins, they will have been redeemed and are here remembered and even honored by the Lord. The inscription of the names "serves explicit notice of the distinct role of national Israel in this eternal city in fulfillment of their distinctive role in history throughout the centuries of their existence (cf. 7:1–8)."[84]

At the gates twelve angels. These are not statues; they are angelic beings symbolically guarding the entrance to eternal Jerusalem.

21:14 And the wall of the city had twelve foundation stones, and on them were the twelve names of the twelve apostles of the Lamb.

The twelve names of the twelve apostles. Just as Israel's twelve tribes are honored, so will the church and its founding apostles be honored and remembered on into eternity. Though Israel and the church represent two different dispensations of history, they are memorialized here in the New Jerusalem; though similar in some ways, they are separate.

21:16 He measured the city with the rod, fifteen hundred miles; its length and width and height are equal.

Fifteen hundred miles. "Using a reed, a measure about ten feet long, the unit of measure common among the Jews, with which to measure the city, its gates, and its walls, the angel finds that the city is square, its length and breadth being the same, twelve thousand furlongs. Since a furlong is equal to 582 feet, the measured distance is equivalent to 1,342 miles, often spoke of roughly as 1,500 miles."[85]

21:18 And the city was pure gold, like clear glass.

Like clear glass. Some speculate that the gold will be pounded down so fine that it will be transparent. There has been nothing like this ever before.

21:19 The first foundation stone was jasper; the second, sapphire; the third, chalcedony; the fourth, emerald.

Jasper. See 21:11.

Sapphire. This could be blue in color.

Chalcedony. This is green in hue.

Emerald. This could also be green.

21:20 The fifth, sardonyx; the sixth, sardius; the seventh, chryso-lite; the eighth, beryl; the ninth, topaz; the tenth, chrysoprase; the eleventh, jacinth; the twelfth, amethyst.

Sardonyx . . . sardius. These are red in color.

Chrysolite. This gem is yellow in hue.

Beryl . . . topaz . . . chrysoprase. These three are green.

Jacinth . . . amethyst. These are blue in tint.

21:21 And the twelve gates were twelve pearls; each one of the gates was a single pearl.

The twelve gates were twelve pearls. These may be natural pearls because pearls can grow large. Or the gates may simply look like the material of which pearls are made. Some suggest that a large pearl will be embedded in the framework of each gate. Whatever the situation, the gates will be a wonderful sight to behold!

21:22 And I saw no temple in it; for the Lord God, the Almighty, and the Lamb, are its temple.

The Lord God . . . and the Lamb, are its temple. Apparently the millennial temple will not be in existence in the eternal state. But since the idea of a temple depicts the meeting place of God and mankind, this verse is telling us there will be no artificial barriers between God and His own.

21:27 And nothing unclean and no one who practices abomination and lying, shall ever come into [the city], but only those whose names are written in the Lamb's book of life.

And nothing unclean . . . shall ever come into [the city]. Some have mistakenly assumed that the verse is saying that sinners are nearby, dwelling just outside the city walls. However, John was simply saying that the issue of sin is over. The sins of the pagan world have been purged forever. We will never look up and see sinful beings coming into this eternal, holy city. See also verse 8.

RENOVATION OF THE
UNIVERSE AND THE FINAL
MESSAGE OF SCRIPTURE

Synopsis

(22:1–5) The river of the water of life that will nourish the tree of life will come from the throne of God and the Lamb. This tree will bear twelve kinds of fruit, and the leaves will be for the healing of the nations. There will no longer be any curse, and the throne of God and the Lamb will be there. His bond-servants will serve Him continually and will see His face. There will no longer be any night, because the Lord God will illumine His own and they will reign forever and ever.

(22:6–19) These words are faithful and true, and these things will shortly take place. "Blessed is he who heeds the words of this prophecy." John was then told not to seal the words of this prophecy, because the time of fulfillment is drawing near. The Lord promised that He is coming quickly to reward men, and He identified Himself as God, the Alpha and the Omega. A blessing is promised for those who have washed their robes: they will have the right to the tree of life and may enter the gates of the New Jerusalem. A final invitation is given for people to "Come" (v. 17), but there is also the warning that no one should add or take away from the words of this prophecy (v. 18). If they do so, God will take away their part from the tree of life (v. 19).

(22:20–21) In the closing benediction the Lord said again that He is coming quickly. Then the Bible closes with the benediction, "The grace of the Lord Jesus be with all. Amen."

22:1 He showed me a river of the water of life . . . coming from the throne of God and of the Lamb.

A river of the water of life. In the new earth there will be no large bodies of water (21:1). Seas and oceans will be gone. Apparently there is only this one body of water, the river of the water of life. Is this a memorial or symbolic body of water, or is it literal? It seems to be refreshing and will sustain the Tree of Life. Johnson believes the water is symbolic. "The sea—the source of the satanic beast (13:1) and the place of the dead (13:1)—will be gone (20:13). Again, the emphasis is not geographical but moral and spiritual. The sea serves as an archetype with connotations of evil. . . . Therefore, no trace of evil in any form will be present in the new creation."[86] However, the more normal interpretation here is to take this as an actual stream of water. Its purpose is described in verse 2. Walvoord states, "The visual picture presented is that the river of life flows down through the middle of the city, and the tree is large enough to span the river, so that the river is in the midst of the street, and the tree is on both sides of the river. It would appear that the pure river of the water of life is not a broad body but a clear stream sufficiently narrow to allow for this arrangement."[87]

22:2 And on either side of the river was the tree of life, bearing twelve kinds of fruit . . . and the leaves of the tree were for the healing of the nations.

And on either side of the river. Since the description is so specific, it would seem that the river is actual and not simply symbolic.

The leaves of the tree were for the healing of the nations. By mentioning the leaves, the verse could simply have in mind that the tree is alive and even flourishing and producing the twelve kinds of fruit. This fruit, however, "feeds" the nations. The Tree of Life in the Garden of Eden (Gen. 3:22, 24) had some sort of life-giving properties so that Adam and Eve, if they had partaken of it, would have lived forever in their fallen state (Gen. 3:22). So here in Revelation this tree has some eternal life-giving value.

The word for "healing" is *therapeian,* from which the English word *therapeutic* is derived, almost directly transliterated from the Greek. Rather than meaning "healing," the word should be understood as "health-giving" or "nourishing," as the verbal form of the word means "to serve or care for." In other words, the leaves of the tree will promote the enjoyment of life in the New Jerusalem. They are not for correcting illnesses, for there will be no sickness.[88]

22:3 There shall no longer be any curse.

There shall no longer be any curse. This is a reference to the original curse that came on the human race and the earth as a result of Adam's sin (Gen. 3:17). By the work of Christ on the cross the curse has ended for those who trust Him. Also, the universal curse caused by sin is finished. "In the new heaven and the new earth, there will be no curse at all and no possibility or need of such divine punishment. This broad statement is justified by the fact that the throne of God and of the Lamb shall be in the new Jerusalem."[89]

22:4 And they shall see His face.

Shall see His face. Four times John saw in a vision both the Father and the Lamb, that is, Christ (21:22–23; 22:1, 3). Obviously this again affirms the deity of Jesus Christ (see also John 1:1–4, 18).

22:5 And there shall no longer be any night; and they shall not have need of the light of a lamp nor the light of the sun, because the Lord God shall illumine them; and they shall reign forever and ever.

The Lord God shall illumine them. God illumines, but also Christ is the lamp of the New Jerusalem (21:23), a fact that again emphasizes the oneness of God the Son with God the Father. Together the Father and the Son replace the former natural light of the physical sun and moon.

They shall reign forever and ever. Several times in this chapter John refers to the fact that the saints are the Lord's bond-servants (vv. 3, 6), that they belong to Him by having His name on their foreheads (v. 4), that they will receive His reward (v. 12), and that they will serve Him (v. 3) and reign with Him forever (v. 5).

22:6 "These words are faithful and true"; and the Lord, the God of the spirits of the prophets, sent His angel to show His bond-servants the things which must shortly take place.

Faithful and true. These words are actually a title of the Messiah (19:11), the living Word of God, but here the reference is to the written Word. The Word of God is both an "alive" written revelation (Heb. 4:12) and the living Son of God.

The God of the spirits of the prophets. As the Lord revealed His Word through the very souls of the ancient prophets, so He revealed His final message through an angel to John and ultimately to His bond-servants regarding future things. From beginning to end the God of the universe has spoken His authoritative revelation through selected prophets to mankind (Heb. 1:1) for their ultimate benefit and salvation.

Which must shortly take place. See 1:1.

> **22:7** And behold, I am coming quickly. Blessed is he who heeds the words of the prophecy of this book.

I am coming quickly. Three times in Revelation Jesus said, "I am coming quickly" (3:11; 22:7, 12). The Greek word *tachu* translated "quickly" has the idea of coming suddenly. That is, when Christ returns, events will take place at a rapid rate—things will fall into place in rapid order. This idea is reinforced by the Lord's statements in 3:3 ("I will come like a thief, and you will not know at what hour I will come upon you") and 16:15 ("I am coming like a thief. Blessed is the one who stays awake and keeps his garments, lest he walk about naked").

Blessed is he who heeds the words of the prophecy of this book. See 1:3.

> **22:8** When I heard and saw, I fell down to worship at the feet of the angel who showed me these things. (See 19:10.)

> **22:9** Worship God. (See 19:10.)

> **22:10** Do not seal up the words of the prophecy of this book, for the time is near.

The time is near. As in 1:3, it is better to translate this statement "The season *[kairos]* is near *[engys]*." By using *kairos* John could be saying that the Lord's next program, or agenda, is ready to take place. Thomas says: "The events of this book are thus identified with the last of the 'critical epoch-making periods foreordained of God.' From the perspective of prophetic anticipation this period is declared to be . . . (*engys,* 'near') (1:3). This declaration echoes and reinforces the . . . (*en tachei,* 'soon') of v. 1."[90]

> **22:11** Let the one who does wrong, still do wrong; and let the one who is filthy, still be filthy; and let the one who is righteous, still practice righteousness; and let the one who holy, still keep himself holy.

Let the one . . . This verse is similar in thought to 13:10. Barnes gives a helpful explanation of this verse. "At the close of this book, and at the close of the whole volume of revealed truth, it was proper to declare, in the most solemn manner, that when these events were consummated, everything would be fixed and unchanging; that all who were then found to be righteous would remain so for ever; and that none who were impenitent, impure, and wicked, would ever change their character or condition. That this is the meaning here seems to me to be plain; and this sentiment accords with all that is said in the Bible of the final condition of the righteous and the wicked."[91]

22:13 I am the Alpha and the Omega.

The Alpha and Omega. See 1:8; 21:6; and page 107.

22:14 Blessed are those who wash their robes, that they may have the right to the tree of life.

Who wash their robes. This speaks of spiritual cleansing that comes about by the shed blood of Christ the Savior, as illustrated by the Tribulation saints, who "washed their robes and made them white in the blood of the Lamb" (7:14).

The tree of life. See 22:2.

22:15 Outside are the dogs and sorcerers and the immoral persons.

Outside. Unbelievers will have no access to the New Jerusalem. See 21:27.

22:16 I am the root and the offspring of David, the bright morning star.

Root and offspring of David. See page 111.

The bright morning star. See page 113.

22:17 And the Spirit and the bride say, "Come." And let the one who hears say, "Come." And let the one who is thirsty come; let the one who wishes take the water of life without cost.

And the Spirit and the bride say, "Come." The Holy Spirit and the bride (that is, believers inhabiting the New Jerusalem) beckon the reader to respond and accept eternal life through Jesus Christ. The sinner's need for salvation is likened to his being thirsty. It would be wrong to say that the purpose of the book of Revelation is to frighten people to turn to Christ, but it would be correct to say that the book portrays the end of history and the judgments that are coming on all humanity. This book sets forth how the world will end. Therefore the invitation to come to salvation is urgent.

Let the one who is thirsty come. This recalls Jesus' encounter with the Samaritan woman in John's Gospel, where He said, "If you knew the gift of God, and who it is who says to you, 'Give Me a drink,' you would have asked Him, and He would have given you living water. . . . but whoever drinks of the water that I shall give him shall never thirst; but the water that I shall give him shall become in him a well of water springing up to eternal life" (John 4:10, 14).

> **22:18–19** I testify to everyone who hears the words of the prophecy of this book: if anyone adds to them, God shall add to him the plagues which are written in this book; and if anyone takes away from the words of the book of this prophecy, God shall take away his part from the tree of life and from the holy city, which are written in this book.

If anyone adds to them. If anyone claims that additional revelation follows after the close of the book of Revelation, they are accursed. That is because with Revelation God closed the biblical canon. So it is presumptuous for someone to say he has additional words from God. Those who say they have been given prophetic knowledge equal to the apostles are liars. Seiss concludes:

> But in the estimate of God, he who adds to or takes away from what it presents, disables all right conception of the system of redemption, and inflicts an injury so great that he who does it need never hope for salvation. How important, therefore, how precious in the eye of heaven, how necessary to the right instruction of God's people, how vital to the proper Christian faith and hope are the unmutilated and unchanged foreshadowings which this Book was given to set forth!
>
> The penalty upon every corrupter of these records also helps to fix and establish the right interpretation of them. "Plagues" constitute one of the prominent subjects; and those "plagues" are to be laid upon each hearer who involves himself in the guilt of adding to or diminishing the contents of the Book.[92]

John's words are similar to the words of Moses in Deuteronomy 4:1–2, 6.

Here the great prophet canonized the words of the Law, and the principles he laid down there are certainly applicable to the entire Old Testament. "Listen to the statues . . . which I am teaching you. . . . You shall not add to the word which I am commanding you, nor take away from it. . . . So keep [the statutes] and do them, for that is your wisdom and your understanding."

Thomas observes, "The relation of the warning of vv. 18–19 to the canonization-formula of Deut. 4:1ff. is another good reason for concluding that John is forbidding any further use of the gift of prophecy. This is a canonizing of the book of Revelation parallel to the way the Deuteronomy passage came to apply to the whole OT canon. Use of the canonical model is equivalent to saying that there was no more room for inspired messages."[93]

See also page 90.

God shall take away his part from the tree of life. Some think John was saying that if a person already had participated in the tree of life but tampers with the Scriptures, he will be removed from it and lose his salvation. But the warning is probably aimed at false prophets, who are "religious" and certainly not born again. They act with great boldness in claiming divine revelation, but if they were God's own children, they would humble themselves before God in light of what He has already written.

22:20 "Yes, I am coming quickly." Amen. Come, Lord Jesus.

I am coming quickly. See verse 7.

Come, Lord Jesus. This should be the cry of all believers. Though in some ways we cling to this earthly life, we know that eternity awaits us and that this is the ultimate "blessed hope" for all of the Lord's children.

ENDNOTES

Chapter 1

1. Joseph A. Seiss, *The Apocalypse* (Grand Rapids: Kregel, 1987), 12–13.
2. John F. Walvoord, *The Revelation of Jesus Christ* (Chicago: Moody, 1966), 14.
3. Ibid., 15
4. Clarence Larkin, *The Book of Revelation* (Glenside, Pa.: Clarence Larkin Estate, 1919), 2.
5. John Peter Lange, *Revelation,* Commentary on the Holy Scriptures, trans. Philip Schaff (Grand Rapids: Zondervan, n.d.), 44.
6. Seiss, *The Apocalypse,* 478.
7. Henry Barclay Swete, *Commentary on Revelation* (Grand Rapids: Kregel, 1977), 278.
8. Paul N. Benware, *Understanding End Times Prophecy* (Chicago: Moody, 1995), 246.
9. Harold W. Hoehner, *Chronological Aspects of the Life of Christ* (Grand Rapids: Zondervan, 1977), 139.
10. Lange, *Revelation,* 38.

Chapter 2

1. Irenaeus, *Against Heresies,* 3.2.2. Unless otherwise stated, all patristic quotations in this study are from A. Roberts and J. Donaldson *The Ante-Nicene Fathers,* 10 vols. (Grand Rapids: Eerdmans, n.d.); or Philip Schaff and H. Wace, *Nicene and Post-Nicene Fathers,* 14 vols. (Grand Rapids: Eerdmans, n.d.).
2. Irenaeus, *Against Heresies,* 5.5.1; cf. 5. 36.1–2. In Irenaeus's *Proof,* he twice cited the elders as his source of information. In chapter 3 he said,

"Now this is what faith does for us, as the elders, the disciples of the apostles, have handed down to us."

3. Irenaeus, *Against Heresies,* 5.33.3.
4. Ibid., 3.3.4; Fragment 3; Eusebius, *Church History,* 5.20.6. The reference in Irenaeus to "a presbyter, a disciple of the apostles [who] reason[ed] with respect to the two testaments, proving that both were truly from one and the same God" (Irenaeus, *Against Heresies,* 4.32.1), is also probably a reference to Polycarp.
5. Ibid., 5.33.4.
6. Justin Martyr, *Dialogue with Trypho,* 81. Even Eusebius, who denied the millenarian doctrine and did not believe that the apostle John was the author of Revelation, acknowledged that, "[Justin] writes also that even down to his time prophetic gifts shone in the Church [see ibid., 82]. And he mentions the Apocalypse of John, saying distinctly that it was the apostle's" (Eusebius, *Church History,* 4.18.8).
7. Irenaeus, *Against Heresies,* 4.30.4.
8. Tertullian, *Against Marcion,* 3.14.
9. Irenaeus quoted or alluded to every chapter of Revelation except chapters 8, 9, 10, and 14. The only chapters not referenced in Tertullian's extant works are 9, 13, and 15. And in Cyprian's writings only chapters 4, 10, 11, 12, and 13 are not represented.
10. Irenaeus, *Against Heresies,* 3.1.1; 3.3.4; Eusebius, *Church History,* 3.1.1; 3.31.1; 5.24.3–4.
11. Irenaeus, *Against Heresies,* 3.3.4. For the connection between John and the early church fathers in Asia Minor, see Larry V. Crutchfield, "The Apostle John and Asia Minor as a Source of Premillennialism in the Early Church Fathers," *Journal of the Evangelical Theological Society* 31 (December 1988): 411–27. Asia Minor was both the scene of the closing years of John's ministry and the fountainhead of premillenarian concepts. It was home to Polycarp, bishop of Smyrna, and Papias, bishop of Hierapolis, and to the apologists Melito of Sardis and Apollinaris of Hierapolis. On his way to a martyr's death in Rome, Ignatius of Antioch paused in Smyrna long enough to become acquainted with Polycarp and to write more than half of his extant epistles. Asia Minor was probably not Justin Martyr's home. But Asia Minor had a marked influence on Justin's life and doctrine, for he was probably converted in Ephesus, and Ephesus was the scene of his famed dialogue with the Jew Trypho. For the polemicist Irenaeus, the last and greatest of the Asiatic fathers, Smyrna was the probable birthplace of both the man and his theology.
12. Irenaeus, *Against Heresies,* 5.33.4.
13. Justin Martyr, *Dialogue,* 80, in Hermigild Dressler et al., eds., *The Fathers of the Church,* 6:277.

14. Justin Martyr, *Dialogue*, 81.
15. J. N. D. Kelly, *Early Christian Doctrines*, rev. ed. (New York: Harper and Row, 1978), 469.
16. Irenaeus, *Against Heresies*, 5.35.1.
17. Ibid., 5.35.1–2.
18. Irenaeus, *First Apology* 30.
19. Ibid., 33.
20. Ibid., 52.
21. Irenaeus, *Against Heresies*, 2.7.
22. Ibid., 5.35.2.
23. Tertullian, *Against Marcion*, 3.25.
24. Tertullian, *On the Resurrection of the Flesh*, 20.
25. Wordsworth, quoted in Seiss, *The Apocalypse*, 21 (italics his). Other second-century fathers who were certainly familiar with the apostle John and his writings were Polycarp (70–155), bishop of Smyrna, and Papias (ca. 60–130), bishop of Hierapolis. Melito (died ca. 190), apologist and bishop of Sardis, wrote a book titled the *Apocalypse of John* (Eusebius, *Church History*, 4.26.2; Jerome, *Lives of Illustrious Men*, 214). The apologist Apollinaris (ca. 175), succeeded Papias as bishop of Hierapolis. All four of these early fathers were church leaders in Asia Minor and most likely premillenarians. According to Eusebius, Theophilus (115–181), bishop of Antioch, produced a work called *Against the Heresy of Hermogenes*, "in which he makes use of testimonies from the Apocalypse of John" (Eusebius, *Church History*, 4.24.1). Some have suggested that there are possible allusions to the Apocalypse in the epistles of Ignatius (ca. 35–107), bishop of Antioch; *The Epistle of Barnabas;* and Hermas's *The Shepherd* (composed apparently in two parts, ca. 96 and 140–150), but the evidence is inconclusive.
26. See Eusebius, *Church History*, 3.28.1–6.
27. For the teachings of the Montanists see ibid., 5.14–19.
28. For Cyprian see *Epistles of Cyprian*, 55.7. And for Hippolytus see *Treatise on Christ and Antichrist*, 36; and *Appendix to the Works of Hippolytus*, 49.3.
29. See Eusebius, *Church History*, 3.28.2 (italics added).
30. Victorinus, *Commentary on the Apocalypse*, 20.11; see also Victorinus, *On the Creation of the World*.
31. See, for example, Clement, *Stromata*, 6.13, and Origen, *Commentary on John*, 5.3.
32. Eusebius, *Church History*, 7.25.7.
33. See, for example, Origen, *De Principiis*, 11.2, and Eusebius, *Church History*, 7.24.1.

34. Eusebius's quotations in chapters 24 and 25 of his *Church History* are the only extant chapters from this work.

35. Ibid., 7.24. Nepos was bishop of Arsinoe, a region on the western bank of the Nile. All we know about this Egyptian church leader and his writings is found here in Eusebius with another brief mention again in Jerome's *Lives of Illustrious Men,* 69. Jerome recorded that Dionysius of Alexandria wrote "two books *Against Nepos the Bishop,* who asserted in his writings a thousand years reign in the body. Among other things he diligently discussed the *Apocalypse of John. . . .*" The two works cited by Jerome appear to be different names for what Eusebius called collectively *On the Promises.*

36. Eusebius, *Church History,* 7.24.2 (italics added).

37. Ibid., 6–9.

38. Ibid., 7.25.1–27.

39. Ibid., 7.25.1, 4.

40. Ibid., 7.25.4–7.

41. Ibid., 7.25.8–27.

42. See for example Henry B. Swete, *The Apocalypse of St. John* (Grand Rapids: Eerdmans, n.d.), cxx–cxxx.

43. In his *Commentary on the Apostle's Creed,* Rufinus, a presbyter and scholar, listed the books of the New Testament canon which included the Revelation of John. He wrote, "These are the books which the Fathers have comprised within the Canon, and from which they would have us deduce the proofs of our faith" (37).

44. See Eusebius, *Church History,* 3.25.

45. Schaff, *History of the Christian Church,* 2:518. Codex Sinaiticus also includes the *Epistle of Barnabas* and Hermas's *The Shepherd.* Emperor Constantine assigned Eusebius the responsibility of producing "fifty copies of the sacred Scriptures" (Eusebius, *Life of Constantine,* 4.36), which helped set the standard for the New Testament canon in the Eastern church.

46. Eusebius, *Church History,* 3.39.3–4.

47. J. Quasten and J. C. Plumpe, eds., *Ancient Christian Writers: The Didache, The Epistle of Barnabas, The Epistles and the Martyrdom of St. Polycarp, The Fragments of Papias, The Epistle to Diognetus,* trans. James A. Kleist (Ramsey, N.J.: Newman, 1946), 6:108; and Schaff, *History of the Christian Church,* 2:697–98.

48. Schaff, *History of the Christian Church,* 2:698.

49. Eusebius, *Church History,* 3.39.12.

50. Athanasius, *Letters,* 39.5. Athanasius said of the twenty-seven books, "These are fountains of salvation, that they who thirst may be satisfied with the living words they contain. In these alone is proclaimed the

doctrine of godliness. Let no man add to these, neither let him take ought from these" (ibid., 39.6).

51. Other Eastern fathers who questioned or rejected Revelation were Cyril of Jerusalem (died 386), Gregory of Nazianzen (died 389), and Amphilochius of Iconium (died after 394).

52. For Augustine's own list of New Testament books see *On Christian Doctrine,* 2.8.

53. Augustine, *City of God,* 20.7.

54. See Gennadius, *Lives of Illustrious Men,* 18.

55. Augustine, *City of God,* 20.8–9.

56. Robert H. Mounce, *The Book of Revelation,* New International Commentary on the New Testament (Grand Rapids: Eerdmans, 1977), 39. Oecumenius's twelve-part commentary took a historical approach to the book of Revelation.

57. Donald Guthrie, *New Testament Introduction* (Downers Grove, Ill.: InterVarsity, 1974), 1:740.

58. Ibid.

59. Eusebius, *Church History,* 3.25.

60. Guthrie, *New Testament Introduction,* 1:741.

61. Among these, Luther included John, Romans, Galatians, Ephesians, 1 Peter, and 1 John.

62. Paul Althaus, *The Theology of Martin Luther* (Philadelphia: Fortress, 1966), 84.

63. Ibid., 85.

64. Ibid.

65. Guthrie, *New Testament Introduction,* 1:741.

66. Ibid.

67. Ibid., 1:742.

68. Ibid.

69. Ned Stonehouse, *The Apocalypse in the Ancient Church* (Goes, Netherlands: Oosterbaan and Le Cointre, n.d.), 154–55.

Chapter 3

1. Raphael Patai, *The Messiah Texts* (Detroit: Wayne State University Press, 1979).

2. Ibid., 220.

3. Ibid.

4. Ibid., 221.

5. Ibid., 224.

6. Ibid., 226.

7. Mike Gendron, "Keys of the Kingdom," in *Dictionary of Premillennial Theology,* ed. Mal Couch (Grand Rapids: Kregel, 1996), 229.

8. Ludwig Ott, *Fundamentals of Catholic Dogma* (St. Louis: B. Herder, 1962), 209.
9. Richard P. Mcbrien, *Catholicism* (San Francisco: Harper San Francisco, 1994), 1135.
10. Ibid.
11. John Peter Lange, *Revelation,* Commentary on the Holy Scriptures, trans. Philip Schaff (Grand Rapids: Zondervan, n.d.), 65.
12. John F. Walvoord, *The Revelation of Jesus Christ* (Chicago: Moody, 1966), 19.
13. Robert L. Thomas, *Revelation 1–7: An Exegetical Commentary* (Chicago: Moody, 1992), 32.
14. W. Boyd Carpenter, "The Revelation," in *Ellicott's Commentary on the Whole Bible,* ed. Charles John Ellicott (reprint, Grand Rapids: Zondervan, 1957), 8:529.
15. J. R. Dummelow, *A Commentary on the Holy Bible* (New York: Macmillan, 1966), 1066.
16. Ibid.
17. Ibid.
18. Amanda J. Burr, quoted in Catherine G. Gonzalez and Justo L. Gonzalez, *Revelation* (Louisville: Knox/Westminster, 1997), 50.

Chapter 4

1. John F. Walvoord, *The Millennial Kingdom* (Findlay, Ohio: Dunham, 1939), 120.
2. Ibid.
3. Ibid., 121.
4. Ibid., 123.
5. John Peter Lange, *Revelation,* Commentary on the Holy Scriptures, trans. Philip Schaff (Grand Rapids: Zondervan, n.d.), 65.
6. Ibid.
7. Ibid.
8. Ibid.
9. For more on how to determine when to take a passage figuratively, see Roy B. Zuck, *Basic Bible Interpretations* (Wheaton, Ill.: Victor, 1991), 145–48.
10. Paul Lee Tan, *The Interpretation of Prophecy* (Rockville, Md.: Assurance, 1988), 162.
11. Ibid., 163.
12. Ibid., 164.
13. W. Milligan, quoted in Robert Tuck, "Revelation," in *The Preacher's Complete Homiletic Commentary* (Grand Rapids: Baker, n.d.), 30:406–7 (italics added).

14. W. Boyd Carpenter, "The Revelation," in *Ellicott's Commentary on the Whole Bible,* ed. Charles John Ellicott (reprint, Grand Rapids: Zondervan, 1957), 8:529.

15. Ibid.

16. Tim LaHaye, *Revelation* (Grand Rapids: Zondervan, 1980), 3.

17. Carpenter, "The Revelation," 8:531–32.

18. Martin Rist, "Revelation: Introduction and Exegesis," in *The Interpreter's Bible,* ed. George A. Buttrick (New York: Abingdon, 1957), 12:354.

19. Hal Lindsey, *The Road to Holocaust* (New York: Bantam, 1989), 10–11.

20. Ibid., 11.

21. Carpenter, "The Revelation," 526.

22. Merrill F. Unger, *Archaeology and the New Testament* (Grand Rapids: Zondervan, 1962), 267.

23. Theodore Zahn, *Introduction to the New Testament* (Minneapolis: Klock and Klock, 1909), 3:183–84.

24. Philip Schaff, *History of the Christian Church* (reprint, Grand Rapids: Eerdmans, 1990), 1:834.

25. John Walvoord, *The Revelation of Jesus Christ* (Chicago: Moody, 1966), 14.

26. A. T. Robertson, *Word Pictures in the New Testament* (Nashville: Broadman, 1933), 6:272–73.

27. Carpenter, "The Revelation," 526.

28. Lindsey, *The Road to Holocaust,* 242.

29. Ibid., 243.

30. Schaff, *History of the Christian Church,* 2:614.

31. Ibid.

32. Ibid., 616–17.

33. Ibid., 617–18.

34. Joseph Wilson Trigg, *Origen* (Atlanta: John Knox, 1983), 121.

35. Ibid., 122.

36. Ibid., 162.

37. Ibid., 212–13 (italics added).

38. Schaff, *History of the Christian Church,* 2:792

39. Robert H. Mounce, *The Book of Revelation,* New International Commentary on the New Testament (Grand Rapids: Eerdmans, 1977), 39.

40. Schaff, *History of the Christian Church,* 618.

41. G. B. Stevens, quoted in Tuck, "Revelation," 30:404–5.

42. S. Cox, quoted in Ibid., 405.

43. Milligan, quoted in Ibid., 406.

44. Ibid. (italics his).

45. George N. H. Peters, *The Theocratic Kingdom* (Grand Rapids: Kregel, 1988), 1:50–51.
46. Michael Avi-Yonah and Zvi Baras, *Society and Religion in the Second Temple Period* (Jerusalem: Massada, 1977), 185–86.
47. Ibid., 159.
48. Raphael Patai, *The Messiah Texts* (Detroit: Wayne State University Press, 1979), 96–97.
49. Ibid., 95–96.
50. Avi-Yonah and Baras, *Society and Religion in the Second Temple Period,* 165.
51. Ibid., 172.
52. Ibid., 173.
53. Ibid., 159.
54. Ibid., 161.
55. Ibid., 154.
56. Ibid., 171.
57. Ibid., 168.
58. Ibid.
59. Moses de Leon, ed., *Zohar,* Vilna ed. (Rome, n.d., 1894). Zohar is the central work in Jewish Kabbalistic (mystical) literature, which consists of homilies, discussions, and parables. It was written in Aramaic in the latter half of the twelfth century in Europe.
60. Michael Wilcock, *The Message of Revelation* (Downers Grove, Ill.: InterVarsity, 1975), 8.
61. Norman Cohn, *The Pursuit of the Millennium* (New York: Oxford University Press, 1970), 29 (italics added).

Chapter 5
1. Henry Barclay Swete, *Commentary on Revelation* (Grand Rapids: Kregel, 1977), cxxv.
2. Ibid., cxxii.
3. Ibid., cxxiii.
4. Ibid., xlvi.
5. Ibid., xlvii.
6. Ibid., liv.
7. John F. Walvoord, *The Revelation of Jesus Christ* (Chicago: Moody, 1966), 25.
8. Ibid., 27.
9. Ibid., 123.
10. Merrill C. Tenney, *Interpreting Revelation* (Grand Rapids: Eerdmans, 1959), 101, 104.
11. Ibid.

12. Swete, *Revelation,* clviii.
13. Henry M. Morris, *The Revelation Record* (Wheaton, Ill.: Tyndale, 1983), 30.
14. Ibid.
15. Ibid., 28–30.
16. Ibid., 31.
17. Ibid.
18. Ibid.
19. Walvoord, *The Revelation of Jesus Christ,* 123.
20. Robert L. Thomas, *Revelation 1–7: An Exegetical Commentary* (Chicago: Moody, 1992), 43.

Chapter 6

1. Robert L. Thomas, *Revelation 8–22: An Exegetical Commentary* (Chicago: Moody, 1992), 377.
2. John F. Walvoord, "Revelation," in *The Bible Knowledge Commentary, New Testament,* ed. John F. Walvoord and Roy B. Zuck (Wheaton, Ill.: Victor, 1983), 975.
3. Thomas, *Revelation 8–22,* 71.
4. Robert L. Thomas, *Revelation 1–7: An Exegetical Commentary* (Chicago: Moody, 1992), 52.
5. John F. Walvoord, *The Revelation of Jesus Christ* (Chicago: Moody, 1966), 35.
6. Ibid., 50.
7. Ibid., 52.
8. Ibid.
9. Thomas, *Revelation 1–7,* 57.
10. Walvoord, *The Revelation of Jesus Christ,* 41.
11. E. W. Bullinger, *Commentary on Revelation* (Grand Rapids: Kregel, 1984), 151.
12. Thomas, *Revelation 1–7,* 90.
13. Horst Balz, "biblion," in *Exegetical Dictionary of the New Testament,* ed. Horst Balz and Gerhard Schneider (Grand Rapids: Eerdmans, 1994), 1:217–18.
14. Walvoord, *The Revelation of Jesus Christ,* 338.
15. Thomas, *Revelation 8–22,* 518.
16. Tim LaHaye, foreword to *Revelation* (Grand Rapids: Zondervan, 1980).

Chapter 7

1. Joseph A. Seiss, *The Apocalypse* (Grand Rapids: Zondervan, n.d.), 28.
2. Leon Morris, *The Revelation of St. John* (Grand Rapids: Eerdmans, 1975), 48 (italics his).

3. Charles C. Ryrie, *Revelation* (Chicago: Moody, 1968), 14.
4. Morris, *The Revelation of St. John,* 86 (italics his).
5. Henry Alford, *The Greek New Testament,* rev. Everett F. Harrison, 4 vols. in 2 (Chicago: Moody, 1958), 4:594.
6. John F. Walvoord, *The Revelation of Jesus Christ* (Chicago: Moody, 1966), 105.
7. Ryrie, *Revelation,* 34.
8. Ibid., 38. Ryrie says, "If the living ones are cherubim, then the scene is one of the redeemed (as represented by the twenty-four elders) joining with the cherubim (representing all the elect angels) in magnifying the worth of the Creator-God. If the living ones represent the attributes of God, then the elders are seen responding with worship to the revelation of God's attributes. In either case the glory of the elders falls before the glory of God, for all that we have as redeemed people is a gift of His grace according to the pleasure of His own will. In heaven we will acknowledge this. It is tragic that we do not do it sooner."
9. Robert P. Lightner, *The God of the Bible and Other Gods* (Grand Rapids: Kregel, 1998), 13 (italics his).
10. See Herbert F. Stevenson, *Titles of the Triune God* (Westwood, N.J.: Revell, 1956), 37–41, for a full discussion of El Shaddai, the Old Testament name for God and the equivalent of "Almighty" in Revelation.
11. J. I. Packer, *Knowing God* (Downers Grove, Ill.: InterVarsity, 1973), 18 (italics his).
12. Ibid., 23–26.

Chapter 8

1. John F. Walvoord, *The Revelation of Jesus Christ* (Chicago: Moody, 1966), 30.
2. Ibid., 31.
3. W. Hall Harris, "A Theology of John's Writings," in *A Biblical Theology of the New Testament,* ed. Roy B. Zuck (Chicago: Moody, 1994), 179.
4. Joseph A. Seiss, *The Apocalypse* (Grand Rapids: Zondervan, 1962), 16 (italics his).
5. Martin Luther, "Preface to the Revelation of St. John," (1522), quoted in John Peter Lange, *Revelation,* Commentary on the Holy Scriptures, trans. Philip Schaff (Grand Rapids: Zondervan, n.d.).
6. Merrill C. Tenney, *Interpreting Revelation* (Grand Rapids: Eerdmans, 1957), 117.
7. See, for example, Graham W. Scroggie, *The Great Unveiling* (Grand Rapids: Zondervan, 1979), 44–46.
8. Donald Guthrie, *New Testament Theology* (Downers Grove, Ill.: InterVarsity, 1981), 300.

9. Walvoord, *The Revelation of Jesus Christ,* 31.

10. Guthrie, *New Testament Theology,* 332.

11. Seiss, *The Apocalypse,* 513.

12. E. Schuyler English, "Christ in Revelation," in *Prophecy in the Seventies,* ed. Charles Lee Feinberg (Chicago: Moody, 1971), 78–79.

13. Guthrie, *New Testament Theology,* 258.

14. The distinction between the Rapture and the Second Coming is discussed in chapter 16.

15. Lewis Sperry Chafer, *Major Bible Themes* (Findlay, Ohio: Dunham, 1953), 62–63.

Chapter 9

1. R. H. Charles, *A Critical and Exegetical Commentary on the Revelation of St. John* (Edinburgh: T & T Clark, 1985), 1:13.

2. Merrill F. Unger, *Zechariah* (Grand Rapids: Zondervan, 1963), 67.

3. Henry M. Morris, *The Revelation Record* (Wheaton: Tyndale, 1983), 37.

4. Tim LaHaye, *Revelation* (Grand Rapids: Zondervan, 1980), 11.

5. Walter Scott, *Exposition of the Revelation of Jesus Christ* (Grand Rapids: Kregel, 1982), 24.

6. Joseph A. Seiss, *The Apocalypse* (Grand Rapids: Kregel, 1987), 27.

7. John Peter Lange, *Revelation,* Commentary on the Holy Scriptures, trans. Philip Schaff (Grand Rapids: Zondervan, n.d.), 91.

8. Unger, *Unger's Commentary on the Old Testament,* 2:1174.

9. Seiss, *The Apocalypse,* 17.

10. A. T. Robertson, *Word Pictures in the New Testament* (Nashville: Broadman, 1933), 6:429.

11. Alan F. Johnson, "Revelation," in *The Expositor's Bible Commentary* (Grand Rapids: Zondervan, 1981), 12:595.

12. Robert L. Thomas, *Revelation 1–7: An Exegetical Commentary* (Chicago: Moody, 1992), 150.

13. John F. Walvoord, *The Holy Spirit,* 3d ed. (Findlay, Ohio: Dunham, 1958), 230.

14. Ed Glasscock, *Matthew* (Chicago: Moody, 1997), 99.

15. Charles Ryrie, *Ryrie Study Bible* (Chicago: Moody, 1986), 1299 (note on Ezekiel 46:1–15).

16. Arnold G. Fruchtenbaum, *Israelology: The Missing Link in Systematic Theology* (Tustin, Calif.: Ariel Ministries, 1992), 810.

17. Charles Lee Feinberg, *The Prophecy of Ezekiel* (Chicago: Moody, 1969), 252.

Chapter 10

1. John F. Walvoord, *The Revelation of Jesus Christ* (Chicago: Moody, 1966), 23.
2. John Peter Lange, *Revelation,* Commentary on the Holy Scriptures, trans. Philip Schaff (Grand Rapids: Zondervan, n.d.), 92.
3. Robert L. Thomas, *Revelation 8–22: An Exegetical Commentary* (Chicago: Moody, 1992), 86–87.
4. Henry M. Morris, *The Revelation Record* (Wheaton, Ill.: Tyndale, 1983), 48.
5. Ibid.
6. Clarence Larkin, *The Book of Revelation* (Glenside, Pa.: Clarence Larkin Estate, 1919), 20.
7. Ibid., 22.
8. Ibid.
9. Ibid., 25.
10. Walvoord, *The Revelation of Jesus Christ,* 119.
11. Robert L. Thomas, *Revelation 1–7: An Exegetical Commentary* (Chicago: Moody, 1992), 127.
12. Walvoord, *The Revelation of Jesus Christ,* 119.
13. Ibid., 248.
14. Thomas, *Revelation 1–7,* 465.

Chapter 11

1. Robert L. Thomas, *Revelation 8–22: An Exegetical Commentary* (Chicago: Moody, 1992), 394–95.
2. Ibid., 401.
3. John F. Walvoord, *The Revelation of Jesus Christ* (Chicago: Moody, 1966), 153.
4. Leon Wood, *A Commentary on Daniel* (Grand Rapids: Zondervan, 1973), 183.
5. David Jeremiah, *The Handwriting on the Wall* (Dallas: Word, 1992), 135.
6. Wood, *A Commentary on Daniel,* 185.
7. Merrill F. Unger, *Unger's Commentary on the Old Testament* (Chicago: Moody, 1981), 2:1648.
8. Walvoord, *The Revelation of Jesus Christ,* 250.
9. Tim LaHaye, *Revelation* (Grand Rapids: Zondervan, 1980), 226–27.
10. Mark Bailey and Tom Constable, *The New Testament Expolorer,* Swindoll Leadership Library (Nashville: Word, 1999), 645–46.
11. W. Leon Tucker, *Studies in Revelation* (Grand Rapids: Kregel, 1980), 346.
12. Robert L. Thomas, *Revelation 1–7: An Exegetical Commentary* (Chicago: Moody, 1992), 189.

13. Ibid., 148.
14. R. C. H. Lenski, *The Interpretation of St. John's Revelation* (Minneapolis: Augsburg, 1963), 90.
15. Henry M. Morris, *The Revelation Record* (Wheaton, Ill.: Tyndale, 1983), 60–61.
16. Walvoord, *The Revelation of Jesus Christ,* 84.
17. Walter Scott, *Exposition of the Revelation of Jesus Christ* (Grand Rapids: Kregel, 1983), 447.

Chapter 12

1. Emery H. Bancroft, *Elemental Theology* (Grand Rapids: Kregel, 1996), 245–46.
2. Ibid., 245.
3. Ibid.
4. Ibid.
5. Ibid., 246.
6. John F. Walvoord, *The Revelation of Jesus Christ* (Chicago: Moody, 1966), 32.
7. Robert L. Thomas, *Revelation 8–22: An Exegetical Commentary* (Chicago: Moody, 1992), 2:507.
8. Alexander Hislop, *The Two Babylons* (New York: Loizeaux Brothers, 1943).
9. H. A. Ironside, *Lectures on the Book of Revelation,* 3d ed. (Neptune, N.J.: Loizeaux Brothers, 1930), 290, 292, 294–95.
10. J. Dwight Pentecost, *Things to Come* (Grand Rapids: Zondervan, 1958), 367–68.

Chapter 13

1. Robert L. Thomas, *Revelation 8–22: An Exegetical Commentary* (Chicago: Moody, 1992), 6–7.
2. Mark Bailey and Tom Constable, *The New Testament Explorer,* Swindoll Leadership Library (Nashville: Word, 1999), 635.
3. R. C. H. Lenski, *The Interpretation of St. John's Revelation* (Minneapolis: Augsburg, 1963), 372–73.
4. *The Wycliffe Bible Commentary,* ed. Charles F. Pfeiffer and Everett F. Harrison (Chicago: Moody, 1962), 622.
5. Merrill F. Unger, *Unger's Commentary on the Old Testament* (Chicago: Moody, 1981), 2:1552–53.
6. Henry M. Morris, *The Revelation Record* (Wheaton, Ill.: Tyndale, 1983), 213.
7. Lewis Sperry Chafer, *Systematic Theology,* 8 vols. in 4 (1948; reprint, Grand Rapids: Kregel, 1993), 2:33–34.

8. Alan F. Johnson, "Revelation," in *The Expositor's Bible Commentary* (Grand Rapids: Zondervan, 1981), 12:493.
9. John F. Walvoord, *The Revelation of Jesus Christ* (Chicago: Moody, 1966), 165.
10. Thomas, *Revelation 8–22*, 2:44.
11. Ibid., 39.
12. Merrill F. Unger, *Biblical Demonology* (Chicago: Scripture Press, 1952), 191–92.

Chapter 14

1. Robert P. Lightner, *Sin, the Savior, and Salvation* (Nashville: Nelson, 1991), 141.
2. Glen W. Barker, "1 John," in *The Expositor's Bible Commentary* (Grand Rapids: Zondervan, 1981), 12:349.
3. Lewis Sperry Chafer, *Systematic Theology,* 8 vols. in 4 (1948; reprint, Grand Rapids: Kregel, 1993), 3:374, 378.
4. Robert L. Thomas, *Revelation 8–22: An Exegetical Commentary* (Chicago: Moody, 1992), 2:502–3.
5. Merrill F. Unger, *Commentary on the Old Testament* (Chicago: Moody, 1982), 1:142.
6. John D. Hannah, "Exodus," in *The Bible Knowledge Commentary, Old Testament,* ed. John F. Walvoord and Roy B. Zuck (Wheaton, Ill.: Victor, 1985), 156.
7. John Peter Lange, *Revelation,* Commentary on the Holy Scriptures, trans. Philip Schaff (Grand Rapids: Zondervan, n.d.), 127.
8. Robert L. Thomas, *Revelation 1–7: An Exegetical Commentary* (Chicago: Moody, 1992), 261.
9. John F. Walvoord, *The Revelation of Jesus Christ* (Chicago: Moody, 1966), 82, 338.
10. Thomas, *Revelation 1–7*, 263.
11. Henry M. Morris, *The Genesis Record* (Grand Rapids: Baker, 1994), 131.
12. Thomas, *Revelation 8–22*, 484.
13. Walvoord, *The Revelation of Jesus Christ,* 338.
14. R. C. H. Lenski, *The Interpretation of St. John's Revelation* (Minneapolis: Augsburg, 1963), 673.
15. Chafer, *Systematic Theology,* 1:93.
16. Joseph A. Seiss, *The Apocalypse* (Grand Rapids: Kregel, 1987), 526–27.

Chapter 15

1. Harold W. Hoehner, *Chronological Aspects of the Life of Christ* (Grand Rapids: Zondervan, 1974), 117.

2. For an excellent discussion on the calculation of Daniel's seventy weeks, see ibid., 115–39.

3. Ibid., 126.

4. John F. Walvoord, "Revelation," in *The Bible Knowledge Commentary, Old Testament,* ed. John F. Walvoord and Roy B. Zuck (Wheaton, Ill.: Victor, 1985), 1364.

5. Robert L. Thomas, *Revelation 1–7: An Exegetical Commentary* (Chicago: Moody, 1992), 481.

6. Robert Tuck, "Revelation," in *The Preacher's Complete Homiletic Commentary* (reprint, Grand Rapids: Baker, n.d.), 31:514.

7. Henry Alford, *The Greek Testament* (reprint, 4 vols. in 2, Chicago: Moody, 1958), 4:624.

8. Albert Barnes, *Notes on the New Testament* (Grand Rapids: Baker, 1983), 173.

9. Alphonse Bossard, *Dictionary of Mary* (Totowa, N.J.: Catholic Book Publishing, 1985), 402.

10. J. Allen, *What the Bible Teaches* (Kilmarnock, Scotland: John Ritchie, 1997), 10:322.

11. Tim LaHaye, *Revelation* (Grand Rapids: Zondervan, 1980), 155.

12. Raphael Patai, *The Messiah Texts* (Detroit: Wayne State University Press, 1979), 220.

13. John Bright, *The Kingdom of God* (New York: Abindgon-Cokesbury, 1953), 17–18.

14. J. Dwight Pentecost, *Things to Come* (Grand Rapids: Zondervan, 1958), 447.

15. Arnold G. Fruchtenbaum, *Israaeology: The Missing Link in Systematic Theology* (Tustin, Calif.: Ariel Ministries, 1992), 810.

Chapter 16

1. Mal Couch, "Rapture, Biblical Study of the," in *Dictionary of Premillennial Theology,* ed. Mal Couch (Grand Rapids: Kregel, 1996), 332.

2. Thomas Ice and Timothy Demy, *Prophecy Watch* (Eugene, Ore.: Harvest House, 1998), 101.

3. Ibid., 101–2.

4. J. F. Strombeck, *First the Rapture* (Grand Rapids: Kregel, 1992), 117.

5. Robert Lightner, *The Last Days Handbook* (Nashville: Nelson, 1997), 94–95.

6. For more critiques of the prewrath view see Gerald B. Stanton, "Review of *The Pre-Wrath Rapture of the Church,*" *Bibliotheca Sacra* 148 (January–March 1991): 909–111; John A. McLean, "Another Look at Rosenthal's 'Pre-Wrath Rapture,'" *Bibliotheca Sacra* 148 (October–

December 1991): 387–98; and Paul S. Karleen, *The Pre-Wrath Rapture of the Church: Is It Biblical?* (Langhorne, Pa.: BF, 1991).

7. Couch, "Rapture, Biblical Study of the," 342.

A Verse-by-Verse Background Guide to the Book of Revelation

1. R. C. H. Lenski, *The Interpretation of St. John's Revelation* (Minneapolis: Augsburg, 1963), 24.

2. Alan F. Johnson, "Revelation," in *The Expositor's Bible Commentary* (Grand Rapids: Zondervan, 1981), 12:424.

3. I. M. Haldeman, *The Tabernacle Priesthood and Offerings* (Old Tappan, N.J.: Revell, n.d.), 214–15.

4. John Peter Lange, *Revelation,* Commentary on the Holy Scriptures, trans. Philip Schaff (Grand Rapids: Zondervan, n.d.), 107.

5. Tim LaHaye, *Revelation* (Grand Rapids: Zondervan, 1980), 27.

6. Robert L. Thomas, *Revelation 1–7: An Exegetical Commentary* (Chicago: Moody, 1992), 153.

7. Lenski, *The Interpretation of St. John's Revelation,* 103–4.

8. Johnson, "Revelation," 12:442.

9. John F. Walvoord, *The Revelation of Jesus Christ* (Chicago: Moody, 1966), 76.

10. Ibid., 77.

11. Ibid.

12. Albert Barnes, *Barnes' Notes on the New Testament* (Grand Rapids: Kregel, 1962), 1566.

13. Ibid.

14. *The Analytical Greek Lexicon* (New York: Harper & Brothers, n.d.), 262.

15. Barnes, *Barnes' Notes on the New Testament,* 96.

16. Heinrich Schlier, "ἀμήν," in *Theological Dictionary of the New Testament,* ed. Gerhard Kittel, trans. Geoffrey W. Bromiley (Grand Rapids: Eerdmans, 1987), 1:336.

17. Thomas, *Revelation 1–7,* 344.

18. Lenski, *The Interpretation of St. John's Revelation,* 172.

19. Ibid.

20. Thomas, *Revelation 1–7,* 353.

21. Ibid., 1:396.

22. Ibid., 430–31.

23. Ibid., 438.

24. Ibid., 454.

25. J. Allen, *Revelation* (Kilmarnock, Scotland: John Ritchie, 1997), 214.

26. R. H. Charles, *The Revelation of St. John* (Edinburgh: Clark, 1985), 1:241.

27. Walvoord, *The Revelation of Jesus Christ,* 166.
28. Henry Barclay Swete, *Commentary on Revelation* (Grand Rapids: Kregel, 1977), 122.
29. Robert L. Thomas, *Revelation 8–22: An Exegetical Commentary* (Chicago: Moody, 1972), 46.
30. Walvoord, *The Revelation of Jesus Christ,* 167.
31. Walter Bauer, William F. Arndt, and F. Wilbur Gingrich, *A Greek-English Lexicon of the New Testament and Other Early Christian Literature,* 2d ed., rev. F. Wilbur Gingrich and Frederick W. Danker (Chicago: Chicago University Press, 1979), 668.
32. Thomas, *Revelation 8–22,* 73.
33. Fritz Rienecker, *Linguistic Key to the Greek New Testament,* ed. Cleon L. Rogers (Grand Rapids: Zondervan, 1980), 836.
34. Ibid.
35. Walvoord, *The Revelation of Jesus Christ,* 176.
36. Lenski, *The Interpretation of St. John's Revelation,* 328.
37. Russell L. Penney, "Zechariah, Eschatology of," in *Dictionary of Premillennial Theology,* ed. Mal Couch (Grand Rapids: Kregel, 1996), 428.
38. Walvoord, *The Revelation of Jesus Christ,* 180.
39. Joseph A. Seiss, *The Apocalypse: Exposition of the Book of Revelation* (Grand Rapids: Kregel, 1987), 264.
40. Bauer, Arndt, and Gingrich, *A Greek-English Lexicon of the Greek New Testament and Other Early Christian Literature,* 591.
41. Ibid.
42. Walvoord, *The Revelation of Jesus Christ,* 183.
43. Ibid., 188.
44. Ibid., 191.
45. Seiss, *The Apocalypse,* 310.
46. Walvoord, *The Revelation of Jesus Christ,* 195.
47. Ibid., 195–96.
48. Ibid., 199.
49. Allen, *Revelation,* 336–37.
50. Ibid., 337.
51. Thomas, *Revelation 8–22,* 177.
52. Walvoord, *The Revelation of Jesus Christ,* 207–8.
53. Thomas, *Revelation 8–22,* 184.
54. James Moffatt, "Revelation," in *The Expositor's Greek Testament,* ed. W. Robertson Nicoll (reprint, Grand Rapids: Eerdmans, 1988), 5:435.
55. William R. Newell, *The Book of Revelation* (Chicago: Moody, 1935), 211.
56. Thomas, *Revelation 8–22,* 193.

57. Lee G. Olsen, "Music," in *Zondervan Pictorial Bible Dictionary* (Grand Rapids: Zondervan, 1967), 563–64.

58. Thomas, *Revelation 8–22*, 196–97.

59. Howard Z. Cleveland, "Sickle," in *Zondervan Pictorial Bible Dictionary* (Grand Rapids: Zondervan, 1967), 792.

60. Rienecker, *A Linguistic Key to the Greek New Testament*, 845.

61. Newell, *The Book of Revelation*, 233 (italics his).

62. Rienecker, *Linguistic Key to the Greek New Testament*, 846.

63. Ibid., 823.

64. Thomas, *Revelation 8–22*, 232.

65. Walvoord, *The Revelation of Jesus Christ*, 228.

66. Thomas, *Revelation 8–22*, 242–43.

67. Walter Scott, *Exposition of the Revelation of Jesus Christ* (Grand Rapids: Kregel, 1982), 337.

68. Ibid.

69. Thomas, *Revelation 8–22*, 292.

70. Ibid., 297.

71. Seiss, *The Apocalypse*, 420.

72. Walvoord, "Revelation," 975.

73. Allen, *Revelation*, 469.

74. Walvoord, *The Revelation of Jesus Christ*, 277.

75. Mal Couch, "Progressive Dispensationalism: Is Christ Now on the Throne of David?—Part III," *Conservative Theological Journal* (September 1998): 276–77. Acts 2:36 says "both Lord and Christ." In Greek "both . . . and" is the Greek conjunction *kai* used twice: *kai kyrios, kai christos*. This conjunction separates the two nouns. In Sharp's Rule VI, he makes this point: "The insertion of the copulative *kai* between nouns of the same case, without articles, . . . denotes that the second noun expresses a different person, thing, or quality, from the preceding noun" (Granville Sharp, *Remarks in the Uses of the Definitive Article . . . Containing Many New Proofs of the Divinity of Christ* [Atlanta: Original Word, 1995], 25).

Thus Peter was saying that "Lord" is a title distinct from "Messiah." "Lord" refers to Psalm 110:1 and Messiah (Christ, the Anointed One) refers to Psalm 2:2. The expression "both *[kai]* Lord and *[kai]* Christ" also supports the idea of Jesus' two different offices. He is now seated as Lord in heaven, and someday He will be the Messiah seated on David's earthly throne in the Millennium.

Though only one person is in view, namely Jesus, His functions are distinct.

76. Hal Lindsey, *There's a New World Coming* (Santa Ana, Calif.: Vision House, 1973), 264.

77. Barnes, *Barnes' Notes on the New Testament*, 1709.
78. Walvoord, *The Revelation of Jesus Christ*, 293.
79. Lindsey, *There's a New World Coming*, 263–64.
80. Lenski, *The Interpretation of St. John's Revelation*, 611–12.
81. Ibid., 619.
82. Ibid., 620.
83. W. Leon Tucker, *Studies in Revelation* (Grand Rapids: Kregel, 1980), 372.
84. Lenski, *The Interpretation of St. John's Revelation*, 624.
85. Thomas, *Revelation 8–22*, 463.
86. Johnson, "Revelation," 12:593.
87. Walvoord, *The Revelation of Jesus Christ*, 323.
88. Ibid., 330.
89. Ibid.
90. Thomas, *Revelation 1–7*, 61.
91. Barnes, *Barnes' Notes on the New Testament*, 459.
92. Seiss, *The Apocalypse*, 526.
93. Thomas, *Revelation 8–22*, 517.